Lecture Notes in Computer Science 16209

Founding Editors

Gerhard Goos
Juris Hartmanis

The series Lecture Notes in Computer Science (LNCS), including its subseries Lecture Notes in Artificial Intelligence (LNAI) and Lecture Notes in Bioinformatics (LNBI), has established itself as a medium for the publication of new developments in computer science and information technology research, teaching, and education.

LNCS enjoys close cooperation with the computer science R & D community, the series counts many renowned academics among its volume editors and paper authors, and collaborates with prestigious societies. Its mission is to serve this international community by providing an invaluable service, mainly focused on the publication of conference and workshop proceedings and postproceedings. LNCS commenced publication in 1973.

Huihui Fang · Meng Wang · Heng Li · Hao Chen ·
Hrvoje Bogunović · Cecilia S. Lee
Editors

Ophthalmic Medical Image Analysis

12th International Workshop, OMIA 2025
Held in Conjunction with MICCAI 2025
Daejeon, South Korea, September 27, 2025
Proceedings

 Springer

Editors
Huihui Fang
Nanyang Technological University
Singapore, Singapore

Meng Wang
National University of Singapore
Singapore, Singapore

Heng Li
Shenzhen University of Advanced
Technology
Shenzhen, China

Hao Chen
Hong Kong University of Science
and Technology
Kowloon, Hong Kong

Hrvoje Bogunović
Medical University of Vienna
Vienna, Wien, Austria

Cecilia S. Lee
University of Washington
Seattle, WA, USA

ISSN 0302-9743   ISSN 1611-3349 (electronic)
Lecture Notes in Computer Science
ISBN 978-3-032-10350-5   ISBN 978-3-032-10351-2 (eBook)
https://doi.org/10.1007/978-3-032-10351-2

Preface

The 12th International Workshop on Ophthalmic Medical Image Analysis (OMIA 2025) was held on September 27th, 2025, in conjunction with the 28th International Conference on Medical Image Computing and Computer-Assisted Intervention (MICCAI). This was hosted in Daejeon, Republic of Korea. This year was an in-person conference.

Age-related macular degeneration, diabetic retinopathy, and glaucoma are the main causes of blindness in both developed and developing countries. The cost of blindness to society and individuals is huge, and many cases can be avoided by early intervention. Early and reliable diagnosis strategies and effective treatments are therefore a world priority. At the same time, there is mounting research on the retinal vasculature and neuro-retinal architecture as a source of biomarkers for several high-prevalence conditions like dementia, cardiovascular disease, and of course complications of diabetes. Automatic and semi-automatic software tools for retinal image analysis are widely used in retinal biomarkers research, and increasingly percolating into clinical practice. Significant challenges remain in terms of reliability and validation, number and type of conditions considered, multi-modal analysis (e.g., fundus, optical coherence tomography, scanning laser ophthalmoscopy), novel imaging technologies, and the effective transfer of advanced computer vision and machine learning technologies, to mention a few. The workshop addressed all these aspects in the ideal interdisciplinary context of MICCAI.

This workshop aimed to bring together scientists, clinicians, and students from multiple disciplines in the growing ophthalmic image analysis community, such as electronic engineering, computer science, mathematics, and medicine, to discuss the latest advancements in the field. A total of *35* papers were submitted to the workshop in response to the call for papers. All submissions are double-blind peer-reviewed by at least three program committee members. The paper selection was based on methodological innovation, technical merit, results, validation, and application potential. Finally, *17* full-length papers were accepted at the workshop and chosen to be included in this Springer LNCS volume.

We are grateful to the Program Committee for reviewing the submitted papers and giving constructive comments and critiques, to the authors for submitting high-quality papers, to the presenters for excellent presentations, and to all the OMIA 2025 attendees from all around the world.

August 2025

Huihui Fang
Meng Wang
Heng Li
Hao Chen
Hrvoje Bogunovic
Cecilia S. Lee

Organization

Steering Committee

Emanuel Trucco	University of Dundee, UK
Huazhu Fu	IHPC, A*STAR, Singapore
Jiang Liu	Southern University of Science and Technology, China
Tom MacGillivray	University of Edinburgh, UK
Yanwu Xu	South China University of Technology, China

Workshop Organizers

Cecilia S. Lee	University of Washington, USA
Hao Chen	Hong Kong University of Science and Technology, China
Heng Li	Shenzhen University of Advanced Technology, China
Huihui Fang	Nanyang Technological University, Singapore
Hrvoje Bogunović	Medical University of Vienna, Austria
Meng Wang	National University of Singapore, Singapore.

Program Committee

Divyadharshini Karthikeyan	Amazon, Seattle, USA
Hanyi Yu	South China University of Technology, Guangzhou, China
Hao Zhang	Shandong University, Jinan, China
Haojin Li	Southern University of Science and Technology, Shenzhen, China
He Zhao	University of Liverpool, Liverpool, UK
Heng Li	Shenzhen University of Advanced Technology, Shenzhen, China
Huihui Fang	Nanyang Technological University, Singapore
Jiangbo Shi	Xi'an Jiaotong University, Xi'an, China
Jingtao Wang	Soochow University, Suzhou, China
Jinhua Liu	Nanyang Technological University, Singapore

Ke Zou	Sichuan University, Chengdu, China
Lei Mou	Cixi Institute of Biomedical Engineering, Ningbo Institute of Materials Technology and Engineering, Chinese Academy of Sciences, Ningbo, China
Lianyu Wang	Nanjing University of Aeronautics and Astronautics, Nanjing, China
Meng Wang	National University of Singapore, Singapore
Mingsi Liu	Assumption University, Bangkok, Thailand
Muthu Rama Krishnan Mookiah	University of Dundee, Dundee, UK
Pengshuai Yin	Guangdong Lab of Artificial Intelligence and Digital Economy (SZ), Shenzhen, China
Qingshan Hou	Northeastern University, Shenyang, China
Qinkai Yu	University of Exeter, Exeter, UK
Shiqi Zhou	South China University of Technology, Guangzhou, China
Ting Xu	National University of Singapore, Singapore
Weiwen Zhang	Hong Kong University of Science and Technology, China
Wenju Cui	University of Science and Technology of China, Hefei, China
Xiang Li	Nanjing University, Nanjing, China
Xiaofeng Lei	Institute of High Performance Computing, A*STAR, Singapore
Xiaoqi Sheng	South China University of Technology, Guangzhou, China
Yaling Tao	South China University of Technology, Guangzhou, China
Yan Hu	Southern University of Science and Technology, Shenzhen, China
Yanyu Xu	Shandong University, Jinan, China
Yi Zhou	Singapore Eye Research Institute, Singapore
Ying Chen	Pazhou Lab, Guangzhou, China
Yuancong Liang	South China University of Technology, Guangzhou, China
Yueqin Diao	South China University of Technology, Guangzhou, China
Yuanyuan Peng	Soochow University, Suzhou, China
Yuhui Ma	Ningbo Institute of Materials Technology and Engineering, Chinese Academy of Sciences, Ningbo, China
Yuning Wang	South China University of Technology, Guangzhou, China

| Yuzhu Cao | University of Science and Technology of China, Hefei, China |
| Zhiwei Liu | South China University of Technology, Guangzhou, China |

Contents

DVIA-Net: Dual-Path Video Information Aggregation Network for Anterior Chamber Angle Analysis

Lingxi Zeng[1,2], Yinglin Zhang[1,2,4], Jialin Li[2], Xiaoli Xing[5], Lingxi Hu[1,2], Chenglin Yao[1,2], Tianhang Liu[1,2], Yi Yue[5], Zunjie Xiao[1,2], Chen Lin[6], Risa Higashita[1,2,3(✉)], and Jiang Liu[1,2,3,4(✉)]

[1] Research Institute of Trustworthy Autonomous Systems, Southern University of Science and Technology, Shenzhen 518055, China
[2] Department of Computer Science and Engineering, Southern University of Science and Technology, Shenzhen 518055, China
[3] Changchun University, Changchun 130022, China
`risa@mail.sustech.edu.cn`
[4] School of Computer Science, University of Nottingham Ningbo China, Ningbo 315100, China
`liuj@sustech.edu.cn`
[5] School of Optometry and Eye Institute, Tianjin Medical University Eye Hospital, Tianjin 300020, China
[6] Shenzhen People's Hospital, Shenzhen 518020, China

Abstract. Anterior chamber angle analysis, especially the appositional angle indicating the early reversibility stage of angle-closure glaucoma, is important for the diagnosis and treatment of the disease. Most existing studies only analyzed the open and closed angle status based on static anterior segment optical coherence tomography (AS-OCT) images, while ignoring the clinically important appositional angle. In this paper, we propose a Dual-path Video Information Aggregation Network (DVIA-Net) based on AS-OCT dynamic video to achieve accurate classification of open, appositional, and synechial angles. Specifically, first, based on the clinical correlation of the above three angle states, we designed a dual-path video information architecture for the feature extraction and aggregation of the iris motion and the open-closed angle stationary status. Secondly, we use a dynamic region recognition (DRR) module to emphasize the salient features during motion. In addition, the open-closed stationary angle information is modeled by the video key-frame structure feature extraction (KSFE) path. Finally, the features of motion and angle stationary status are aggregated to achieve accurate classification. To verify the effectiveness of DVIA-Net, we collected an AS-OCT dynamic video dataset that records the changes in chamber angle state. Compared with the state-of-the-art methods, experimental results show that the proposed DVIA-Net not only achieves the best overall performance but also makes an improvement on the appositional angle classification.

L. Zeng and Y. Zhang—Contribute equally to this work.

© The Author(s), under exclusive license to Springer Nature Switzerland AG 2026
H. Fang et al. (Eds.): OMIA 2025, LNCS 16209, pp. 1–10, 2026.
https://doi.org/10.1007/978-3-032-10351-2_1

Keywords: Anterior chamber angles Classification · AS-OCT videos ·
Angle-closure glaucoma · Appositional angle

1   Introduction

Glaucoma is one of the primary causes of irreversible blindness, with an esti-
mated 112 million people being affected worldwide by 2040 [15,17]. Based on
the status of the Anterior Chamber Angle (ACA), glaucoma is typically classified into open-angle and angle-closure types. The latter encompasses varying
degrees of severity in cases of appositional and synechial angle closure. [2] Appositional angle, representing the reversible angle-closure state in the early stage
of the disease, may still offer the possibility of medical intervention [13]. Thus,
accurate assessment of the angle closing progression is important for clinical
diagnosis and treatment.

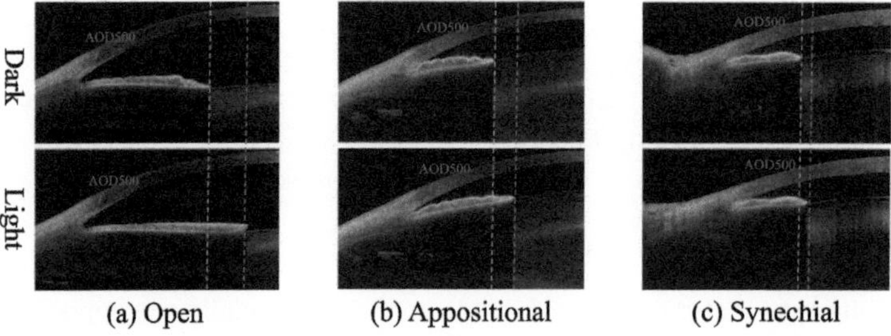

Fig. 1. The illustration of open, appositional, and synechial anterior chamber angles
(ACAs) in AS-OCT video frames. The first and second rows show the frames under dark
and bright conditions. Columns (a), (b), and (c) correspond to different ACA types.
AOD500 point indicates the anterior chamber open distance 500 microns. The green
and blue dash lines indicate the end of the iris at the darkest and lightest moments.

Recently, many classification algorithms have utilized anterior segment optical coherence tomography (AS-OCT) images, which enabling high-resolution
observation of anterior segment structures with non-contact and good repeatabil-
ity [5], to assess the status of the anterior chamber angle. Most existing methods
achieve open-closed ACA binary classification based on static AS-OCT images.
Xu *et al.* [19] used multi-scale HOG features for open-closed classification. Fu
et al. [4] and Xu *et al.* [18] developed more accurate automatic detection algorithms using convolutional neural networks. MLDN-Net [5] combined global and
local angle features to enhance performance. Fu *et al.* [6] and Hao *et al.* [8]
segmented the main ocular structures in AS-OCT images and calculated clinical parameters to support clinical assessment. MT network [10] first applied
the AS-OCT video in open-closed ACAs classification. And they further calculated some clinical parameters based on AS-OCT video for classification [11].
However, the aforementioned methods primarily discussed the open-closed ACA

status, without considering the appositional ACA. Only few methods address the open-appositional-synechial classification task. MSDN-net [7] learned spatial representations of paired bright and dark AS-OCT images. Hao *et al.* [9] used AS-OCT images to capture 3D iris structure for the classification. However, the key difference between open-appositional-synechial ACA is whether the anterior chamber open distance 500 microns (AOD500) can be observed, as shown in Fig. 1, which both the static and dynamic change information is important for the judgment. The previous work does not focus on the AOD500, and they did not consider combining this two information. In this work, we combine them to make a better judgment and classification for the ACA status.

In this paper, considering the open-appositional-synechial ACA, we proposed a DVIA-Net based on AS-OCT dynamic videos for the anterior chamber angle closing progression assessment. By using the AS-OCT dynamic videos, the classification performance is improved, making it possible to replace the gonioscope detection in existing clinical workflows. When using AS-OCT video to classify the status of the anterior chamber angles (ACAs), we need to extract two key types of information: 1) the dynamic changes of the iris morphological structure; 2) the open-closed stationary status of the anterior chamber angle. The main contributions are as follows:

1. To achieve accurate ACA classification, we proposed a dual-path video information network architecture to model the iris motion and the open-closed angel stationary status. To our knowledge, this is the first classification of open, appositional, and synechial ACA states using AS-OCT videos.
2. We used the dynamic region recognition (DRR) module to strengthen the salient features during motion. At the same time, the video key-frame structure feature (KSFE) extraction path is used to extract the open-closed stationary information of the anterior chamber angle.
3. To verify the effectiveness of our method, we collected an AS-OCT video dataset, which recorded the movement of iris during the light-dark-light illumination change process. Extensive experiments suggest that the proposed DVIA-Net not only achieves the best overall classification performance, but also improves the classification accuracy of the appositional angle.

2   Method

As shown in Fig. 2, this paper proposes a Dual-path Video Information Aggregation Network (DVIA-Net) for open, appositional, and synechial angles classification based on dynamic AS-OCT video. First, we cut each AS-OCT video frame in half from the middle, as our goal is to classify ACA. After that, key-frame extraction is performed on the cropped video frames set $\mathcal{V} = \{I_1, \cdots, I_T\}$ where I_i means the ith frame in the set $\mathcal{V}$. Secondly, the iris motion information and open-closed stationary information of ACAs are extracted. For iris motion information, the Dynamic Region Recognition (DRR) module uses the difference map of key-frames to calculate the attention map set $\mathcal{M} = \{m_1, \cdots, m_t\}$ for set

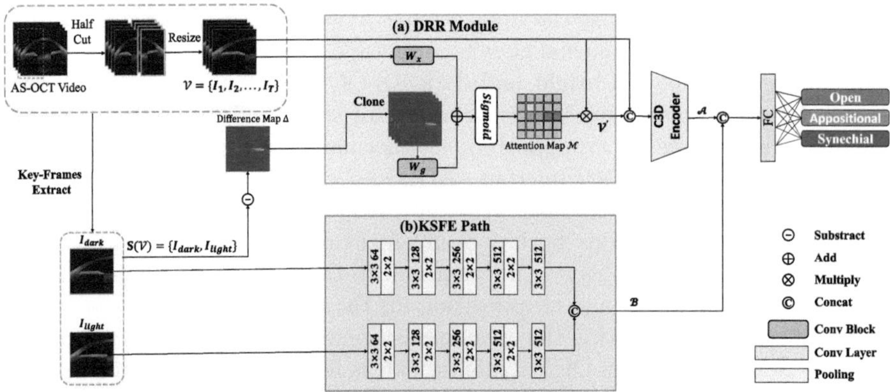

Fig. 2. Overview of the proposed Dual-path Video Information Aggregation Network (DVIA-Net) based on AS-OCT videos. We used the dynamic region recognition (DRR) module to strengthen the salient features in the iris motion information path. At the same time, the keyframe structure feature extraction (KSFE) path is used to extract the open-closed stationary information of the anterior chamber angle.

$\mathcal{V}$. We enhance the video frames I_i by attention map m_i, getting the enhanced frames set $\mathcal{V}' = \{I'_1, \cdots, I'_T\}$. The enhanced frames set is then concatenated with $\mathcal{V}$. This module can help the network recognize the dynamic changed area in the video. The key-frame structure feature extraction (KSFE) path is used to derive the open-close stationary information from key frames under dark and light conditions. Finally, the features from two path are concatenated and a fully connected layer is used to obtain the classification results for open, appositional, and synechial angles.

2.1 Dynamic Region Recognition Module

The key-frames I_{light} and I_{dark} are determined at the moments where the diameter of the pupil is smallest and biggest in the AS-OCT video. The two key frames are shown in Fig. 2.

$$(I_{dark}, I_{light}) = \mathbf{S}(\mathcal{V}) \tag{1}$$

To help the network recognize the dynamic changed area in the video, we propose a DRR module, as illustrated in Fig. 2(a), based on the two key frames.

We use the difference map $\Delta = I_{dark} - I_{light}$ between key frames I_{dark} and I_{light} to help the model focus on these critical regions. In this part, we first calculate the difference map between the extracted key frames. Then we use two convolution blocks W_g and W_x to encode the difference map and the AS-OCT video.

After that, the encoded feature is added together. And then a sigmoid function σ is used to get the attention weight map m_i.

$$m_i = \sigma(W_g * \Delta + W_x * I_i) \tag{2}$$

The attention weight map effectively integrates the areas of change, directing the model's focus toward these dynamic regions. It enhances the model's ability to discern subtle variations that are critical for accurate classification. And finally, we can get the enhanced features as $\mathcal{V}' = \{I_1', \cdots, I_T'\}$ where $I_i' = I_i \cdot m_i$. We then concatenate the enhanced features $\mathcal{V}'$ with the original input $\mathcal{V}$, and feed them $[\mathcal{V}; \mathcal{V}']$ to the C3D backbone to extract the final dynamic change features $\mathcal{A}$, as formulated in Eq. 3.

$$\mathcal{A} = \mathbf{C3D}([\mathcal{V}; \mathcal{V}']) \tag{3}$$

2.2   Key-Frame Structure Feature Extraction

The dynamic changes in open and appositional anterior chamber angles exhibit similar patterns, as shown in Fig. 1. Therefore, the stationary structure information of ACA is nessesary for the classification of appositional angle.

In the key-frame structure feature extraction path, we apply two convolutional networks Θ_1 and Θ_2 to separately extract features from the two frames. These two networks are two-dimension version of the C3D network. Then a concatenation operation is used to fuse the feature vectors of the key frames to get feature $\mathcal{B}$ as follows:

$$\mathcal{B} = [\Theta_1(I_{dark}); \Theta_2(I_{light})] \tag{4}$$

Finally, the feature $\mathcal{A}$ and $\mathcal{B}$ is fused to improve the overall classification performance of the network.

$$Logits = \mathbf{FC}([\mathcal{A}; \mathcal{B}]) \tag{5}$$

2.3   Loss Function

The cross-entropy loss is used in this work, as shown in Eq. 6.

$$L = -\sum_{i=1}^{N} w_i y_i log\left(\frac{e^{z_i}}{\sum_{j=1}^{N} e^{z_j}}\right) \tag{6}$$

where $N = 3$ is the number of classes, y_i is the one-hot label for class i, z_i and z_j is the model output logits for class i and j. We empirically set $w_0 = 1.00$, $w_1 = 3.00$, and $w_2 = 1.30$ according to the classes distribution.

3   Experimental Results

3.1   Dataset

AS-OCT Video Dataset. We first collected an AS-OCT Video Dataset. All AS-OCT videos in our dataset were acquired using a CASIA-2 machine (Tomey Inc., Japan) from 205 patients (326 eyes). For each eye, videos were acquired in the horizontal and vertical direction, resulting in a total of 652 videos. To enable the network to focus on a single ACA, each video was split in half, yielding a total of 1304 videos, all of which were with open, appositional, and synechial gradings annotated by dynamic gonioscopic examinations (616 with open ACA, 208 with appositional ACA, and 480 with synechial ACA). The videos were captured under a darkâĂŞlightâĂŞdark illumination protocol over a 10-second interval, with each video comprising 101 frames that are fully utilized in our network. The original resolution of each split frame is 2133×622 pixels. In our experiments, we divided the dataset into a training set of 912 videos, a validation set of 136 videos, and a testing set of 256 videos by hierarchy random sampling. Videos from the same eye were not split across different sets.

AS-OCT Images Dataset. To explore the difference between AS-OCT video data and AS-OCT image data in the classification of ACAs, we also collect a AS-OCT Images Dataset from the same group as the video data. The dataset includes 1304 dark-light AS-OCT image pairs which are captured at the same horizontal and vertical direction, in the dark room and under natural light respectively. The dataset distribution is the same as the Video Dataset.

3.2   Implementation Details and Metrics

We implement all models using PyTorch 2.2.0 on an NVIDIA GeForce RTX A6000 and trained for 50 epochs with the SGD optimization strategy. We adopt an initial learning rate of 1e-5 and a batch size of 10. Empirically, we select frame 0 and frame 50 as key-frames in our experiment. All input frames were resized to 192×192. Refer to [7,10], we use macro sensitivity(M-Sen), balanced accuracy (B-Acc), and macro specificity (M-Spe) as the primary metrics to evaluate classification performance. Kappa coefficient and F1 score are also considered.

3.3   Comparison with SOTA Methods

We compared the proposed model with other state-of-the-art (SOTA) methods, such as Vision Transformer (ViT) [1,3], ResNet-34 [12], C3D [16], and ConvLSTM [14], as well as two networks specifically designed for chamber angle classification: MSDN [7], which uses light and dark AS-OCT images, and MT [10], which performs open-closed binary classification using dynamic video.

As shown in Table 1, our proposed DVIA-Net demonstrates an overall performance gain with a B-Acc of 0.822, a M-Sen of 0.749, and a M-Spe of 0.895, outperforming all the compared methods. To explore its generalization ability, we conducted experiments using two types of backbone networks: C3D [16] and ResNet34 [12]. The results in Table 1 indicate that the performance of both has been improved. Since our model with the C3D backbone achieves the best performance, unless otherwise specified, the DVIA-Net mentioned in this paper refers to the model with C3D backbone.

ViT [1,3], ResNet-34 [12], C3D [16], and ConvLSTM [14] were trained on both AS-OCT image and video datasets. The improvement of their classification performance by AS-OCT videos, especially for the appositional angle, as shown in Fig. 3, proves our hypothesis that dynamic videos provide additional

Table 1. The classification comparison of ACAs with other SOTA methods. The best scores are in **bold**. The second best are in <u>underline</u>.

Methods	Dataset	B-Acc	M-Sen	M-Spe	Kappa	F1
ViT [3]	Images	0.664	0.526	0.802	0.378	0.524
ResNet34 [12]	Images	0.754	0.645	0.864	0.546	0.641
C3D [16]	Images	0.769	0.664	0.874	0.574	0.660
ConvLSTM [14]	Images	0.666	0.524	0.809	0.357	0.492
MSDN [7]	Images	0.782	0.679	0.886	**0.625**	0.679
ViT [1]	Video	0.751	0.644	0.858	0.541	0.641
ResNet34	Video	0.764	0.672	0.856	0.514	0.643
C3D	Video	0.779	0.691	0.868	0.539	0.661
ConvLSTM	Video	0.727	0.691	0.868	0.451	0.577
MT [10]	Video	0.782	0.688	0.877	0.611	0.689
Ours (ResNet34)	Video	<u>0.813</u>	<u>0.737</u>	<u>0.889</u>	<u>0.623</u>	**0.715**
Ours (C3D)	Video	**0.822**	**0.749**	**0.895**	**0.625**	<u>0.713</u>

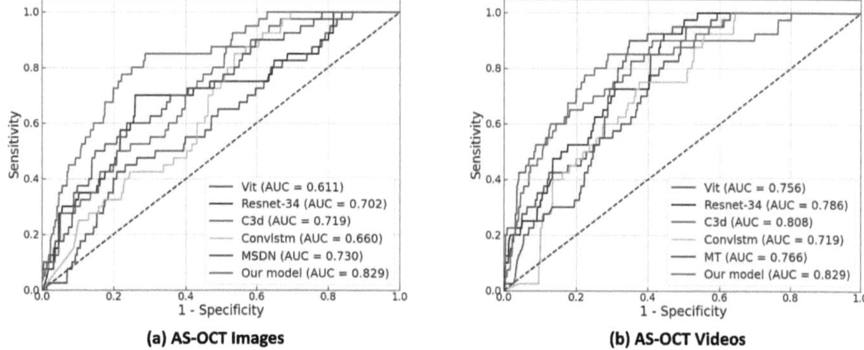

Fig. 3. The ROC curve comparison with other SOTA methods in the classification of appositional ACA. To compare with the methods trained on AS-OCT images more intuitively, we also draw the ROC curve of our DVIA-Net in (a).

information over static images. Although MT [10] is also designed for ACA classification using AS-OCT video, its performance is still lower than that of our proposed DVIA-Net. This is mainly because they do not fully utilize the stationary chamber angle structural information. In subsequent ablation stuy, we will show that only by considering both the dynamic changes and the open-closed stationary status of ACA in the video can we achieve the best performance in open, appositional, and synechial classification.

To show that the proposed DVIA-Net improves the appositional classification performance, we use the ROC curve to comprehensively evaluate the trade-off between the sensitivity and specificity rates of the appositional angle classification across various thresholds. As shown in Fig. 3, the DVIA-Net produces the best performance, achieving an AUC of 0.829 for classifying appositional ACAs.

3.4 Ablation Study

Table 2. Ablation study of DRR and KSFE module on AS-OCT Video.

Backbone	DRR	KSFE	Kappa	F1	B-Acc	Sensitivities			M-Sen	M-Spe
						Open	Appositional	Synechial		
C3D	–	–	0.539	0.661	0.779	0.717	0.700	0.656	0.691	0.868
C3D	✓	–	**0.632**	0.710	0.808	**0.875**	0.600	0.698	0.724	0.893
C3D	–	✓	0.597	0.667	0.773	0.858	0.375	**0.771**	0.668	0.878
C3D	✓	✓	0.625	**0.714**	**0.822**	0.858	**0.775**	0.615	**0.749**	**0.895**

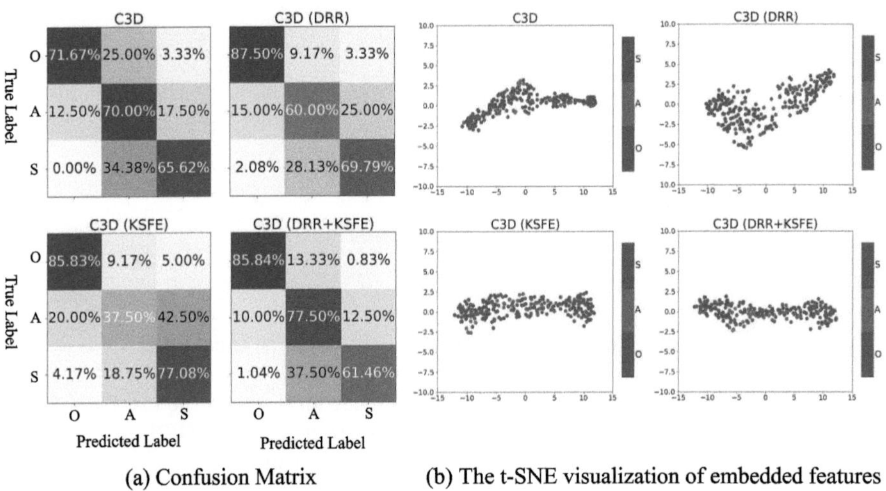

(a) Confusion Matrix   (b) The t-SNE visualization of embedded features

Fig. 4. The visualization of the confusion matrix (a) and embedded feature distribution (b) for the classification of Open (O), Appositional (A), and Synechial (S) ACAs.

To evaluate the contribution of each module, we conducted the ablation study as shown in Table 2. Adding the DRR and KSFE modules separately improves overall performance, but the sensitivity of the appositional angle decreased. When only stationary chamber angle structure information is emphasized by KFSE, appositional angle sensitivity drops to 37.5%, which aligns with clinical knowledge that it's distinguishable only in the dynamic process. In contrast, when the DRR and KSFE modules are added simultaneously, all metrics are improved, particularly for the appositional ACA classification. This further validates the importance of two key video information: dynamic changes of the iris and the open-closed stationary status of ACA. Focusing on either one of them is insufficient, as it tends to boost performance by simply improving the classification of easily distinguishable open and synechial angles. The confusion matrix and the embedded feature distribution for classification are displayed in Fig. 4 (a) and (b). What we can additionally observe is that only when DRR and KFSE are used simultaneously does the feature distribution of the appositional angle is relatively distinguishable, which indicates a better classification robustness.

4   Conclusion

This paper proposes a Dual-path Video Information Aggregation Network (DVIA-Net) for classifying open, appositional, and synechial anterior chamber angles based on AS-OCT videos. We emphasize the importance of aggregating two types of video information and design DRR and KSFE modules to help capture the dynamic change of iris and stationary ACA structure status. Extensive comparison and ablation studies support our hypothesis and demonstrate the effectiveness of DVIA-Net.

Acknowledgements. This study was funded by General Program of National Natural Science Foundation of China (Grant No.82272086) and Shenzhen Medical Research Fund (Grant No. D2402014).

Disclosure of Interests. The authors have no competing interests to declare that are relevant to the content of this article.

References

1. Arnab, A., Dehghani, M., Heigold, G., Sun, C., Lucic, M., Schmid, C.: ViViT: a video vision transformer. In: IEEE/CVF International Conference on Computer Vision (ICCV), pp. 6816–6826 (2021)
2. Baig, N., Kam, K.W., Tham, C.C.: Managing primary angle closure glaucoma-the role of lens extraction in this era. Open Ophthalmol. J. **10**, 86 (2016)
3. Dosovitskiy, A.: An image is worth 16x16 words: Transformers for image recognition at scale. arXiv preprint arXiv:2010.11929 (2020)
4. Fu, H., et al.: A deep learning system for automated angle-closure detection in anterior segment optical coherence tomography images. Am. J. Ophthalmol. **203**, 37–45 (2019)
5. Fu, H., et al.: Angle-closure detection in anterior segment OCT based on multilevel deep network. IEEE Trans. Cybernet. **50**(7), 3358–3366 (2019)
6. Fu, H., et al.: Segmentation and quantification for angle-closure glaucoma assessment in anterior segment OCT. IEEE Trans. Med. Imaging **36**(9), 1930–1938 (2017)
7. Hao, H., et al.: Angle-closure assessment in anterior segment OCT images via deep learning. Med. Image Analy. **69**(101956) (2021)

8. Hao, J., et al.: Reconstruction and quantification of 3D iris surface for angle-closure glaucoma detection in anterior segment OCT. In: Medical Image Computing and Computer Assisted Intervention (MICCAI), pp. 704–714 (2020)
9. Hao, J., et al.: Hybrid variation-aware network for angle-closure assessment in AS-OCT. IEEE Trans. Med. Imaging **41**(2), 254–265 (2021)
10. Hao, L., Hu, Y., Higashita, R., JQ Yu, J., Zheng, C., Liu, J.: Multiview volume and temporal difference network for angle-closure glaucoma screening from AS-OCT videos. J. Healthcare Eng. **2022**(1), 2722608 (2022)
11. Hao, L., et al.: Dynamic analysis of iris changes and a deep learning system for automated angle-closure classification based on AS-OCT videos. Eye and Vision **9**(1), 41 (2022)
12. He, K., Zhang, X., Ren, S., Sun, J.: Deep residual learning for image recognition. In: IEEE Conference on Computer Vision and Pattern Recognition (CVPR), pp. 770–778 (2016)
13. Shang, Q., et al.: Automated iris segmentation from anterior segment OCT images with occludable angles via local phase tensor. In: Annual International Conference of the IEEE Engineering in Medicine and Biology Society (EMBC), pp. 4745–4749 (2019)
14. Shi, X., Chen, Z., Wang, H., Yeung, D.Y., Wong, W.K., Woo, W.C.: Convolutional LSTM network: A machine learning approach for precipitation nowcasting. In: Advances in Neural Information Processing Systems (NeurIPS), vol. 28 (2015)
15. Tham, Y.C., Li, X., Wong, T.Y., Quigley, H.A., Aung, T., Cheng, C.Y.: Global prevalence of glaucoma and projections of glaucoma burden through 2040: a systematic review and meta-analysis. Ophthalmology **121**(11), 2081–2090 (2014)
16. Tran, D., Bourdev, L., Fergus, R., Torresani, L., Paluri, M.: Learning spatiotemporal features with 3D convolutional networks. In: IEEE International Conference on Computer Vision (ICCV), pp. 4489–4497 (2015)
17. Xiang, L., Chan, E., Liao, J., Wong, T., Aung, T., Cheng, C.Y.: Number of people with glaucoma in Asia in 2020 and 2040: a hierarchical bayesian meta-analysis. Investigative Ophthalmol. Vis. Sci. **54**(15), 2656–2656 (2013)
18. Xu, B.Y., Chiang, M., Chaudhary, S., Kulkarni, S., Pardeshi, A.A., Varma, R.: Deep learning classifiers for automated detection of gonioscopic angle closure based on anterior segment OCT images. Am. J. Ophthalmol. **208**, 273–280 (2019)
19. Xu, Y., et al.: Anterior chamber angle classification using multiscale histograms of oriented gradients for glaucoma subtype identification. In: Annual International Conference of the IEEE Engineering in Medicine and Biology Society (EMBC), pp. 3167–3170. IEEE (2012)

BEAM: Boosting Fundus Image Enhancement via Adapted Text-to-Image Models

Ziheng Wang[1]([✉]), Pujin Cheng[2,3], and Xiaoying Tang[2]

[1] School of Artificial Intelligence, The Chinese University of Hong Kong, Shenzhen, China
`zihengwang3@link.cuhk.edu.cn`
[2] Department of Electronic and Electrical Engineering, Southern University of Science and Technology, Shenzhen, China
[3] Department of Electrical and Electronic Engineering, The University of Hong Kong, Hong Kong SAR, China

Abstract. High-quality fundus images are crucial in the diagnosis of ophthalmic diseases. However, these images in real-world settings often suffer from degradation due to motion blur, illumination irregularities, and artifacts. Existing enhancement methods that rely on paired datasets or simplified degradation models have difficulty addressing the complex degradations commonly observed in clinical realities. We state that pre-trained large-scale text-to-image models contain rich image priors to enhance fundus images to high-quality ones, and we can take low-quality images directly as input with the skip-connection maintaining structure consistency, reducing the ambiguity brought from random noise sampling while simultaneously eliminating the need for additional controlling modules. We then fine-tune the pre-trained network in a single step with a small fraction of trainable parameters to adapt it to the fundus image enhancement task, and show the superiority of BEAM through extensive experiments over other state-of-the-art approaches. Moreover, we expanded our framework to an unpaired scheme and showcased its capacity to generate a realistic paired simulation dataset. The source code and dataset are available at https://github.com/wangzh1/BEAM.

Keywords: Fundus Image Enhancement · Text-to-Image Models · Diffusion Models

1 Introduction

The quality of fundus images is crucial for the accurate diagnosis and management of various ophthalmic conditions. The ability to identify subtle signs of disease greatly relies on clear and high-quality fundus images, in turn enabling early diagnosis and more effective treatment [6]. However, obtaining such images is often challenging due to factors that degrade image quality, such as glare from

© The Author(s), under exclusive license to Springer Nature Switzerland AG 2026
H. Fang et al. (Eds.): OMIA 2025, LNCS 16209, pp. 11–20, 2026.
https://doi.org/10.1007/978-3-032-10351-2_2

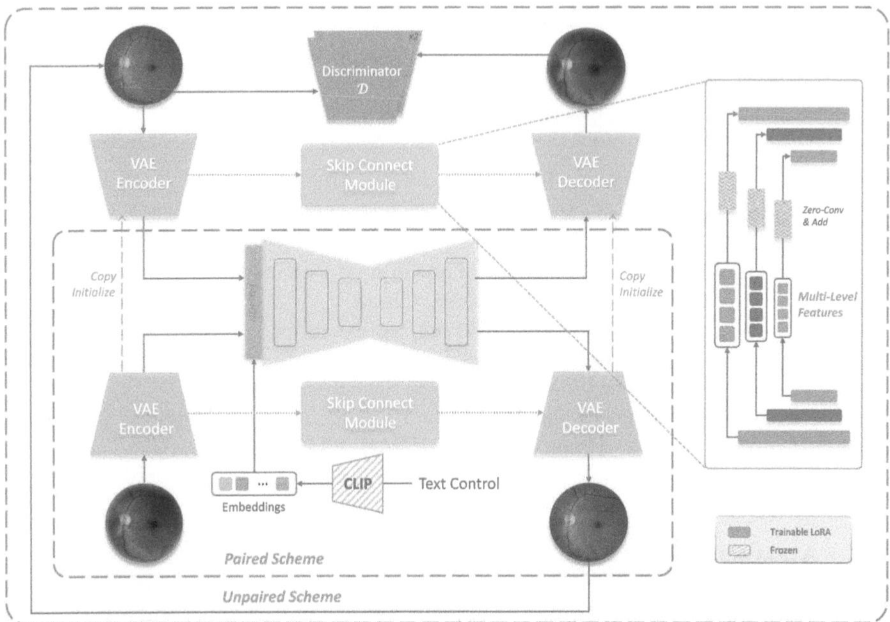

Fig. 1: **Pipeline of BEAM.** BEAM is a framework using a pre-trained latent diffusion model, VAE encoder-decoder, and text encoder for fundus image enhancement. It takes low-quality images as input, retrains with a skip connect module for detail retention, and supports unpaired training via introducing duplicated trainable VAE and adversarial training.

light sources, patient movement causing motion blur, poor illumination, and retinal artifacts. These degradations can obscure critical diagnostic information and hinder the performance of automated analysis systems.

To address these issues, traditional solutions often rely on operations in the transform domain. For instance, Cheng et al. [2] applied a structure-preserving guided filtering technique to deblur fundus images, while Cao et al. [1] removed low-frequency components in the root domain to obtain clearer results. However, these methods struggle with more complex degradations. Therefore, recent research has shifted towards learning-based enhancement approaches, focusing both on realistically simulating the degradation process to synthesize paired datasets and on effectively enhancing low-quality images. Shen et al. proposed an restoration network with an artificial degradation pipeline on frequency domain [22] to synthesize paired dataset, but it was not enough to simulate complex realistic degradation factors. Using this degradation pipeline, Liu et al. developed the Pyramid Constraint Network [14] to improve the representation of clinically significant features. Similarly, Li et al. introduced the Structure-Consistent Restoration Network [12] for cataract fundus images, grounding their approach in preserving high-frequency component consistency. Li et al. [13]

and Cheng et al. [4] introduced frequency self-supervision and importance-guided self-supervision with synthesized data supervision, respectively, to further improve the network's ability of domain adaption. However, these methods are all strongly biased by the artificial degradation simulation. Cheng et al. [3] utilized a diffusion model to learn the enhancement process, but it also needed a data-driven degradation model and was quantitatively inferior to other state-of-the-art (SOTA) methods in terms of low-level features. On the other hand, Zhao et al. [28] directly employed an unpaired training manner to enhance fundus images using Generative Adversarial Network and cycle consistency [29].

We realize that due to the significant intersections between fundus image enhancement and clinical knowledge, this challenge not only lies at a low-level processing layer, but also needs high-level features and semantic understandings. Recent development of text-to-image (T2I) models in the computer vision field [18,20] offer a promising avenue for this task. Therefore, we propose to take advantage of their rich diffusion priors to better facilitate the transfer between low-quality and high-quality fundus images. In this paper, we dedicate to adapt pre-trained T2I models to enhance fundus images. Successful applications adapting T2I diffusion for downstream tasks [23,24] introduced additional modules such as ControlNet and regularizers. While these techniques maintain the efficiency of the original latent representation, they complicate the process by duplicating network parameters, significantly increasing memory overhead. To further reduce computational cost, we replace input noise with image itself and utilize skip-connections, which have proven to be effective in preserving detailed features [19]. However, this shift requires retraining in the image space, which can be costly with hundreds or thousands of steps of fine-tuning. Leveraging recent advances in few-step T2I diffusion using distillation and adversarial training [21] and successful cases of one-step diffusion fine-tuning [23,25], we also demonstrate the effectiveness of single-step adaptation in our task. Moreover, we show that our pipeline can be easily extended to an unpaired scheme by duplicating another pair of VAE and introduce adversarial training.

The main contribution of BEAM can be summarized as follows: (1) We present a simple but effective pipeline to adapt T2I models to the task of fundus image enhancement without changing the main structure or adding additional controlling modules. (2) We demonstrate that fine-tuning a very small fraction of the parameters in a pre-trained T2I model is sufficient to outperform existing methods. (3) Through unpaired training, we use BEAM to synthesize a realistic degraded fundus image dataset and make it public.

2   Method

In this section, we detail how we adapt a pre-trained text-to-image model for fundus image enhancement. An overview of the BEAM framework is presented in Fig. 1. By adapting the structure of the pre-trained text-to-image model, our method originally supports paired training, when high-quality and low-quality image pairs are available. Additionally, we extend the framework by introducing an duplicated VAE encoder-decoder pair and discriminators for adversarial training.

2.1 BEAM Pipeline

Our approach provides a simple yet efficient solution for adapting text-to-image models to enhance fundus images. We employ a distilled version of Stable Diffusion 2.1 [21] as the backbone, retaining its core components: a frozen CLIP [17] text encoder, a VAE encoder-decoder pair, and a latent diffusion network. To maintain structural integrity, such as the preservation of blood vessels, we introduce a skip-connect module that has been proved to be effective [19] to transfer features from the VAE encoder to the decoder.

Unlike conventional diffusion methods that initialize with random noise, our pipeline directly uses the degraded image as input. This eliminates the need for additional modules such as ControlNet [26], significantly reduces the number of trainable parameters. Inspired by the success of Low-Rank Adaptation (LoRA) [9] in fine-tuning large text-to-image diffusion models for various downstream tasks [16,23,24], we also adopt LoRA to accelerate the training process. Furthermore, since the original backbone was trained using adversarial diffusion distillation with very few steps and has proven effective with a single step [21], we implement a single-step training approach, which also boosts the training efficiency. Together, these make it possible for BEAM to outperform SOTA methods with only 3M trainable parameters.

2.2 Paired Training

In the paired training scheme, BEAM is trained for an enhancement mapping $\mathcal{T} : \mathcal{X} \rightarrow \mathcal{Y}$ using pairs of high-quality and synthetically degraded fundus images.

Loss Functions. We use the Learned Perceptual Image Patch Similarity (LPIPS) loss [27] to measure perceptual differences between the enhanced and high-quality images. To preserve fine details, such as the sharpness of blood vessels, we introduce a high-frequency loss by applying a high-pass filter $\mathcal{H}$ to both the enhanced image $\hat{\mathbf{x}}$ and the ground truth $\mathbf{y}$, minimizing their L-1 difference:

$$\mathcal{L}_{\text{high-freq}} = \|\mathcal{H}(\hat{\mathbf{x}}) - \mathcal{H}(\mathbf{y})\|_1 . \tag{1}$$

To prevent over-enhancement and ensure stability when processing already high-quality images, we include an identity loss to penalize deviations from the input when enhancement is unnecessary:

$$\mathcal{L}_{\text{idt}} = \mathbb{E}_{\mathbf{y} \sim \mathcal{y}} \left[\|\mathcal{T}(\mathbf{y}) - \mathbf{y}\|_1 \right], \tag{2}$$

where $\mathcal{T}$ denotes the enhancement function. The total loss for paired training is a weighted combination of these terms:

$$\mathcal{L}_{\text{paired}} = \lambda_{\text{LPIPS}}\mathcal{L}_{\text{LPIPS}} + \lambda_{\text{high-freq}}\mathcal{L}_{\text{high-freq}} + \lambda_{\text{idt}}\mathcal{L}_{\text{idt}}. \tag{3}$$

2.3   Unpaired Training

Our unpaired training includes two domain translations $\mathcal{T}(\mathbf{x}, t_{\mathcal{Y}}) : \mathcal{X} \rightarrow \mathcal{Y}$ and $\mathcal{T}(\mathbf{y}, t_{\mathcal{X}}) : \mathcal{Y} \rightarrow \mathcal{X}$, where $t_{(.)}$ denotes the text description for the corresponding target domain.

Cycle Consistency Loss. We utilize a pixel-wise loss $\mathcal{L}_{\text{rec}}$ combining L-1 norm and LPIPS [27] between input image $\mathbf{x}$ and reconstructed $\hat{\mathbf{x}}$ from $\mathbf{y}$:

$$\mathcal{L}_{\text{rec}}(\mathbf{x}, \hat{\mathbf{x}}) = \lambda_1 \|\mathbf{x} - \hat{\mathbf{x}}\|_1 + \lambda_{\text{LPIPS}} \mathcal{L}_{\text{LPIPS}}(\mathbf{x}, \hat{\mathbf{x}}). \tag{4}$$

The cycle consistency loss can be described as:

$$\mathcal{L}_{\text{cycle}} = \mathbb{E}_{\mathbf{x} \sim \mathcal{X}} \left[\mathcal{L}_{\text{rec}} \left(\mathcal{T} \left(\mathcal{T} \left(\mathbf{x}, t_{\mathcal{Y}} \right), t_{\mathcal{X}} \right), \mathbf{x} \right) \right] \quad + \mathbb{E}_{\mathbf{y} \sim \mathcal{Y}} \left[\mathcal{L}_{\text{rec}} \left(\mathcal{T} \left(\mathcal{T} \left(\mathbf{y}, t_{\mathcal{X}} \right), t_{\mathcal{Y}} \right), \mathbf{y} \right) \right]. \tag{5}$$

Adversarial Loss. We employ adversarial losses [7], with discriminators $\mathcal{D}_{\mathcal{X}}$ and $\mathcal{D}_{\mathcal{Y}}$ using CLIP backbone [11]. The adversarial loss for domain mapping function $\mathcal{X} \rightarrow \mathcal{Y}$ can then be defined as:

$$\mathcal{L}_{\text{adv}}^{\mathcal{X} \rightarrow \mathcal{Y}} = \mathbb{E}_{\mathbf{y} \sim \mathcal{Y}} \left[\log \mathcal{D}_{\mathcal{Y}}(\mathbf{y}) \right] + \mathbb{E}_{\mathbf{x} \sim \mathcal{X}} \left[\log \left(1 - \mathcal{D}_{\mathcal{Y}} \left(\mathcal{T} \left(\mathbf{x}, t_{\mathcal{Y}} \right) \right) \right) \right]. \tag{6}$$

Identity Loss. To ensure that the model does not over-enhance or distort images unnecessarily, we incorporate an identity loss:

$$\mathcal{L}_{\text{idt}} = \mathbb{E}_y [\mathcal{L}_{\text{rec}}(\mathcal{T}(\mathbf{y}, t_{\mathcal{X}}), \mathbf{y})] + \mathbb{E}_x [\mathcal{L}_{\text{rec}}(\mathcal{T}(\mathbf{x}, t_{\mathcal{Y}}), \mathbf{x})]. \tag{7}$$

Total Loss The total loss function for BEAM is a combination of the losses with corresponding coefficient λ:

$$\mathcal{L}_{\text{unpaired}} = \mathcal{L}_{\text{cycle}} + \lambda_{\text{adv}} \mathcal{L}_{\text{adv}} + \lambda_{\text{idt}} \mathcal{L}_{\text{idt}}. \tag{8}$$

3   Experiments

3.1   Training BEAM

Dataset. We utilize the EyeQ dataset [6], which comprises 28,792 fundus images categorized into three quality grades: Good, Usable, and Reject. For paired training, we select all images labeled as "Good" to serve as our high-quality dataset and generate a corresponding low-quality image by applying synthetic degradations, including Gaussian blur, additive noise, and contrast reduction, based on the degradation model [22]. These degradation parameters are randomly sampled to mimic diverse real-world degradation scenarios. The dataset is divided into training and test sets following the original EyeQ split.

Table 1: **Comparison with SOTA supervised methods on paired dataset.** Note that BEAM-B and BEAM-S both have ∼1B parameters in total.

Method	Full-Reference Trainable Params ↓	PSNR ↑	SSIM ↑	VSD ↑	Non-Reference DRA ↑	FIQA ↑
Original	–	–	–	–	0.7236	0.1502
Degraded [22]	–	19.37	0.7794	0.7189	0.5841	–
pix2pix [10]	211M	24.28	0.7619	0.6521	0.6146	0.5093
SCRNet [12]	341M	27.84	0.8594	0.7244	0.6465	0.7364
GFENet [13]	341M	28.79	0.8759	0.7367	0.6849	0.7499
I-SECRET [4]	151M	28.22	0.8692	0.7351	0.6823	0.8025
PCENet [14]	102M	27.43	0.8471	0.7367	0.6245	0.7163
BEAM-S (ours)	3M	29.58	0.8946	**0.7824**	0.7068	0.7910
BEAM-B (ours)	133M	**30.08**	**0.8982**	**0.7824**	**0.7104**	**0.8255**

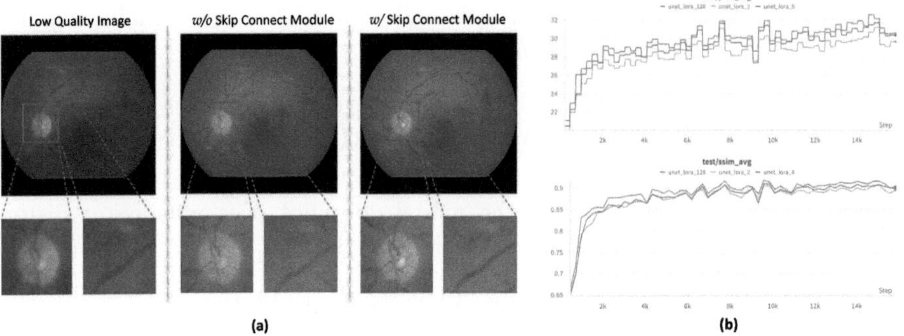

Fig. 2: (a) Performance comparison of intermediate training result with and without skip connect module. The skip connect module keeps more structure details and improve the sharpness of the enhanced vessels. (b) Quantitative comparison between different sizes of BEAM.

Implementation Details. We utilize PyTorch-Lightning [5] as the framework for training BEAM. We use the AdamW optimizer with a base learning rate of 1.5×10^{-5} and a weight decay of 1×10^{-2}. All training processes are conducted on NVIDIA A40 GPU(s). For the paired scheme, the model is trained for 30 epochs with a batch size of 4 on 4 GPUs within 15 h. For the unpaired scheme, the model is trained for 5 epochs with a batch size of 1 on a single GPU within 19 h. We use LoRA rank 2 for training BEAM-S, while rank 128 for BEAM-B. For both model, we set the LoRA rank of VAE to 4. For more details, please refer to our code release.

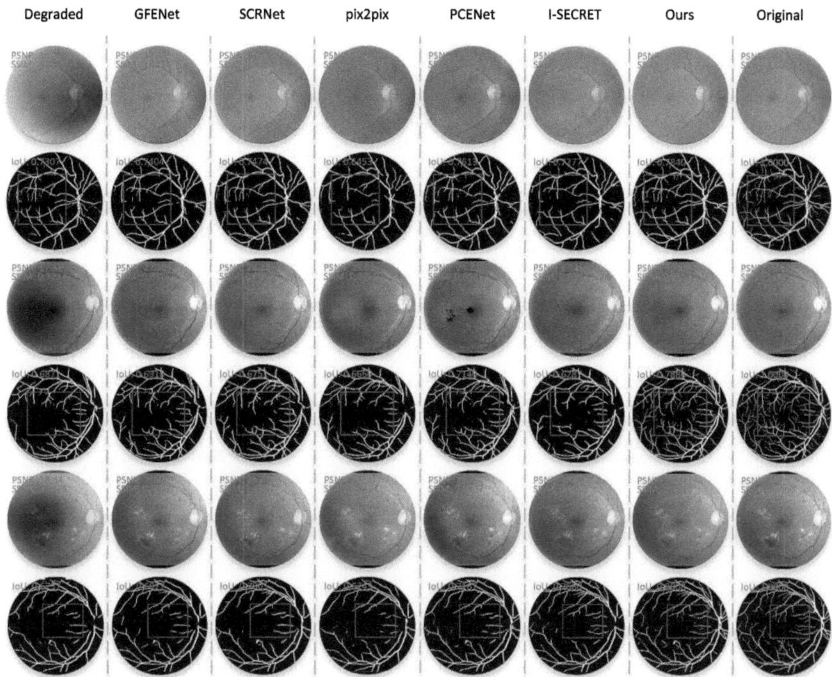

Fig. 3: Comparison of retinal fundus images before and after enhancement by different methods: GFENet [13], SCRNet [12], pix2pix [10], PCENet [14], and I-SECRET [4].

3.2   Evaluation

We first conduct ablation experiments with different sizes of BEAM to show the power of the image priors embedded in the pre-trained text-to-image model. Specifically, we train BEAM with LoRA ranks of UNet ranging from 2 to 128. Selected performance curves are as shown in Fig. 2(b). The results demonstrate that fine-tuning only a minimal number of parameters enables us to effectively adapt a pre-trained text-to-image model for our task of fundus image enhancement. Furthermore, in Fig. 2(a), we highlight the effectiveness of the skip connect module in preserving detailed structures.

Paired Evaluation. For full-reference evaluation, we conduct quantitative analysis on the test set mentioned in Sect. 3.1, against SOTA approaches requiring paired datasets (e.g., pix2pix [10], SCRNet [12], GFENet [13], I-SECRET [4], PCENet [14]). We employ PSNR and SSIM image quality metrics [8]. Furthermore, we segment images with a segmentation network [15] and use Vessel Segmentation Dice (VSD) to assess the enhancement of the structural vascular details. To quantify clinically meaningful enhancement effects, we measure Diabetic Retinopathy detection Accuracy (DRA) using the DR detection method

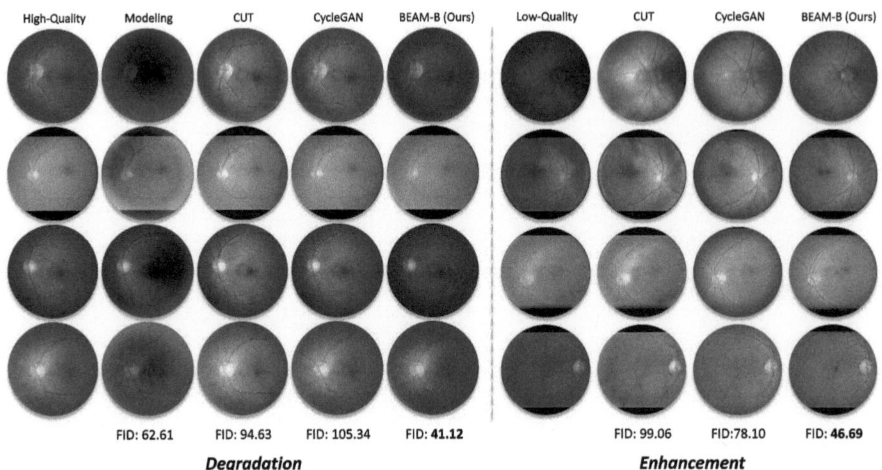

Fig. 4: **Evaluation of unpaired training.** Left: Comparison of degradation results; Right: Comparison of enhancement results.

stated in [3]. Figure 3 shows sample comparisons between other SOTA methods. Our BEAM is particularly superior to other methods in terms of structural details and achieves better metric results.

For non-reference evaluation, we use images labeled as "Usable" from the EyeQ test set and apply MCF-Net [6] to evaluate quality. The proportion of enhanced images assessed as "Good" was defined as the Fundus Image Quality Assessment Score (FIQA).

Unpaired Evaluation. Generating realistic low-quality images through degradation is also crucial for creating paired datasets to train robust enhancement models. So, we evaluate BEAM on both degradation and enhancement tasks. For a fair comparison, we select unpaired domain translation methods, CycleGAN [29] and CUT [30]. Figure 4 demonstrates BEAM's superiority in both tasks. Due to complex degradation, CUT struggles to deblur low-quality images, while CycleGAN fails to preserve vessel structure consistency. In contrast, BEAM effectively removes low-level degradation while retaining vessel details. We also compare BEAM with a mathematical modeling method [22] in degradation. Qualitative results reveal that BEAM generates the most realistic outcomes in both degradation and enhancement, while achieving the lowest FID score.

4 Conclusion

This paper introduces BEAM, a framework adapting pre-trained text-to-image models for fundus image enhancement. The proposed BEAM directly takes image as input without introducing random noise or adding controlling branches, thus allowing for fine-tuning in a single step with minimal parameters while outperforming SOTA methods. Furthermore, through extending BEAM to unpaired training, it performs realistic transformation between high-quality and low-quality fundus images, also beneficial for creating paired datasets.

Acknowledgments. This work was supported in part by the HPC Platform of ShanghaiTech University.

References

1. Cao, L., Li, H., Zhang, Y.: Retinal image enhancement using low-pass filtering and α-rooting. Signal Process. **170**, 107445 (2020)
2. Cheng, J., Li, Z., Gu, Z., Fu, H., Wong, D.W.K., Liu, J.: Structure-preserving guided retinal image filtering and its application for optic disk analysis. IEEE Trans. Med. Imaging **37**(11), 2536–2546 (2018)
3. Cheng, P., Lin, L., Huang, Y., He, H., Luo, W., Tang, X.: Learning Enhancement From Degradation: A Diffusion Model For Fundus Image Enhancement (Mar 2023). https://doi.org/10.48550/arXiv.2303.04603
4. Cheng, P., Lin, L., Huang, Y., Lyu, J., Tang, X.: I-SECRET: importance-guided fundus image enhancement via semi-supervised contrastive constraining. In: de Bruijne, M., et al. (eds.) MICCAI 2021. LNCS, vol. 12908, pp. 87–96. Springer, Cham (2021). https://doi.org/10.1007/978-3-030-87237-3_9
5. Falcon, W.: ff. The PyTorch Lightning team: PyTorch Lightning **2**, 1–2 (2019). https://doi.org/10.5281/zenodo.3828935, https://github.com/Lightning-AI/lightning
6. Fu, H., et al.: Evaluation of retinal image quality assessment networks in different color-spaces. In: Shen, D., et al. (eds.) Medical Image Computing and Computer Assisted Intervention - MICCAI 2019, pp. 48–56. Springer International Publishing, Cham (2019)
7. Goodfellow, I., et al.: Generative adversarial nets. In: Ghahramani, Z., Welling, M., Cortes, C., Lawrence, N., Weinberger, K. (eds.) Advances in Neural Information Processing Systems, vol. 27. Curran Associates, Inc. (2014)
8. Hore, A., Ziou, D.: Image quality metrics: PSNR vs. SSIM. In: 2010 20th International Conference on Pattern Recognition, pp. 2366–2369. IEEE, Istanbul, Turkey (Aug 2010). https://doi.org/10.1109/ICPR.2010.579
9. Hu, E.J., et al.: LoRA: low-Rank Adaptation of Large Language Models (Oct 2021). https://doi.org/10.48550/arXiv.2106.09685
10. Isola, P., Zhu, J.Y., Zhou, T., Efros, A.A.: Image-to-image translation with conditional adversarial networks. In:2017 IEEE Conference on Computer Vision and Pattern Recognition (CVPR) (2017)
11. Kumari, N., Zhang, R., Shechtman, E., Zhu, J.Y.: Ensembling off-the-shelf models for gan training. In: Proceedings of the IEEE/CVF Conference on Computer Vision and Pattern Recognition (CVPR) (June 2022)
12. Li, H., et al.: Structure-consistent restoration network for cataract fundus image enhancement (2022). https://arxiv.org/abs/2206.04684
13. Li, H., et al.: A generic fundus image enhancement network boosted by frequency self-supervised representation learning. arXiv preprint arXiv:2309.00885 (2023)

14. Liu, H., et al.: Degradation-invariant enhancement of fundus images via pyramid constraint network. In: International Conference on Medical Image Computing and Computer-Assisted Intervention. pp. 507–516. Springer (2022). https://doi.org/10.1007/978-3-031-16434-7_49

15. Liu, W., et al.: Full-resolution network and dual-threshold iteration for retinal vessel and coronary angiograph segmentation. IEEE J. Biomed. Health Inform. **26**(9), 4623–4634 (2022). https://doi.org/10.1109/JBHI.2022.3188710

16. Parmar, G., Park, T., Narasimhan, S., Zhu, J.Y.: One-Step Image Translation with Text-to-Image Models (Mar 2024). https://doi.org/10.48550/arXiv.2403.12036

17. Radford, A., et al.: Learning transferable visual models from natural language supervision (2021). https://arxiv.org/abs/2103.00020

18. Rombach, R., Blattmann, A., Lorenz, D., Esser, P., Ommer, B.: High-resolution image synthesis with latent diffusion models (2021)

19. Ronneberger, O., Fischer, P., Brox, T.: U-net: Convolutional networks for biomedical image segmentation (2015). https://arxiv.org/abs/1505.04597

20. Saharia, C., et al.: Photorealistic text-to-image diffusion models with deep language understanding (2022). https://arxiv.org/abs/2205.11487

21. Sauer, A., Lorenz, D., Blattmann, A., Rombach, R.: Adversarial diffusion distillation. In: Leonardis, A., Ricci, E., Roth, S., Russakovsky, O., Sattler, T., Varol, G. (eds.) Computer Vision – ECCV 2024, vol. 15144, pp. 87–103. Springer Nature Switzerland, Cham (2025). https://doi.org/10.1007/978-3-031-73016-0_6

22. Shen, Z., Fu, H., Shen, J., Shao, L.: Modeling and enhancing low-quality retinal fundus images. IEEE Trans. Med. Imaging **40**(3), 996–1006 (2021). https://doi.org/10.1109/TMI.2020.3043495

23. Wu, R., Sun, L., Ma, Z., Zhang, L.: One-Step Effective Diffusion Network for Real-World Image Super-Resolution (Oct 2024). https://doi.org/10.48550/arXiv.2406.08177

24. Wu, R., Yang, T., Sun, L., Zhang, Z., Li, S., Zhang, L.: SeeSR: towards Semantics-Aware Real-World Image Super-Resolution (Jun 2024). https://doi.org/10.48550/arXiv.2311.16518

25. Yin, T., et al.: One-step diffusion with distribution matching distillation. In: CVPR (2024)

26. Zhang, L., Rao, A., Agrawala, M.: Adding Conditional Control to Text-to-Image Diffusion Models (Nov 2023). https://doi.org/10.48550/arXiv.2302.05543

27. Zhang, R., Isola, P., Efros, A.A., Shechtman, E., Wang, O.: The unreasonable effectiveness of deep features as a perceptual metric. In: CVPR (2018)

28. Zhao, H., Yang, B., Cao, L., Li, H.: Data-driven enhancement of blurry retinal images via generative adversarial networks. In: Shen, D., et al. (eds.) Medical Image Computing and Computer Assisted Intervention – MICCAI 2019, vol. 11764, pp. 75–83. Springer International Publishing, Cham (2019). https://doi.org/10.1007/978-3-030-32239-7_9

29. Zhu, J., Park, T., Isola, P., Efros, A.A.: Unpaired image-to-image translation using cycle-consistent adversarial networks. CoRR abs/ arXiv: 1703.10593 (2017). http://arxiv.org/abs/1703.10593

30. Zhu, J.Y., Park, T., Isola, P., Efros, A.A.: Unpaired image-to-image translation using cycle-consistent adversarial networks (2020). https://arxiv.org/abs/1703.10593

Multimodal Fusion Framework Using Contrastive Learning for Exposure Keratopathy

Gyutae Oh[1], Yeokyoung Won[2,3], Donghui Lim[2,3,4], and Jitae Shin[1]($\boxtimes$)

[1] Department of Electrical and Computer Engineering, Sungkyunkwan University, Suwon 16419, Republic of Korea
`alswo740012@g.skku.edu, jtshin@skku.edu`
[2] SNU Eye Clinic, Seoul 06035, Republic of Korea
`wyk900105@hanmail.net`
[3] Department of Ophthalmology, Samsung Medical Center, Sungkyunkwan University School of Medicine, Seoul 06351, Republic of Korea
[4] Samsung Advanced Institute for Health Sciences and Technology, Sungkyunkwan University, Seoul 03063, Republic of Korea

Abstract. In this study, we propose a two-stage multimodal fusion learning framework for the automated grading of exposure keratopathy using four complementary imaging modalities: broad-beam, slit-beam, scatter, and blue-light, collected directly at a tertiary care center. In stage 1 (Grade Based Learning&Beam Based Learning), a backbone network is trained to capture and fuse the unique anatomical and pathological features inherent to each modality. In stage 2 (Dynamic Feature Fusion), we leverage the stage 1 pretrained backbone to train a modality agnostic classifier that, given only a single broad-beam image at inference time, implicitly exploits the rich multispectral information of the other three modalities. Experimental results demonstrate that our method achieves an average improvement of over 16% in both F1 score and overall accuracy (ACC) compared to single modality baselines. Ablation studies confirm the significant contribution of each component. By requiring only a single modality at inference, this framework is expected to maintain high diagnostic performance in real-world clinical settings while substantially reducing imaging requirements and patient burden. The code is publicly available at https://github.com/GYUGYUT/Multimodal-Fusion-Framework-Using-Contrastive-Learning-for-Exposure-Keratopathy.

Keywords: Exposure keratopathy · Multimodal Fusion · Contrastive Learning

---

G. Oh and Y. Won—These authors contributed equally as co-first authors.
D. Lim and J. Shin—These authors jointly supervised this work as co-corresponding authors.

H. Fang et al. (Eds.): OMIA 2025, LNCS 16209, pp. 21–31, 2026.
https://doi.org/10.1007/978-3-032-10351-2_3

1   Introduction

Exposure keratopathy is characterized by inflammation and damage to the cornea resulting from prolonged exposure of the ocular surface [16,18]. It commonly occurs due to incomplete eye closure, as seen in conditions such as facial nerve palsy and eyelid malpositions, or reduced blink reflex [16,18]. Elderly and critically ill patients, especially those in intensive care units (ICUs), are at significantly higher risk, due to factors such as compromised tear production, reduced blinking, lagophthalmos, and changes in vascular permeability, all of which exacerbate corneal exposure [16,23,25,27]. Studies have reported that 20~42% of ICU patients, and up to 57% of ventilated patients, experience exposure keratopathy [16,18,23]. Early diagnosis and prompt treatment of exposure keratopathy are essential, as the condition can often be effectively managed with simple interventions such as artificial tears or lubricating ointments [17]. However, in reality, many elderly and ICU patients face limited access to ophthalmologic care, making timely detection and management particularly challenging [19,29]. For example, in long-term care facilities, ophthalmologists are often unavailable onsite, and patients may need to be transferred to external facilities for specialized evaluation. This logistic barrier frequently delays diagnosis and treatment, leading to disease progression and vision-threatening complications such as persistent epithelial defects, corneal opacification, perforation, or even endophthalmitis [3]. In the diagnosis of corneal diseases, including exposure keratopathy, accurate assessment of lesion characteristics, including severity, location, depth, and the presence of infiltration requires dynamic examination using various illumination techniques under a slit-beam microscope. Thus, unlike fundus images, which typically involve a single, standardized imaging modality, anterior segment images inherently comprise multiple modalities that vary according to the slit-beam illumination methods: broad-beam [30], slit-beam [5], scatter [7], and blue-light [1] images. Accordingly, artificial intelligence (AI) diagnostic models for retinal diseases, such as those by Ebrahimi et al. [8] and Pao et al. [26], are based on uniform fundus images. In contrast, the diagnosis of corneal diseases demand a more flexible imaging approach that integrates diverse modalities to capture the full spectrum of pathological features. Nevertheless, most existing AI studies on corneal diseases have utilized only a single imaging modality. For instance, Li et al. [20] and Hung et al. [12] proposed infectious keratitis classification models based solely on broad-beam images. In parallel, there is growing interest in multimodal approaches in medial AI, where diagnostic models integrate several types of data to enhance diagnostic performance [9,13,32]. For example, Ma et al. [21] significantly improved the accuracy of early biliary atresia diagnosis by combining ultrasound images with clinical data, and Kaczmarczyk et al. [14] demonstrated that a multimodal AI model fusing images and clinical data outperforms single-modal models. Hou et al. [11] reported similar findings. However, prior studies have predominantly focused on combining text-based clinical information (e.g., electronic medical records) with a single imaging modality or with large language models, offering limited examples of leveraging the unique characteristics of the diverse imaging actually used in clinical settings [2,10].

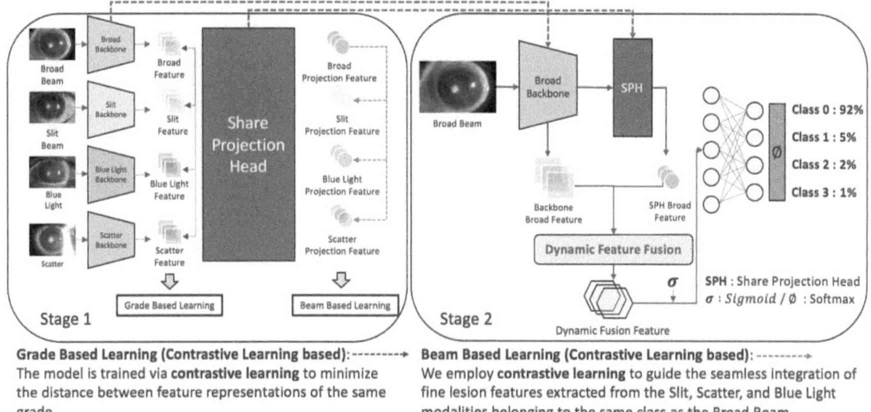

Grade Based Learning (Contrastive Learning based): ┄┄┄→
The model is trained via **contrastive learning** to minimize the distance between feature representations of the same grade.

Beam Based Learning (Contrastive Learning based): ┄┄┄→
We employ **contrastive learning** to guide the seamless integration of fine lesion features extracted from the Slit, Scatter, and Blue Light modalities belonging to the same class as the Broad Beam.

Fig. 1. This figure illustrates the overall architecture, showing the general workflow and example images for the broad-beam, slit-beam, blue-light, and scatter modalities. However, because the data used in this experiment are strictly prohibited from external distribution, we obtained prior permission from the first and corresponding authors to use similar images from [31] (Color figure online) (CC BY 4.0) as alternatives.

Therefore, we aimed to propose a two-stage AI framework for the diagnosis and severity prediction of exposure keratopathy based on four types of anterior segment images. In the first stage, we employ a contrastive learning-based approach to train the backbone network to effectively learn each modality specific features, enabling the detection of early lesion signs that may not be visible with a single modality alone [6,28]. However, in medically underserved settings, acquiring all four modalities is often impractical due to limitations in time, cost, and equipment availability. To address this, the second stage of our framework introduces a classifier trained to use only a single imaging modality broad-beam image, which represents the most common format captured by standard cameras or smartphones at inference time, while implicitly leveraging the information learned from the other modalities during training. To our knowledge, this is the first work in exposure keratopathy to combine multimodal image fusion with single modality based classification.

2   Method

The method proposed in this paper comprises two sequential training stages. The overall training process is illustrated in Fig. 1. In the first stage, we employ two contrastive learning techniques (Grade Based Learning and Beam Based Learning) to ensure that the broad-beam features corresponding to the same grade naturally incorporate the fine lesion characteristics extracted from the slit-beam, scatter, and blue-light modalities of the same grade. To maximize the efficacy of contrastive learning, the grade composition within each modality's mini-batch is configured to match the broad-beam mini-batch in both quantity and positional arrangement. In the second stage, we introduce a Dynamic Feature Fusion strategy that adaptively integrates the features extracted by the backbone with those produced by a shared projection head. This fusion mechanism is designed to allow complementary interactions between heterogeneous feature representations, thereby enhancing the overall performance of the downstream classifier.

Grade Based Learning(GBL, Stage 1): As shown in Fig. 1, we define four imaging modalities broad-beam (b), slit-beam (s), blue-light (bl), and scatter (sc) as $\mathcal{M} = \{b, s, bl, sc\}$, $\mathcal{M} \subset \mathbb{R}^{H \times W}$. For any modality $m \in \mathcal{M}$, let I_m denote the input image of modality m, and B_m denote the modality specific backbone. The feature extracted through the backbone is expressed as $F_m = B_m(I_m) \in \mathbb{R}^{C \times H \times W}$. In this study, we partially modify the SupCon loss [15] by defining positive pairs as samples from different modalities sharing the same grade label as the broad-beam grade and training them to be close in the embedding space. The embeddings $\mathbf{F}_{b,i}, \mathbf{F}_{M,i} \in \mathbb{R}^{H \times W}$ obtained from two modalities are flattened and unit normalized to form $\mathbf{f}_{b,i}, \mathbf{f}_{M,i} \in \mathbb{R}^D$, and a loss is defined to reduce the distance between samples with the same grade label as follows: Here, N denotes the total number of normalized embedding vectors, i indexes the anchor embedding vector, j indexes positive candidates sharing the same grade as anchor i, and k indexes all embedding vectors compared against anchor i, including both positive and negative samples. Additionally, the embedding vector f_b is fixed as the anchor. $\tau > 0$ is the temperature parameter (set to 0.5), and the indicator function $\mathbb{I}[y_i = y_j] = \begin{cases} 1, & \text{if } y_i = y_j \\ 0, & \text{otherwise} \end{cases}$ is used. y is labels. By maximizing the exponentiated inner product between embeddings of the same grade, the distances between embeddings within each grade are effectively reduced. We refer to this as Grade Based Learning.

$$\mathcal{L}_{GBL(f_b, f_m)} = -\frac{1}{N} \sum_{i=1}^{N} \frac{\sum_{j=1}^{N} \mathbb{I}[y_{b,i} = y_j] \exp\left(\mathbf{f}_{b,i}^{\top} \mathbf{f}_j / \tau\right)}{\sum_{k=1}^{N} \exp\left(\mathbf{f}_{b,i}^{\top} \mathbf{f}_k / \tau\right)}, \tag{1}$$

Beam Based Learning (BBL, Stage 1): This section explains the method by which broad-beam features of the same grade obtained in Stage 1 implicitly reflect the fine lesion characteristics extracted from the slit-beam, scatter, and blue-light modalities of the same grade. The Shared Projection Head (SPH) used for Feature Embedding Projection follows [4], where a nonlinear projection layer is added after the Backbone output. This separates the Backbone representation from the contrastive loss space, encouraging the Backbone to learn more generalizable features. The SPH is shared across all B_m, and after passing through the SPH, the projection is expressed as $P_m = \text{SPH}(F_m) \in \mathbb{R}^{B \times d}$, where d is the projection dimension and B is the batch size, both of which

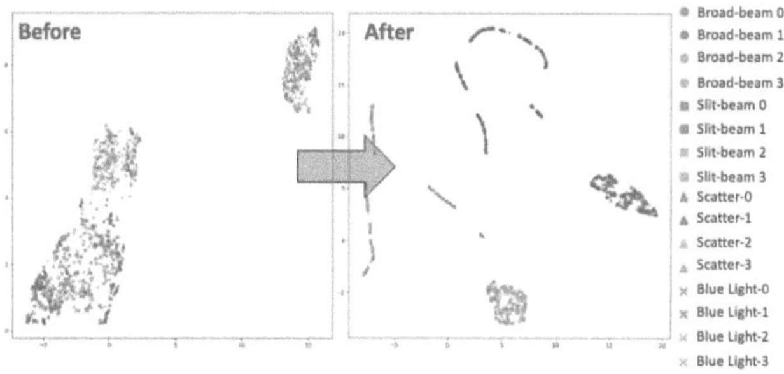

Fig. 2. This figure uses UMAP [24] to visualize the features before and after training with our proposed method for each independently trained backbone, grouped by modality and grade. Detailed information for each modality and grade is shown on the right side of the figure. Identical colors represent the same grade, and identical shapes represent the same modality.

are configurable. Additionally, we partially modify the NT-Xent loss from [4] to enable P_b to implicitly learn the fine lesion features of other P_m. Applying L_2 normalization to both P_b and P_m, we generate unit vectors $z_b, z_m \in \mathbb{R}^{B \times d}$, which are stacked to form a matrix $R \in \mathbb{R}^{2B \times d}$. The cosine similarity matrix is then computed by $S = RR^\top \in \mathbb{R}^{2B \times 2B}$. A temperature parameter τ is applied to S. Since we need to compare positives and negatives, self similarity entries are masked to prevent interference during training. For indices, if $i \leq B$, the positive sample index is defined as $i^+ = i + B$, and if $i > B$, $i^+ = i - B$. The positive similarity is $s_i^+ = S_{i,i^+}$, and the negative similarity is $s_{ij}^- = S_{i,j}$, $j = 1,\ldots,2B$, $j \neq i$, $j \neq i^+$. The general form of the loss function is as follows:

$$\mathcal{L}_{BBL}(P_b, P_m) = \frac{1}{2B} \sum_{i=1}^{2B} \left[-\log \frac{\exp(s_i^+)}{\sum_{\substack{j=1 \\ j \neq i}}^{2B} \exp(S_{i,j})} \right]. \tag{2}$$

However, when performing Beam Based Learning, unlike the conventional NT-Xent method, the model is encouraged solely to generate feature vectors where the broad-beam modality is similar to other modalities without considering grade labels. This increases the likelihood that the model will fail to classify grades correctly. Therefore, to mitigate this issue, Grad Based Learning, which clusters samples of the same grade, is conducted beforehand. Consequently, the overall loss used in stage 1 can be defined as follows, where λ controls the influence of Beam Based Learning:

$$\mathcal{L}_{Stage1} = \sum_{m \in \{s, bl, sc\}} \mathcal{L}_{GBL}(f_b, f_m) + \lambda \sum_{m \in \{s, bl, sc\}} \mathcal{L}_{BBL}(P_b, P_m). \tag{3}$$

Dynamic Feature Fusion(Stage 2): Stage 2 introduces the method for training the classifier. We use only the B_b and SPH models learned in stage 1 and discard the other components. Accordingly, the training utilizes only data from the broad-beam modality. Through Grade Based Learning, we trained F_b to generate similar embedding vectors when it shares the same grade with F_s, F_{bl}, F_{sc}. Also, via Beam Based Learning, P_b was encouraged to have a distribution similar to P_s, P_{bl}, P_{sc}. This enables B_b to have robust characteristics for grade classification, and P_b, even when using only broad-beam as input, to generate features implicitly reflecting fine lesion characteristics from the slit-beam, scatter, and blue-light modalities. Therefore, to effectively utilize these two characteristics, we propose Dynamic Feature Fusion. First, since $f_b \in \mathbb{R}^D$ and $P_b \in \mathbb{R}^d$, we transform both embeddings to a common dimension D' via a simple MLP. The transformed embeddings are expressed as $h_1, h_2 \in \mathbb{R}^{D'}$ where D' is a tunable dimension. Next, the concatenated vector of h_1 and h_2 is passed through a sigmoid function to compute the weight α, and the features are finally fused as follows: where α is a scalar weight applied to each embedding vector.

$$h_{\text{fused}} = \alpha \cdot h_1 + (1 - \alpha) \cdot h_2 \tag{4}$$

Dynamic Feature Fusion is not simply an averaging of h_1 and h_2, but a method that dynamically adjusts the contribution of each feature through a learnable parameter α. This allows the model to autonomously assess the importance of the input features and combine them effectively. The extracted h_{fused} is first passed through a sigmoid activation(σ), and the resulting value is then used as the input to the final classifier.

Table 1. Train/Val/Test Data Distribution for Four Imaging Modalities

Split	Photo 1 (Broad-beam)					Photo 2 (Slit-beam)					Photo 3 (Blue-light)					Photo 4 (Scatter)				
	Total	0	1	2	3	Total	0	1	2	3	Total	0	1	2	3	Total	0	1	2	3
train	346	83	93	88	82	1035	149	398	238	250	603	76	256	184	87	552	121	212	142	77
val	43	10	12	11	10	129	19	50	29	31	75	9	32	23	11	69	15	26	18	10
test	44	11	12	11	10	130	18	50	30	32	76	10	32	23	11	69	15	27	18	9

3 Experiments

3.1 Experiment Data Collection and Setting

The study was approved by the Institutional Review Board (IRB) of the Samsung Medical Center (IRB no. 2024-12-004). This study retrospectively collected data from 61 patients diagnosed with and treated for exposure keratopathy at the department of ophthalmology, Samsung Medical Center, between April 2008 and February 2025. All patients had multiple follow-up visits over the course

Table 2. Comparison of Individual and Combined Training Results for broad-beam, slit-beam, scatter, and blue-light Using Supervised Learning and Our Method.

Train_Method	Train_Data	Accuracy	Specificity	Sensitivity	F1 Score
Supervised	Broad-beam	0.7045	0.9008	0.7015	0.7049
Supervised	Slit-beam	0.6692	0.8787	0.6686	0.6510
Supervised	Blue-light	0.6447	0.8758	0.6407	0.6368
Supervised	Scatter	0.6957	0.8900	0.6685	0.6729
Supervised	Total	0.6865	0.8880	0.6783	0.6789
Ours	**Stage 1:Total/Stage2:Broad**	**0.8409**	**0.9462**	**0.8382**	**0.8379**

of their illness, during which various types of anterior segment images were obtained. Images were captured using the SL-D7 (Topcon Healthcare Solutions, Inc.) and D850 (Nikon, Inc.) cameras. Each image was annotated by two ophthalmology specialists according to the severity of exposure keratopathy, and the labels were categorized into four grades, which were used for model training. : Grade 0 (Normal) - no fluorescein staining with intact corneal surface; Grade 1 (Mild) - punctate epithelial erosions; Grade 2 (Moderate) - epithelial defects without stromal involvement; and Grade 3 (Severe) - corneal ulceration with stromal involvement or melting [22]. For normal data, the fellow eyes of patients diagnosed with exposure keratopathy, that were confirmed to have no abnormal findings upon examination, were included in the dataset. The entire collected dataset was split into training, validation, and test sets in an 8:1:1 ratio. The number of samples in each split is summarized in Table 1. For experimental consistency, all experiments were conducted under the following settings: image size of 224×224, GPU V100, batch size of 16, learning rate of 0.0001, early stopping patience of 10, embedding dimensions D, d, $D' = 256$, weighting parameter λ = 0.1, temperature parameter $\tau = 0.5$, DenseNet-121 as the backbone network, Adam optimizer, ReduceLROnPlateau learning rate scheduler, and PyTorch version 2.4.1+cu118. Additionally, evaluations were performed every 100 iterations.

3.2   Experiment Results

This section demonstrates that the proposed method more effectively integrates various image modalities compared to other approaches, leading to superior results. All experimental settings, including backbone architectures and hyperparameters, strictly followed the configurations described in Sect. 3.1 to ensure a fair comparison. The results of training on each single modality individually and the combined training on all four modalities are presented in Table 2. The baseline supervised training used for the comparative experiments in Table 2 was conducted using the Cross-Entropy loss. These results show that training with individual modalities generally yields suboptimal performance, and surprisingly, the combined training using all modalities (Total experiment), despite the substantially increased data volume, fails to achieve meaningful performance improvements. This suggests that conventional supervised learning alone is insufficient to effectively capture the complex lesion characteristics present across multiple image modalities. In contrast, the proposed method achieved an average improvement of over 16% in accuracy and an average improvement of 13% across other evaluation metrics. Notably, while most modalities exhibit F1-scores in the range of 60 to 70, the proposed method demonstrates superior performance, exceeding 83, strongly validating the necessity and effectiveness of integrated learning across multiple image modalities. Furthermore, despite the data imbalance evident in Table 1, the proposed method achieved outstanding training results. As shown in Fig. 2, the proposed approach not only effectively learns the complex lesion characteristics across multiple image modalities but also enables clear separation between severity grades.

Table 3. Ablation Study: Performance Evaluation by Removing Grade Based Learning (GBL), Beam Based Learning (BBL), and Dynamic Feature Fusion (DFF).

Method			Metrics			
GBL	BBL	DFF	Accuracy	Specificity	Sensitivity	F1 Score
✓			0.7500	0.9154	0.7492	0.7563
	✓		0.7727	0.9235	0.7700	0.7710
✓		✓	0.7727	0.9232	0.7678	0.7685
	✓	✓	0.7954	0.9315	0.7969	0.7958
✓	✓		0.6590	0.8858	0.6640	0.6634
✓	✓	✓	**0.8409**	**0.9462**	**0.8382**	**0.8167**

3.3   Ablation Study

We evaluated the impact of our proposed techniques on performance. All experiments were conducted under the same hyperparameter settings specified in Sect. 3.1. In experiments without dynamic feature fusion, the features extracted by the SPH module were fed into the final layer; for a fair comparison, we also evaluated the results of applying the GBL and BBL modules individually after SPH. In Table 3, checkmarks (✓) in the "Method" column indicate which modules were used in each experiment. The ablation studies showed that performance was maximally enhanced when all modules were used together, whereas individual application prevented effective feature fusion, yielding only marginal gains or even degraded performance. These results confirm that the combined use of our proposed techniques produces the optimal outcome.

4   Conclusion

This study addresses not only multimodal research but also the integration of multiple imaging modalities in a manner that closely reflects real-world diagnostic workflows. The proposed framework jointly learns complex features from multiple imaging modalities in stage 1, followed by the application of Dynamic Feature Fusion in stage 2 to effectively integrate these diverse representations. Remarkably, our method achieves an accuracy exceeding 84.09%, significantly outperforming existing approaches. Furthermore, it demonstrates that even in the absence of all imaging modalities, accurate diagnosis can still be achieved using only a single broad-beam image. Comprehensive ablation studies further validate that the strategic combination of the proposed components leads to substantial performance gains. In conclusion, this study presents a practical and efficient framework for the rapid and accurate diagnosis of exposure keratopathy in clinical settings. The proposed method requires only a single-modal input at inference yet achieves superior classification performance compared to existing approaches, enabling early diagnosis that minimizes corneal damage and facilitates timely treatment.

Acknowledgment. This work was supported by SMC-SKKU Future Convergence Research Program Grant and by the BK21 FOUR Project.

Disclosure of Interests. The authors have no competing interests to declare that are relevant to the content of this article.

References

1. Bandamwar, K.L., Papas, E.B., Garrett, Q.: Fluorescein staining and physiological state of corneal epithelial cells. Cont. Lens Anterior Eye **37**(3), 213–223 (2014)
2. Bhattacharya, S., Prusty, S., Pande, S.P., Gulhane, M., Lavate, S.H., Rakesh, N., Veerasamy, S.: Integration of multimodal imaging data with machine learning for improved diagnosis and prognosis in neuroimaging. Front. Hum. Neurosci. **19**, 1552178 (2025)
3. Bird, B., Dingley, S., Stawicki, S.P., Wojda, T.R.: Exposure keratopathy in the intensive care unit: Do not neglect the unseen. In: Vignettes in Patient Safety-Volume 2. IntechOpen (2018)
4. Chen, T., Kornblith, S., Norouzi, M., Hinton, G.: A simple framework for contrastive learning of visual representations. In: International Conference on Machine Learning, pp. 1597–1607. PmLR (2020)
5. Clover, J.: Slit-lamp biomicroscopy. Cornea **37**, S5–S6 (2018)
6. Curiel, L., Chopra, R., Hynynen, K.: Progress in multimodality imaging: truly simultaneous ultrasound and magnetic resonance imaging. IEEE Trans. Med. Imaging **26**(12), 1740–1746 (2007)
7. Denion, E., Béraud, G., Marshall, M.L., Denion, G., Lux, A.L.: Sclerotic scatter. J. Fr. Ophtalmol. **41**(1), 62–77 (2018)
8. Ebrahimi, B., et al.: Assessing spectral effectiveness in color fundus photography for deep learning classification of retinopathy of prematurity. J. Biomed. Opt. **29**(7), 076001–076001 (2024)
9. Fukuzawa, F., et al.: Importance of patient history in artificial intelligence-assisted medical diagnosis: comparison study. JMIR Med. Educ. **10**, e52674 (2024)
10. Hegselmann, S., et al.: Large language models are powerful electronic health record encoders. arXiv preprint arXiv:2502.17403 (2025)

11. Hou, C., Huang, T., Hu, K., Ye, Z., Guo, J., Zhou, H.: Artificial intelligence-assisted multimodal imaging for the clinical applications of breast cancer: a bibliometric analysis. Dis. Oncol. **16**(1), 537 (2025)
12. Hung, N., et al.: Using slit-lamp images for deep learning-based identification of bacterial and fungal keratitis: model development and validation with different convolutional neural networks. Diagnostics **11**(7), 1246 (2021)
13. Ji, H., Kim, S., Sunwoo, L., Jang, S., Lee, H.Y., Yoo, S., et al.: Integrating clinical data and medical imaging in lung cancer: feasibility study using the observational medical outcomes partnership common data model extension. JMIR Med. Inform. **12**(1), e59187 (2024)
14. Kaczmarczyk, R., Wilhelm, T.I., Martin, R., Roos, J.: Evaluating multimodal ai in medical diagnostics. npj Digital Med. **7**(1), 205 (2024)
15. Khosla, P.: Supervised contrastive learning. Adv. Neural. Inf. Process. Syst. **33**, 18661–18673 (2020)
16. Kousha, O., Kousha, Z., Paddle, J.: Exposure keratopathy: Incidence, risk factors and impact of protocolised care on exposure keratopathy in critically ill adults. J. Crit. Care **44**, 413–418 (2018)
17. Kousha, O., Kousha, Z., Paddle, J.: Incidence, risk factors and impact of protocolised care on exposure keratopathy in critically ill adults: a two-phase prospective cohort study. Crit. Care **22**, 1–8 (2018)
18. Kuruvilla, S., et al.: Incidence and risk factor evaluation of exposure keratopathy in critically ill patients: a cohort study. J. Crit. Care **30**(2), 400–404 (2015)
19. Labreche, T., Stolee, P., McLeod, J.: An optometrist-led eye care program for older residents of retirement homes and long-term care facilities. Canadian Geriatrics J. CGJ **14**(1), 8 (2011)
20. Li, Z., et al.: Deep learning for multi-type infectious keratitis diagnosis: a nationwide, cross-sectional, multicenter study. NPJ Digital Med. **7**(1), 181 (2024)
21. Ma, Y., et al.: Development of an artificial intelligence-based multimodal diagnostic system for early detection of biliary atresia. BMC Med. **23**(1), 127 (2025)
22. Mackie, I.: Neuroparalytic keratitis. Current Ocular Therapy. Philadelphia, PA, USA: WB Saunders, pp. 452–454 (1995)
23. McHugh, J., Alexander, P., Kalhoro, A., Ionides, A.: Screening for ocular surface disease in the intensive care unit. Eye **22**(12), 1465–1468 (2008)
24. McInnes, L., Healy, J., Melville, J.: Umap: Uniform manifold approximation and projection for dimension reduction. arXiv preprint arXiv:1802.03426 (2018)
25. Ousler, G.W., III., Hagberg, K.W., Schindelar, M., Welch, D., Abelson, M.B.: The ocular protection index. Cornea **27**(5), 509–513 (2008)
26. Pao, S.I., Lin, H.Z., Chien, K.H., Tai, M.C., Chen, J.T., Lin, G.M.: Detection of diabetic retinopathy using bichannel convolutional neural network. Journal of Ophthalmology **2020**(1), 9139713 (2020)
27. Patel, V., Daya, S.M., Lake, D., Malhotra, R.: Blink lagophthalmos and dry eye keratopathy in patients with non-facial palsy: clinical features and management with upper eyelid loading. Ophthalmology **118**(1), 197–202 (2011)
28. Rodríguez-Palomares, J.F., Fernández, G., et al.: Integrating multimodal imaging in clinical practice: the importance of a multidisciplinary approach. Revista Espanola de Cardiologia (English ed.) **69**(5), 477–479 (2016)
29. Sommer, A., et al.: Challenges of ophthalmic care in the developing world. JAMA Ophthalmol. **132**(5), 640–644 (2014)
30. Witmer, M.T., Kiss, S.: Wide-field imaging of the retina. Surv. Ophthalmol. **58**(2), 143–154 (2013)

31. Won, Y.K., et al.: Deep learning-based classification system of bacterial keratitis and fungal keratitis using anterior segment images. Front. Med. **10**, 1162124 (2023)
32. Yang, L., Wan, Y., Pan, F.: Enhancing chest x-ray diagnosis with a multimodal deep learning network by integrating clinical history to refine attention. J. Imaging Inform. Med., 1–16 (2025)

GARD: Gamma-Based Anatomical Restoration and Denoising for Retinal OCT

Botond Fazekas[1,2]([✉]) [iD], Thomas Pinetz[2] [iD], Guilherme Aresta[1,2] [iD],
Taha Emre[2] [iD], and Hrvoje Bogunović[1,2] [iD]

[1] Christian Doppler Laboratory for Artificial Intelligence in Retina, Center for Medical Data Science, Medical University of Vienna, 1090 Vienna, Austria
[2] Institute of Artificial Intelligence, Center for Medical Data Science, Medical University of Vienna, 1090 Vienna, Austria
`botond.fazekas@meduniwien.ac.at`

Abstract. Optical Coherence Tomography (OCT) is a vital imaging modality for diagnosing and monitoring retinal diseases. However, OCT images are inherently degraded by speckle noise, which obscures fine details and hinders accurate interpretation. While numerous denoising methods exist, many struggle to balance noise reduction with the preservation of crucial anatomical structures. This paper introduces GARD (Gamma-based Anatomical Restoration and Denoising), a novel deep learning approach for OCT image despeckling that leverages the strengths of diffusion probabilistic models. Unlike conventional diffusion models that assume Gaussian noise, GARD employs a Denoising Diffusion Gamma Model to more accurately reflect the statistical properties of speckle. Furthermore, we introduce a Noise-Reduced Fidelity Term that utilizes a pre-processed, less-noisy image to guide the denoising process. This crucial addition prevents the reintroduction of high-frequency noise. We accelerate the inference process by adapting the Denoising Diffusion Implicit Model framework to our Gamma-based model. Experiments on a dataset with paired noisy and less-noisy OCT B-scans demonstrate that GARD significantly outperforms traditional denoising methods and state-of-the-art deep learning models in terms of PSNR, SSIM, and MSE. Qualitative results confirm that GARD produces sharper edges and better preserves fine anatomical details.

Keywords: Denoising · Gamma · Diffusion models · OCT · Retina

1 Introduction

Optical Coherence Tomography (OCT) provides cross-sectional images of the retina and other ocular structures [10], allowing the diagnosis and monitoring of a wide range of diseases, from age-related macular degeneration and diabetic retinopathy to glaucoma and optic nerve disorders [8]. However, OCT imaging

© The Author(s), under exclusive license to Springer Nature Switzerland AG 2026
H. Fang et al. (Eds.): OMIA 2025, LNCS 16209, pp. 32–42, 2026.
https://doi.org/10.1007/978-3-032-10351-2_4

relies on the interference of backscattered light, making it inherently susceptible to speckle noise. This noise arises from the constructive and destructive interference of coherent light waves scattered from the microscopic structures within the tissue, manifesting as a granular pattern superimposed on the OCT image [26].

Speckle noise significantly degrades image quality, obscuring fine details and reducing the contrast between different tissue layers. This can hinder diagnosis, particularly in the early stages of the disease, and can make it difficult to monitor subtle changes over time [16]. Reducing noise levels is therefore highly desirable. One can use repeated acquisitions and average them over time; however, this procedure prolongs acquisition times and introduces registration artifacts in case of patient movements. A reliable OCT denoiser would allow for faster image acquisition times, as fewer scans would be needed to achieve an acceptable signal-to-noise ratio, and potentially allowing similar diagnostic quality with lower-cost, lower-power OCT devices compared to the state-of-the-art. This latter point is especially relevant in developing countries, where access to advanced ophthalmic imaging technology is often limited [28].

Speckle removal (or denoising) in OCT, i.e., the process of suppressing unwanted noise while preserving the essential features, is an active research topic. Early approaches included anisotropic diffusion filtering [23,25], non-local means denoising [1,31], block matching non-local means denoising (BM3D) [4], wavelet transform-based methods [12,29], and low-rank decomposition-based methods [3,14]. Traditional methods have been developed for natural images and therefore have a hard time distinguishing noise from signal in the medical domain, where structures often look vastly different.

Convolutional neural networks (CNNs) are a promising alternative, with, e.g., the conditional General Adversarial Network (cGAN) for OCT despeckling [19] outperforming traditional methods. However, such supervised approaches usually require a substantial number of noisy/clean pairs for training, which are difficult to acquire in practice. One prominent approach is self-supervised learning, exemplified by Noise2Void (N2V) [15] and its extensions, which eliminates the need for clean target data. A significant advancement in this area is Noise2Void2 (N2V2) [11], introducing key modifications to mitigate the checkerboard artifacts often observed with N2V. SCUNet [30], another state-of-the-art method for various image restoration tasks including denoising, leverages a Swin Transformer-based architecture within a U-Net framework and employs a self-supervised data synthesis technique.

Recently, denoising diffusion probabilistic models (DDPMs) have been successfully applied to medical images [5]. DDPMs operate by learning to reverse a process that gradually adds noise to an image, i.e. the denoising process can then be viewed as estimating an intermediate step in this reverse process, given a noisy input. However, standard DDPMs typically assume a Gaussian noise distribution, which is a suboptimal approximation for OCT, where the image is formed by measuring the interference of backscattered light waves. This interference process leads to speckle noise, which is more accurately modeled by a Gamma distribution [22] due to its ability to capture the positive-only and skewed distribution of intensity fluctuations inherent in coherent imaging [6]. As an approximation, others have attempted to capture the noise characteristics of OCT images via a DDPM in the logarithmic domain using an entropy based data fidelity term to maintain content consistency [17]. However, this fidelity term can inadvertently reinforce noise in the input image. In contrast, Nachmani*et al.*[20] have already introduced Gamma-based DDPMs (DDGM), demonstrating their effectiveness on synthetic data and natural image inpainting tasks, however, DDGMs have not yet been explored for medical image restoration in particular.

We introduce **GARD** (**G**amma-based **A**natomical **R**estoration and **D**enoising) to explore the potential of DDGMs for medical imaging denoising, showcasing its applicability in retinal OCT. In particular: i) we adapt and apply a **Gamma-distribution based DDPM for OCT**, which more accurately models the statistical properties of speckle noise compared to the commonly used Gaussian assumption, ii) we propose the **Noise-Reduced Fidelity Term (NRFT)** that leverages a less noisy image (obtained through techniques like averaging multiple acquisitions) to guide the denoising process, and iii) we evaluate our method on a dataset containing paired sets of OCT images with high and low levels of noise, providing a more **objective and reliable assessment of denoising performance.**

2   Model Architecture

Gamma Diffusion Process. Our approach adapts the diffusion probabilistic model framework [9] to address the specific statistical properties of speckle noise in OCT images. The intensity of speckle noise is well-modeled by a Gamma distribution [22]. While other statistical models like the Rayleigh distribution have also been proposed to describe speckle [13,18], the Gamma distribution is particularly advantageous for our framework. It not only accurately captures the positive-only and skewed nature of intensity fluctuations inherent in coherent imaging but also possesses mathematical properties that make it highly suitable for the proposed diffusion formulation. Therefore, instead of the standard Gaussian noise used in DDPMs, we employ the Denoising Diffusion Gamma Model (DDGM) process formulated by Nachmani*et al.*[20].

While speckle noise is physically multiplicative in raw, linear-scale OCT data, our model operates on post-processed, display-ready images. These images typically undergo a logarithmic or fourth-square root transformation for dynamic range compression, which renders the noise approximately additive in the domain where our model operates. Consequently, the additive nature of the DDGM forward process is a physically motivated and appropriate choice for OCT denoising.

The forward noising process is characterized by the following equation:

$$\mathbf{x}_t = \sqrt{1-\beta_t}\mathbf{x}_{t-1} + (g_t - \mathbb{E}[g_t]) \tag{1}$$

where $\mathbf{x}_t$ is the noisy image at timestep t, $\mathbf{x}_{t-1}$ is from the previous timestep. β_t is part of a predefined noise schedule. $g_t \sim \Gamma(k_t, \theta_t)$ is a Gamma-distributed random variable with shape parameter $k_t = \frac{\beta_t}{\alpha_t \theta_0^2}$ and scale parameter $\theta_t = \sqrt{\bar{\alpha}_t}\theta_0$. Here, θ_0 is a hyperparameter controlling the initial noise level, and β_t is part of a predefined noise schedule (similar to DDPMs). This formulation, and the crucial property that the sum of independent Gamma-distributed variables with the same scale is also Gamma-distributed, allows for efficient sampling of the noisy image $\mathbf{x}_t$ at any timestep t directly from the original image $\mathbf{x}_0$.

The reverse process in the DDGM, as derived in [20], aims to estimate x_{t-1} from x_t. A neural network, ϵ_θ, is trained to predict the noise component. The reverse process step is given by:

$$x_{t-1} = \frac{x_t - \frac{1-\alpha_t}{\sqrt{1-\bar{\alpha}_t}}\epsilon_\theta(x_t, t)}{\sqrt{\bar{\alpha}_t}} + \sigma_t \frac{\bar{g}_t - \mathbb{E}[\bar{g}_t]}{\sqrt{\mathbb{V}[\bar{g}_t]}} \tag{2}$$

where σ_t controls stochasticity, $\mathbb{V}$ is variance and $\bar{g}_t \sim \Gamma(\bar{k}_t, \theta_t)$ with $\bar{k}_t = \sum_{i=1}^{t} k_i$.

To accelerate the reverse process during inference time (denoising), we adapt the Denoising Diffusion Implicit Model (DDIM) sampling approach [27] to the Gamma diffusion model. Following the DDIM methodology, we achieve deterministic sampling and enable larger denoising steps by setting $\sigma_t = 0$ in Eq. 2. This eliminates the stochastic component of the reverse process, allowing us to skip timesteps during inference.

Noise-Reduced Fidelity Term. Previous work, e.g. [17], has incorporated fidelity terms into the diffusion process to improve data consistency and prevent the generation of spurious artifacts. These terms penalize deviations between the denoised output and the original *noisy* input image. However, there is a significant drawback, as it can inadvertently reinforce the noise present in the original input, hindering the denoising process.

To overcome this limitation, we propose the *Noise-Reduced Fidelity Term* (NRFT). Our approach intentionally deviates from a traditional MAP estimation framework; instead of enforcing fidelity to the original noisy image, the NRFT leverages a pre-processed, less-noisy estimate to guide the model towards the underlying anatomy. The core idea is to use the fidelity term to primarily retain low-frequency information from the original image, while allowing the diffusion model to generate realistic high-frequency details. Instead of comparing the denoised output to the original noisy image $\mathbf{y}_s$, we compare it to a pre-processed version, $\tilde{\mathbf{y}}$, obtained by applying a non-local means (NLM) filter [2] to $\mathbf{y}$:

$$\tilde{\mathbf{y}} = \text{NLM}(\mathbf{y}) \tag{3}$$

NLM filtering effectively reduces noise while preserving edges and larger structures, making $\tilde{\mathbf{y}}_s$ a more reliable reference for assessing the fidelity of the denoised image. This pre-processing step provides a cleaner target for the fidelity term, guiding the reverse diffusion process towards a solution that is both consistent with the underlying structure and free from higher-frequency noise. The

NLM filter was chosen for this pre-processing step due to its practical advantages: it is computationally efficient and requires no separate training process, unlike deep learning-based alternatives.

During inference, we incorporate the NRFT by iteratively applying the DDGM reverse process (Eq. 2) and then refining the result using the fidelity term. Following [17], the fidelity term is incorporated by solving the following optimization problem at each reverse step:

$$\tilde{x}^{t-1} \leftarrow \arg\min_z \left(z + e^{\tilde{y}-z} + \mu \left\| z - x^{t-1} \right\|^2 \right) \tag{4}$$

where x^{t-1} is the output of the DDGM reverse process step (Eq. 2), $\tilde{y}$ is the NLM-filtered image (Eq. 3), $\tilde{x}^{t-1}$ is the refined estimate at timestep $t-1$ and μ is a weighting parameter controlling the strength of the fidelity term. We use a Newton's optimization method [21] to find the solution to this optimization problem. The refined estimate, $\tilde{x}^{t-1}$, then becomes the input, x^t, for the next DDGM reverse step.

3   Experiments

Datasets. Our models were trained in a large and unique dataset with 2 000 volumes from an investigational High-Res Spectral-Domain OCT device (Heidelberg Engineering, Germany), totaling 86 819 cross-sectional B-scans.

Quantitative evaluation was done on a prospectively collected dataset with 13 OCT volumes acquired with a commercial Spectralis device (Heidelberg Engineering, Germany), containing pairs of noisy and less-noisy B-scans. Noisy B-scans were obtained from single OCT sweeps, while corresponding less-noisy versions from 30 registered B-scans acquired at the identical anatomical location using the device's *automated real time averaging* (ART). Each volume has 19 B-scans, each with the single-acquisition (noisy) and an averaged, less-noisy version. The perfect registration within each set of B-scans enables a direct pixel-wise comparison, offering a near "gold-standard" for denoising evaluation.

Additionally, a qualitative evaluation dataset was used, comprising Cirrus (Carl Zeiss Meditec, Dublin, CA, USA), Topcon (Topcon Healthcare, Tokyo, Japan), and Spectralis OCT scans from the same patients at the same visit. This dataset was specifically chosen to compare the denoising performance on images from Cirrus and Topcon devices against the less-noisy output of the Spectralis device, which utilizes ART for noise reduction. However, due to differences in acquisition devices and processes, these scans are not registered, limiting their use to visual assessment of denoising results across different OCT platforms.

Baselines and Ablation Studies. We compare our proposed model GARD against several baselines. We included a non-deep learning method: Non-Local Means (NLM), and three state-of-the-art image restoration algorithms SCUNet [30], Speckle2Speckle [7] and N2V2 [11] with their publicly available pre-trained weights, to evaluate their off-the-shelf performance. In addition to these baselines, we performed an ablation study by testing various diffusion model configurations, including standard Gaussian DDPMs and our Gamma-based DDGMs, both with and without our proposed NRFT and the CDPM fidelity term from [17].

Implementation and Training Details. All diffusion models use a U-Net architecture [24]. Both Gaussian and Gamma models used a linear β_t schedule from 10^{-4} to 0.02 over $T = 1000$ timesteps. Also for Gamma, $\theta_0 = 0.1$ resulted in a noise most similar to typical OCT noise.

The models were trained with the AdamW optimizer (learning rate $= 10^{-5}$, batch size $= 8$) for $500\,000$ iterations. Random horizontal flip was used for data augmentation. Models were implemented in PyTorch and trained on one NVIDIA A100 GPU[1]. For non-local-mean filtering we used the fast implementation from the scikit-image package. In NRFT μ was set to 10 to ensure high consistency with the input image. Instead of performing the full reverse process from $t = T$ to $t = 0$, we started the denoising process at $t = 70$ and sampled every 10th timestep. This significantly reduces the number of inference steps required without sacrificing image quality.

Evaluation Metrics. We quantitatively assessed denoising performance using three standard metrics: Peak Signal-to-Noise Ratio (PSNR), Structural Similarity Index (SSIM), and Mean Square Error (MSE).

In addition, we performed Wilcoxon signed-rank tests to determine the statistical significance of the observed differences in performance between GARD and the baselines.

4   Results and Discussion

GARD achieves the best performance in all metrics (Table 1), outperforming traditional methods (NLM), state-of-the-art deep learning methods (SCUNet, N2V2), specialized self-supervised speckle denoisers (Speckle2Speckle), and other diffusion-based models (DDPM, CPDM, and their variants). Notably, our method achieves a PSNR improvement of 0.31 dB over SCUNet, 0.34 dB over the standard DDPM and 0.23 dB over the vanilla DDGM. This demonstrates the combined effectiveness of the Gamma diffusion process and our proposed Noise-Reduced Fidelity Term (NRFT) for OCT image despeckling. GARD is significantly better for all metrics and methods with $p < 0.01$.

The ablation studies, comparing DDGM, DDGM+CPDM and GARD highlight the contribution of the NRFT. The vanilla DDGM already shows competitive performance, ranking second best across all metrics. The fidelity term of [17] (CPDM) negatively impacts performance because it enforces consistency with the noisy input, effectively reintroducing the high-frequency noise that the diffusion process aims to eliminate. In contrast, our NRFT significantly improves performance over the vanilla DDGM, demonstrating its benefit. Interestingly,

---

[1] The source code of our project is available at https://github.com/ABotond/GARD

while the NRFT significantly boosts the performance of the DDGM, it results in a minor performance degradation for the standard DDPM (Table 1). This suggests a potential synergistic effect between our proposed fidelity term and the Gamma-based diffusion process. The NLM-filtered image, by preserving anatomical edges, appears to provide a more effective structural guide for the Gamma model which better aligns with the underlying speckle statistics. Conversely, for the mismatched Gaussian assumption in the standard DDPM, this specific form of guidance may be less compatible, failing to yield a similar improvement. These results validate our hypothesis about using a noise-reduced image for fidelity.

Table 1. Performance on the paired dataset. Mean (standard-deviation) shown for SSIM, PSNR (dB), and MSE. Bold indicates the best performance, underlined indicates the second best. The different configurations are compared against their less-noisier counterparts with higher ART number. * denotes statistically significant difference from GARD with $p < 0.01$.

Model	SSIM ↑	PSNR ↑	MSE ↓
Noisy input	0.43* (0.04)	24.80* (1.15)	222.52* (56.86)
NLM [2]	0.52* (0.10)	26.96* (1.95)	144.78* (67.28)
Speckle2Speckle [7]	0.49* (0.07)	26.59* (1.06)	147.08* (38.13)
N2V2 [11]	0.31* (0.06)	24.76* (1.26)	226.69* (66.75)
SCUNet [30]	0.55* (0.08)	28.10* (1.55)	107.89* (45.93)
DDPM [5]	0.54* (0.08)	27.85* (1.38)	112.04* (35.28)
DDPM [5] + CPDM	0.51* (0.07)	27.21* (1.51)	130.78* (42.56)
DDPM [5] + NRFT	0.53* (0.08)	27.62* (1.54)	119.52* (42.58)
CPDM [17]	0.44* (0.04)	25.39* (1.12)	194.03* (48.72)
CPDM [17] + NRFT	0.47* (0.07)	26.10* (1.59)	170.07* (61.16)
DDGM	<u>0.56</u>* (0.08)	<u>28.16</u>* (1.46)	<u>105.39</u>* (39.92)
DDGM + CPDM	0.53* (0.08)	27.69* (1.55)	118.24* (45.76)
GARD	**0.58** (0.09)	**28.25** (1.54)	**103.95** (41.91)

Visual inspection (Fig. 1) supports the quantitative findings. The noisy input exhibits substantial speckle. SCUNet reduces noise but still leaves some fine structures missing, especially small regions with high reflectivity. DDPM shows considerable improvement, but some fine structures are still missing. GARD delivers the visually best result, with sharper edges and better preservation of subtle anatomical details, confirming the potential for improved diagnostic utility. We visually evaluated our method on scans from different device vendors (Fig. 2), and it considerably improves their quality. However, due to the lack of appropriate metrics, we present these results only for illustrative purposes.

While GARD shows superior performance on our paired dataset and promising qualitative results on scans from different vendors, we acknowledge that the quantitative evaluation was conducted on data from a single device type.

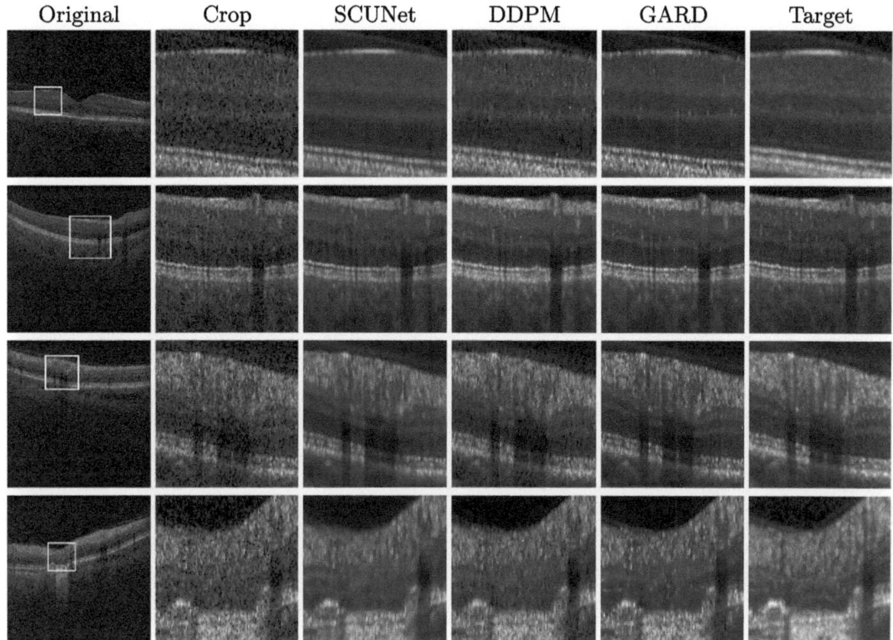

Fig. 1. Qualitative denoising results on a OCT B-scan. Columns: Original noisy image with crop region indicated, Cropped noisy image, and the results for the best performing baseline model SCUNet, DDPM, GARD (Ours), and less-noisy reference target. GARD provides the sharpest edges and best detail preservation.

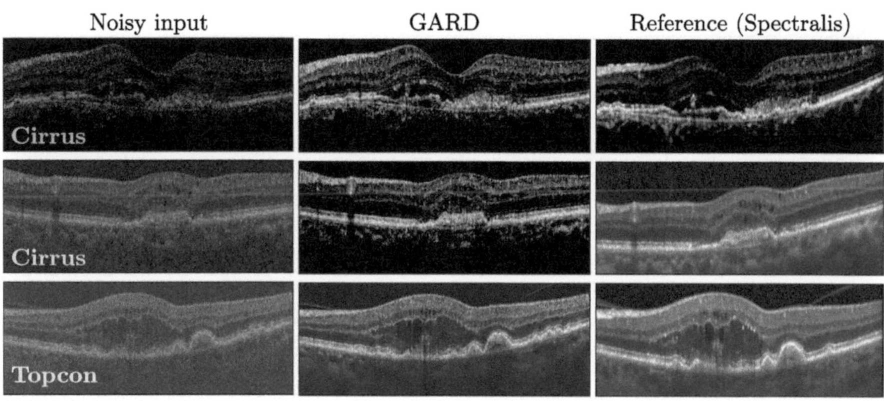

Fig. 2. Qualitative comparison of GARD denoising on OCT scans from different devices. Each row represents a different eye. Spectralis scans were acquired with ART and serve as less-noisy references.

This is primarily due to the difficulty in acquiring perfectly registered noisy and less-noisy paired scans from multiple commercial devices. Therefore, extensive validation on a wider range of devices and clinical conditions remains a key direction for future work.

5   Conclusion

We introduced GARD, a denoising diffusion gamma model (DDGM) with a noise-reduced fidelity term (NRFT) for speckle reduction in retinal OCT images. Our approach, leveraging the Gamma distribution for accurate noise modeling, demonstrated superior quantitative and qualitative performance compared to traditional and deep learning baselines, including other diffusion model variants. The NRFT, utilizing a pre-processed less-noisy image, proved crucial for avoiding noise reinforcement, leading to sharper edges and better fine detail preservation. This improved image quality has the potential to enhance diagnostic accuracy of retinal diseases, especially in underserved regions where lower-cost OCT devices, enhanced by our denoising method, could provide clinically useful images. While promising, our quantitative evaluation was performed on a single, specialized dataset due to the rarity of paired noisy and less-noisy OCT data. Future work will focus on validating our method on diverse datasets and exploring its applicability to other imaging modalities affected by speckle noise.

Acknowledgements. The financial support by the Christian Doppler Research Association, Austrian Federal Ministry of Economy, Energy and Tourism, the National Foundation for Research, Technology and Development, and Heidelberg Engineering is gratefully acknowledged.

References

1. Aum, J., hyun Kim, J., Jeong, J.: Effective speckle noise suppression in optical coherence tomography images using nonlocal means denoising filter with double gaussian anisotropic kernels. Appl. Opt. **54**(13), D43–D50 (2015). https://doi.org/10.1364/AO.54.000D43
2. Buades, A., Coll, B., Morel, J.M.: A non-local algorithm for image denoising. In: 2005 IEEE Computer Society Conference on Computer Vision and Pattern Recognition (CVPR 2005), vol. 2, pp. 60–65 (Jun 2005). https://doi.org/10.1109/CVPR.2005.38, iSSN: 1063-6919
3. Cheng, J., et al.: Speckle Reduction in 3D Optical Coherence Tomography of Retina by A-Scan Reconstruction. IEEE Trans. Med. Imaging **35**(10), 2270–2279 (2016). https://doi.org/10.1109/TMI.2016.2556080
4. Chong, B., Zhu, Y.K.: Speckle reduction in optical coherence tomography images of human finger skin by wavelet modified BM3D filter. Optics Commun. **291**, 461–469 (2013). https://doi.org/10.1016/j.optcom.2012.10.053
5. Chung, H., Lee, E.S., Ye, J.C.: MR image denoising and super-resolution using regularized reverse diffusion. IEEE Trans. Med. Imaging **42**(4), 922–934 (2023). https://doi.org/10.1109/TMI.2022.3220681

6. Goodman, J.W.: Speckle phenomena in optics: theory and applications. Roberts and Company Publishers (2007)

7. Göbl, R., Hennersperger, C., Navab, N.: Speckle2speckle: Unsupervised learning of ultrasound speckle filtering without clean data (2022)

8. Hee, M.R., et al.: Optical coherence tomography of the human retina. Arch. Ophthalmol. **113**(3), 325–332 (1995)

9. Ho, J., Jain, A., Abbeel, P.: Denoising Diffusion Probabilistic Models. In: Advances in Neural Information Processing Systems, vol. 33, pp. 6840–6851. Curran Associates, Inc. (2020)

10. Huang, D., et al.: Optical coherence tomography. Science **254**(5035), 1178–1181 (1991)

11. Höck, E., Buchholz, T.O., Brachmann, A., Jug, F., Freytag, A.: N2V2 - fixing noise2void checkerboard artifacts with modified sampling strategies and a tweaked network architecture. In: Computer Vision – ECCV 2022 Workshops, pp. 503–518. Springer Nature Switzerland, Cham (2023). https://doi.org/10.1007/978-3-031-25069-25933

12. Kafieh, R., Rabbani, H., Selesnick, I.: Three dimensional data-driven multi scale atomic representation of optical coherence tomography. IEEE Trans. Med. Imaging **34**(5), 1042–1062 (2015). https://doi.org/10.1109/TMI.2014.2374354

13. Karamata, B., Hassler, K., Laubscher, M., Lasser, T.: Speckle statistics in optical coherence tomography. J. Opt. Soc. Am. A **22**(4), 593–596 (2005). https://doi.org/10.1364/JOSAA.22.000593

14. Kopriva, I., Shi, F., Chen, X.: Enhanced low-rank + sparsity decomposition for speckle reduction in optical coherence tomography. J. Biomed. Opt. **21**(7), 076008 (2016). https://doi.org/10.1117/1.JBO.21.7.076008

15. Krull, A., Buchholz, T.O., Jug, F.: Noise2void - learning denoising from single noisy images. In: Proceedings of the IEEE/CVF Conference on Computer Vision and Pattern Recognition (CVPR) (June 2019)

16. Leitgeb, R.A., Werkmeister, R.M., Blatter, C., Schmetterer, L.: Doppler optical coherence tomography. Prog. Retin. Eye Res. **41**, 26–43 (2014). https://doi.org/10.1016/j.preteyeres.2014.03.004

17. Li, S., Higashita, R., Fu, H., Li, H., Niu, J., Liu, J.: Content-preserving diffusion model for unsupervised AS-OCT image despeckling. In: MICCAI 2023, pp. 660–670. Springer Nature Switzerland, Cham (2023). https://doi.org/10.1007/978-3-031-43990-2_62

18. Liba, O., et al.: Speckle-modulating optical coherence tomography in living mice and humans. Nat. Commun. **8**(1), 15845 (2017). https://doi.org/10.1038/ncomms15845

19. Ma, Y., Chen, X., Zhu, W., Cheng, X., Xiang, D., Shi, F.: Speckle noise reduction in optical coherence tomography images based on edge-sensitive cGAN. Biomed. Opt. Express **9**(11), 5129–5146 (2018). https://doi.org/10.1364/BOE.9.005129

20. Nachmani, E., Roman, R.S., Wolf, L.: Denoising Diffusion Gamma Models (Oct 2021). https://doi.org/10.48550/arXiv.2110.05948, arXiv:2110.05948 [eess]

21. Nocedal, J., Wright, S.J.: Numerical optimization. Springer (1999)

22. Pircher, M., Götzinger, E., Leitgeb, R.A., Fercher, A.F., Hitzenberger, C.K.: Speckle reduction in optical coherence tomography by frequency compounding. J. Biomed. Opt. **8**(3), 565–569 (2003). https://doi.org/10.1117/1.1578087

23. Puvanathasan, P., Bizheva, K.: Interval type-II fuzzy anisotropic diffusion algorithm for speckle noise reduction in optical coherence tomography images. Opt. Express **17**(2), 733–746 (2009). https://doi.org/10.1364/OE.17.000733

24. Ronneberger, O., Fischer, P., Brox, T.: U-Net: convolutional networks for biomedical image segmentation. In: MICCAI 2015. pp. 234–241. LNCS, Springer International Publishing, Cham (2015). https://doi.org/10.1007/978-3-319-24574-24428
25. Salinas, H.M., Fernandez, D.C.: Comparison of PDE-based nonlinear diffusion approaches for image enhancement and denoising in optical coherence tomography. IEEE Trans. Med. Imaging **26**(6), 761–771 (2007). https://doi.org/10.1109/TMI.2006.887375
26. Schmitt, J.: Optical coherence tomography (OCT): a review. IEEE J. Sel. Top. Quantum Electron. **5**(4), 1205–1215 (1999). https://doi.org/10.1109/2944.796348
27. Song, J., Meng, C., Ermon, S.: Denoising diffusion implicit models. In: International Conference on Learning Representations (2021)
28. WHO: World Population Ageing 2020 - Highlights, chap. Introduction, p. 3. World Health Organization (2020)
29. Zaki, F., Wang, Y., Su, H., Yuan, X., Liu, X.: Noise adaptive wavelet thresholding for speckle noise removal in optical coherence tomography. Biomed. Opt. Express **8**(5), 2720–2731 (2017). https://doi.org/10.1364/BOE.8.002720
30. Zhang, K., Zhang, K., et al.: Practical blind image denoising via Swin-Conv-UNet and data synthesis. Mach. Intell. Res. **20**(6), 822–836 (2023). https://doi.org/10.1007/s11633-023-1466-0
31. Zhang, X., Li, L., Zhu, F., Hou, W.W., Chen, X.: Spiking cortical model–based nonlocal means method for speckle reduction in optical coherence tomography images. J. Biomed. Opt. **19**(6), 066005 (2014). https://doi.org/10.1117/1.JBO.19.6.066005

Anomaly Detection in Anterior Eye Segment Using Self-supervised Siamese Autoencoders

Philippe Baumstimler[1]([✉]), Sébastien Gagné[2,3], Mathieu Champagne[2], Jean-Mathieu Gagnon[2], Clément Playout[1], and Lama Séoud[1]

[1] Polytechnique Montréal, Montreal, Canada
[2] LightX Innovations, Montreal, Canada
[3] Institut de l'Oeil des Laurentides, Boisbriand, Canada

Abstract. Reconstruction-based anomaly detection models are widely used in medical imaging for their ability to provide both image- and pixel-level anomaly estimations, enhancing interpretability. However, in complex medical scenarios, these models often capture generic features, leading to the unintended reconstruction of anomalies and ultimately failing in the anomaly detection task. In this study, we investigate the application of reconstruction-based methods to anterior eye segment (AES) anomaly detection and propose a novel training framework based on Self-Supervised (SSL) Siamese Autoencoders to enhance normality representation learning. We introduce a combined self-distillation and restoration objective using pseudo-anomalies to mitigate overgeneralization, while leveraging perceptual and structural reconstruction losses for improved reconstruction quality. We evaluated our model on a private dataset of 2,647 external photographs of the AES - including clinical samples and 36 identified diseases such as cataracts, hemorrhages, pinguecula, and pterygium - and on a public dataset of 3,200 retinal fundus images with 46 annotated pathologies. Experimental results demonstrate superior quantitative and qualitative performance compared to baseline methods on both datasets. Our approach shows strong generalization capabilities and holds promise for non-invasive AES biomarker discovery. This work marks, to the best of our knowledge, the first attempt to apply unsupervised anomaly detection models to external ocular photographs, a non-invasive and cost-effective ophthalmic imaging modality. Code is available at: https://github.com/VisionICLab/AnoSiamAE.

Keywords: Anomaly Detection · Anterior Eye Segment · Siamese Autoencoders

1 Introduction

Early diagnosis of ocular pathologies is crucial for preventing vision loss. Anterior eye segment (AES) photography is an inexpensive, accessible and non-invasive

H. Fang et al. (Eds.): OMIA 2025, LNCS 16209, pp. 43–53, 2026.
https://doi.org/10.1007/978-3-032-10351-2_5

imaging modality. Recent studies using supervised learning have demonstrated impressive performances in predicting AES-related diseases including cataracts, keratitis, keratoconus and primary-angled closure glaucoma [24]. Furthermore, recent studies conducted by Babenko et al. [2] and Lang et al. [15] have provided evidence that AES images may reveal systemic biomarkers linked to diabetic retinopathy, poor blood sugar control and elevated lipids. However, supervised models lack interpretability and rely on predefined labels, which restricts their ability to detect novel anomalies. In this work, we address AES image analysis as an unsupervised anomaly detection problem.

Among anomaly detection models, reconstruction-based methods are particularly popular. These are designed to learn to reconstruct normal samples only, making them unable to accurately reconstruct out-of-distribution (OOD) samples. This approach has been widely applied to various medical imaging modalities, including brain MRIs [5], chest X-rays [14], lymph node sections [20] and fundus images [27]. However, these methods suffer from overgeneralization, leading to the unintended reconstruction of anomalies and ultimately failing in the anomaly detection task [7]. Consequently, these models face a fundamental trade-off: improved reconstruction quality against better anomaly detection performance.

In this study, we explore reconstruction-based approaches for anomaly detection in AES photographs while addressing the overgeneralization problem, ensuring both strong anomaly detection and reconstruction performance. Inspired by the work of Chen et al. [9] and Baier et al. [3], we propose a novel anomaly detection training framework that improves representation learning of normal attributes in reconstruction-based approaches through Self-Supervised Learning (SSL) Siamese Autoencoders. Our key contributions are as follows: (1) We investigate the application of reconstruction-based methods for anomaly detection in AES imaging and demonstrate their limitations. (2) We propose a novel anomaly detection training framework for reconstruction-based approaches that enhances in-distribution representation learning through the combination of self-distillation and pseudo-anomaly restoration. (3) We demonstrate how our

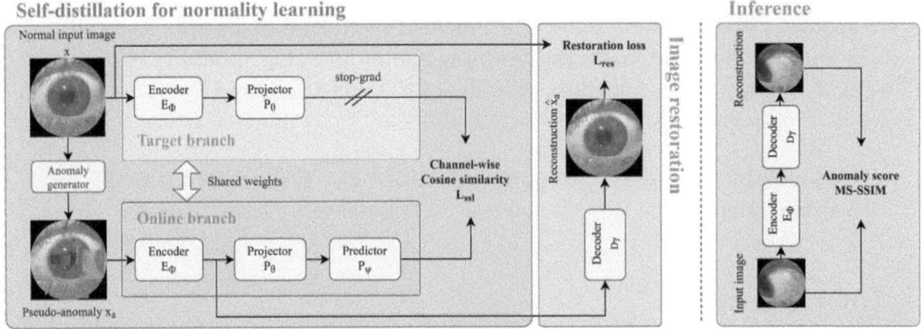

Fig. 1. Overview of the proposed SSL Siamese Autoencoder training and inference frameworks

method effectively enhances anomaly detection while ensuring strong reconstruction capabilities without overgeneralization. An overview of the proposed framework is provided in Fig. 1.

2 Methodology

2.1 Pseudo-Anomaly Generation

In this work, our goal is to generate a large pool of OOD samples that are as varied as possible. By doing so, we encourage the model to focus on learning normality in AES images.

As in [25], pseudo-abnormal generation consists in randomly sampling, augmenting and blending up to $N = 20$ patches from the original normal image x. To encourage both low and high-level feature restoration, each patch is assigned a random ratio ranging from 0.05 to 0.4 times the corresponding dimension of x. Inspired by CutPaste [16] and DRAEM [25], we enhance the robustness of the model's reconstructions to AES anomalies by applying random augmentations from the following set: {*flip, blur, dropout, brightness, saturation, hue, erase*}. This pseudo-anomaly generator produces a wide variety of pseudo-anomalies within a single normal image.

2.2 Image Restoration

Following the theory of reconstruction-based models, training is conducted exclusively on normal images. To prevent overgeneralization, we frame our task as a restoration problem by learning to maximize similarity between the normal input x and the reconstructed output $\hat{x}_a$ obtained from its pseudo-abnormal counterpart x_a. We define a restoration loss $\mathcal{L}_{res}$ combining a perceptual loss that is efficient in generation tasks [11], and a structural loss that is efficient in complex reconstruction scenarios [8], as follow:

$$\mathcal{L}_{res}(x, \hat{x}_a) = \frac{1}{2}\mathcal{L}_{ssim}(x, \hat{x}_a) + \frac{1}{2}\mathcal{L}_{Perc}(x, \hat{x}_a) \tag{1}$$

We employ the relative perceptual loss $\mathcal{L}_{perc}$ introduced by Shvetsova et al. [20], which has been successfully applied to diverse medical imaging and is defined as:

$$\mathcal{L}_{Perc}(x, \hat{x}_a) = \frac{||\tilde{f}(\hat{x}_a) - \tilde{f}(x)||_1}{||\tilde{f}(x)||_1} \tag{2}$$

where $\tilde{f}$ are the normalized intermediate features of a pretrained VGG19 [17]. To ensure the reconstruction of fine-grained anatomical structures, we incorporate a structural similarity loss $\mathcal{L}_{ssim}$, defined as:

$$\mathcal{L}_{ssim}(x, \hat{x}_a) = \frac{1}{H \times W} \sum_{i=1}^{H} \sum_{j=1}^{W} 1 - SSIM(x_{ij}, \hat{x}_{a,ij}) \tag{3}$$

$$SSIM(a, b) = [l(a, b)]^{\alpha} \cdot [c(a, b)]^{\beta} \cdot [s(a, b)]^{\gamma} \tag{4}$$

where H and W are the image height and width, and x_{ij}, $\hat{x}_{a,ij}$ are corresponding patches centered at coordinates (i, j) in the original and reconstructed images from a sliding window of size 11. The $SSIM$ represents the structural similarity metric, based on the scaled product of the luminance l, the contrast c and the structure s measurements between two given patches a and b. We adopt the original implementation from [23], fixing $\alpha = \beta = \gamma = 1$.

The reconstruction $\hat{x}_a$ is obtained by forwarding the pseudo-abnormal input x_a through the encoder-decoder pipeline, as depicted in Fig. 1. The autoencoder used is a lightweight ($\sim$ 2.3M parameters) fully convolutional network, converting $3 \times 256 \times 256$ inputs to $4 \times 32 \times 32$ latent representations, then back to the input format.

2.3 Self-distillation for Normality Learning

Consider a normal sample x and its pseudo-abnormal counterpart x_a. In the context of anomaly detection, since both share the same underlying features except for synthetic anomalies, an ideal model should enforce similar latent representations, i.e. $E_\phi(x) \simeq E_\phi(x_a)$. For that, we leverage self-distillation-based methods [4] to constrain the latent representation.

Following the methodology of [3,9], we adopt a Siamese framework with shared online and target branches, as shown in Fig. 1. By applying the channel-wise cosine distance D_{cos}, we aim to minimize the distance between similar samples. Specifically for anomaly detection, we adapt this framework by dedicating the target branch $T(\cdot)$ exclusively to normal samples and the online branch $O(\cdot)$ to pseudo-abnormal samples. The objective is to pull pseudo-abnormal features toward normal ones, enforcing a latent space that captures only normality. The tailored Siamese SSL loss $\mathcal{L}_{ssl}$ is defined by:

$$\mathcal{L}_{ssl}(x, x_a) = D_{cos}(O(x_a), T(x)) \tag{5}$$

As in [9], we prevent model collapse by only backpropagating gradients through the online branch. The projector and the predictor are used only for training, and are eventually discarded at inference time. The final loss of the model is given by:

$$\mathcal{L}(x, x_a, \hat{x}_a) = \alpha\mathcal{L}_{ssl}(x, x_a) + (1 - \alpha)\mathcal{L}_{res}(x, \hat{x}_a) \tag{6}$$

where $\alpha \in [0, 1]$ controls the relative contributions of the restoration and self-distillation tasks.

2.4 Anomaly Score

AES images are complex objects, containing both high-level and fine-grained structures and textures. To account for this, and since our model is trained using the SSIM loss for restoration, we use the multi-scale version of SSIM (MS-SSIM) as our anomaly score at inference time, where:

$$\mathcal{A}(x, \hat{x}) = \frac{1}{H \times W} \sum_{i=1}^{H} \sum_{j=1}^{W} 1 - \text{MS-SSIM}(x_{ij}, \hat{x}_{ij}) \tag{7}$$

$$\text{MS-SSIM}(a, b) = [l_M(a, b)]^{\alpha_M} \prod_{m=1}^{M} [c_m(a, b)]^{\beta_m} \cdot [s_m(a, b)]^{\gamma_m} \tag{8}$$

according to the same nomenclature as in Eq. 3 and 4. Following the original implementation [22], the MS-SSIM is computed as the product of scaled luminance l_m, contrast c_m and structure s_m measurements between two given patches a and b. Each of the M scales is derived iteratively by applying a low-pass filter followed by a factor 2 down-sampling interpolation. The hyperparameters α_M, β_m and γ_m are set according to [22]. This metric evaluates the structural similarities at multiple scales and smoothing levels, thereby enabling the model to capture anomalies across different levels.

3   Experiments and Results

3.1   Implementation Details

Data: We trained and evaluated our approach on a private dataset of 2,647 high-resolution AES photographs. These images were collected, after ethics review board approval (CER-2223-75-D), from 154 patients at two clinics, *l'Institut de l'Oeil des Laurentides* and *l'Ecole d'Optométrie de Montréal*, and from 100 students at Polytechnique Montréal university, using two smartphones mounted on a slit lamp designed by *LightX Innovations*. Images were annotated by a senior ophthalmologist, with 2,411 labeled as normal and 236 containing at least one pathological sign among 35 distinct labels. The dataset was split into training, validation and test sets and stratified at patient level. Normal samples were split into 60% for training, 20% for validation, and 20% for testing. Since training does not require abnormal samples, the latter were equally distributed into the validation and test sets. To assess robustness across imaging modalities, we also trained our approach on the RFMiD dataset [18], a public collection of 3,200 retinal fundus images annotated with 46 pathologies. It includes 1,920 training images (of which only the 400 normal images were used for training), and 640 images each for validation and testing. All images from both datasets were downsampled to 256×256 pixels and cropped to retain only the region of interest before training.

Baselines: For a fair comparison, each baseline was re-implemented using the same unified autoencoder architecture as our approach, and was trained from scratch. We identified four reconstruction-based categories from which we selected the following baselines:

Autoencoders: We first considered pure autoencoder-based methods. We evaluated the Mean Absolute Error (AE_{MAE}) [5] and SSIM (AE_{SSIM}) [8]

48   P. Baumstimler et al.

Autoencoders, as well as the Deep Perceptual Autoencoder (DPA) [20] with a refined perceptual loss for medical anomaly detection.

Restoration Model: We then considered restoration-based approaches, first the Denoising Autoencoder (DAE) [12], which adds Gaussian noise to the inputs, and then DRAEM [25], which also employs hand-crafted pseudo-anomalies.

Variational Models: To evaluate our latent constraint scheme, we compared it with a β-Variational Autoencoder (β-VAE) [5,14], which is commonly used to learn the underlying data distribution.

Generative Adversarial Networks: Finally, we selected Generative Adversarial Networks (GANs) for their strong generative capabilities. This included AnoVAEGAN [6], which combines GANs with the VAE training process, and GANomaly [1], which introduces an additional encoder to learn a feature distance metric for anomaly detection.

Table 1. Comparative performance scores computed over 3 runs between defined baselines and our approach. **In bold:** best results. <u>Underlined</u>: second best results

Models	AES						RFMiD					
	Anomaly detection		Reconstruction		Restoration		Anomaly detection		Reconstruction		Restoration	
	AUROC↑	AP↑	SSIM↑	LPIPS↓	SSIM↑	LPIPS↓	AUROC↑	AP↑	SSIM↑	LPIPS↓	SSIM↑	LPIPS↓
AE_{MAE}	0.593	0.275	0.849	0.250	0.786	0.308	0.515	0.833	0.799	0.423	0.771	0.442
AE_{SSIM}	0.706	0.398	**0.877**	0.204	0.808	0.275	0.428	0.765	**0.856**	0.266	0.820	0.319
DPA	0.795	0.449	0.745	**0.155**	0.691	0.236	0.464	0.817	0.744	**0.156**	0.709	0.228
DAE	0.783	0.408	0.764	0.388	0.751	0.395	0.452	0.805	0.773	0.465	0.768	0.464
DRAEM	0.796	0.358	<u>0.866</u>	0.232	**0.847**	0.252	0.543	0.834	<u>0.844</u>	0.289	**0.834**	0.310
β-VAE	0.632	0.293	0.825	0.283	0.778	0.321	0.468	0.813	0.787	0.465	0.779	0.466
AnoVAEGAN	0.587	0.270	0.783	0.280	0.725	0.333	0.483	0.806	0.785	0.348	0.752	0.365
GANomaly	0.745	0.339	0.671	0.350	0.596	0.399	0.586	0.843	0.675	0.387	0.626	0.411
Ours ($\alpha = 0.1$)	0.824	0.483	0.850	<u>0.159</u>	<u>0.831</u>	**0.184**	0.610	0.867	0.836	<u>0.182</u>	<u>0.825</u>	**0.206**
Ours ($\alpha = 0.3$)	0.853	<u>0.506</u>	0.846	0.167	0.828	<u>0.190</u>	<u>0.613</u>	<u>0.868</u>	0.830	0.188	0.821	<u>0.210</u>
Ours ($\alpha = 0.5$)	**0.868**	**0.519**	0.839	0.184	0.822	0.204	**0.625**	**0.874**	0.823	0.201	0.814	0.222
Ours ($\alpha = 0.7$)	<u>0.863</u>	0.501	0.829	0.206	0.813	0.225	0.566	0.844	0.808	0.231	0.799	0.252
Ours ($\alpha = 0.9$)	0.830	0.453	0.786	0.299	0.774	0.313	0.466	0.808	0.753	0.415	0.751	0.415

Training Setup: All models were trained for 150 epochs, using Adam optimizer [13] with a learning rate starting at 1×10^{-3}, then following a cosine reduction schedule until reaching 1×10^{-4}. Training was conducted on a single NVIDIA GeForce RTX 3080 with batch size of 8, and repeated using 3 random seeds.

3.2   Results

Anomaly Detection, Reconstruction and Restoration: Models were evaluated on the anomaly detection task by calculating the area under the receiver-operator curve (AUROC) and the average precision score (AP). We also evaluated the reconstruction capabilities by computing structural similarity (SSIM) and perceptual similarity (LPIPS) [26] on normal test samples. For restoration, we added an unseen random elastic augmentation on up to 5 random patches of each normal test sample, and compared the output image with the original version. All scores are reported in Table 1 on both AES and RFMiD datasets.

On AES images, our method achieves the best anomaly detection performance while maintaining competitive reconstruction capabilities, on par with pure reconstruction-based approaches such as AE_{MAE}, AE_{MAE} and DPA. In terms of restoration, our approach ranks second to DRAEM in SSIM and first in LPIPS. Interestingly, the best anomaly detection results are obtained with a weighting factor α of 0.5, whereas extrema ($\alpha \in \{0.1, 0.3\}$ and $\alpha \in \{0.7, 0.9\}$) lead to performance degradation. This highlights the importance of a balanced relative contribution between restoration and self-distillation, which directly governs the trade-off between restoration fidelity and anomaly detection effectiveness. The results on the RFMiD dataset, shown in the second half of Table 1, support the observations made on AES and further demonstrate the generalization capability of our method. While baselines tend to suffer from performance trade-offs, our approach consistently performs well across all tasks.

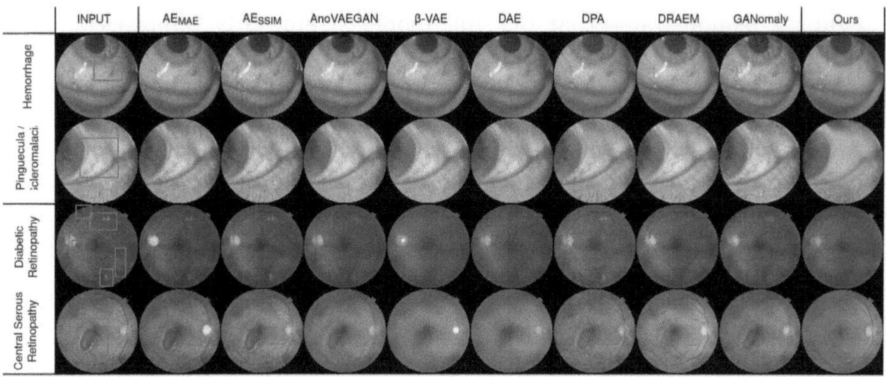

Fig. 2. Abnormal samples and their respective reconstructions from baselines and our model. Anomalies are highlighted by the red bounding boxes. (Color figure online)

Furthermore, on real anomalies, our method demonstrates significantly better qualitative performance, as illustrated in Fig. 2. It effectively replaces abnormal structures with healthy features while maintaining high reconstruction capability in healthy regions. In AES images, hemorrhages and scleromalacia are effectively replace by sclera. Similarly, in retinal fundus images, exudates, cotton wool spots and other lesions are accurately corrected by the model. While DRAEM also produces strong qualitative results on retina fundus images, it struggles to fully remove hemorrhages in the AES sample. Besides, DRAEM relies on a secondary U-Net to compute its anomaly score, making it heavier ($\sim$ 3.5M parameters) compared to our more lightweight approach ($\sim$ 2.3M parameters). Although our approach exhibits strong perceptual reconstruction capabilities, it still struggles with complex fine-grained structures such as veins, eyelashes, and skin texture.

This often results in failed predictions due to lower reconstruction scores in these regions.

Ablation Studies: We conducted ablation studies to further evaluate the contributions of the overall framework (Table 2) and the pseudo-anomaly generation strategy (Table 3) on AES anomaly detection.

Table 2. Ablation study: global framework - **In bold**: best results for each metric.

Experiment	Anomaly detection		Reconstruction		Restoration	
	AUROC↑	AP↑	SSIM↑	LPIPS↓	SSIM↑	LPIPS↓
1) AE $\mathcal{L}_{perc} + \mathcal{L}_{ssim}$	0.699	0.390	**0.854**	**0.142**	0.790	0.225
2) 1 + Restoration ($\alpha = 0$)	0.817	0.458	0.850	0.157	**0.830**	**0.184**
3) 1 + 2 + SSL (Ours)	**0.868**	**0.519**	0.839	0.184	0.822	0.204

Table 2 demonstrates that our full model significantly improves anomaly detection, compared to a pure restoration model (2), with only a slight drop in restoration metrics. Despite lower reconstruction scores compared to a traditional AE (1), its reconstruction capability remains higher than most of the baselines. This reveals that strong anomaly detection relies on more than just reconstruction, and that our combined self-distillation and restoration framework better models normality.

Table 3. Ablation study: pseudo-anomaly generation - **In bold**: best results for each metric. <u>Underlined</u>: second best results.

Generation strategies			Anomaly detection		Reconstruction		Restoration	
Shape	Source	Blend	AUROC↑	AP↑	SSIM↑	LPIPS↓	SSIM↑	LPIPS↓
rectangle	input	simple	**0.868**	**0.519**	**0.839**	<u>0.184</u>	<u>0.822</u>	<u>0.204</u>
rectangle	input	Poisson	0.750	0.396	0.788	0.247	0.751	0.301
rectangle	DTD	simple	<u>0.857</u>	0.484	0.827	0.202	0.813	0.219
rectangle	DTD	Poisson	0.837	0.483	0.827	0.198	0.808	0.222
Perlin	input	simple	0.844	<u>0.507</u>	**0.839**	**0.179**	**0.824**	**0.199**
Perlin	input	Poisson	0.715	0.382	0.796	0.229	0.755	0.284
Perlin	DTD	simple	0.834	0.491	0.826	0.197	0.813	0.213
Perlin	DTD	Poisson	0.847	0.503	<u>0.829</u>	0.189	0.812	0.211

We explored several pseudo-anomaly generation strategies by varying shapes (rectangles, Perlin noise [19,25]), sources (input, DTD texture dataset [10]) and blending techniques (simple interpolation, Poisson image interpolation [21]). As shown in Table 3, our strategy - rectangle patches from input images blended via simple interpolation - achieves the best anomaly detection score and second-best in reconstruction and restoration. Interestingly, subtler anomalies created using Poisson interpolation lead to a notable performance drop, likely because the pseudo-anomalous images closely resemble the originals, making the restoration loss $\mathcal{L}_{res}$ nearly equivalent to the reconstruction loss. Perlin noise-based shapes improve reconstruction and restoration scores, possibly due to reduced bias towards specific gradient orientations, but yield weaker anomaly detection compared to rectangle shapes. Although simple, the implementation of rectangular patches allow us to apply distinct sets of augmentations in each region, creating diverse anomalies within a single image, which likely contributes to the performance gain. Lastly, using input-derived anomalies instead of DTD-based textures [10] exposes the model to domain-specific patterns, enhancing its ability to encode and restore normal structures.

4   Conclusion

Our tailored anomaly detection framework for AES, combining a SSL Siamese framework and restoration objectives, has demonstrated superior in-distribution representation learning compared to baselines models. Our framework enables high anomaly detection performance while preserving strong reconstruction capabilities, thus enhancing both the reliability and the interpretability of our model. Notably, our approach maintains a lightweight architecture at inference, supporting potential on-device and real-time anomaly detection in AES. However, our method is primarily limited by the pseudo-anomalies generation and anomaly scoring. Since the generated pseudo-anomalies may not capture the full spectrum of real anomalies, detecting fine-grained abnormalities remains challenging: measuring perceptual differences between the original and the reconstructed image is difficult, especially in complex areas of interest, as these differences are often obscured by normal reconstruction errors. Future work will focus on developing a learned domain-specific anomaly score and improving the pseudo-anomaly generation strategy for more robustness to unknown abnormalities. This study paves the way for unsupervised anomaly detection in AES photographs by introducing a novel SSL Siamese Autoencoder framework that bears potential in pathological biomarker discovery.

Acknowledgements. This work was supported by Mitacs as part of the Mitacs Accelerate program.

Disclosure of Interests. The authors have no competing interests to declare that are relevant to the content of this article.

References

1. Akcay, S., Atapour-Abarghouei, A., Breckon, T.P.: GANomaly: semi-supervised anomaly detection via adversarial training. In: Jawahar, C.V., Li, H., Mori, G., Schindler, K. (eds.) ACCV 2018. LNCS, vol. 11363, pp. 622–637. Springer, Cham (2019). https://doi.org/10.1007/978-3-030-20893-6_39

2. Babenko, B., et al.: Detection of signs of disease in external photographs of the eyes via deep learning. Nat. Biomed. Eng. **6**(12), 1370–1383 (2022)

3. Baier, F., Mair, S., Fadel, S.G.: Self-supervised Siamese autoencoders. In: Miliou, I., Piatkowski, N., Papapetrou, P. (eds.) Advances in Intelligent Data Analysis XXII, pp. 117–128. Springer Nature Switzerland, Cham (2024). https://doi.org/10.1007/978-3-031-58547-0_10

4. Balestriero, R., et al.: A cookbook of self-supervised learning (2023). https://arxiv.org/abs/2304.12210

5. Baur, C., Denner, S., Wiestler, B., Navab, N., Albarqouni, S.: Autoencoders for unsupervised anomaly segmentation in brain MR images: a comparative study. Med. Image Anal. **69**, 101952 (2021)

6. Baur, C., Wiestler, B., Albarqouni, S., Navab, N.: Deep autoencoding models for unsupervised anomaly segmentation in brain MR images. In: Crimi, A., Bakas, S., Kuijf, H., Keyvan, F., Reyes, M., van Walsum, T. (eds.) Brainlesion: Glioma, Multiple Sclerosis, Stroke and Traumatic Brain Injuries, pp. 161–169. Springer International Publishing, Cham (2019)

7. Bercea, C.I., Rueckert, D., Schnabel, J.A.: What do we learn? debunking the myth of unsupervised outlier detection (2023). https://arxiv.org/abs/2206.03698

8. Bergmann, P., Löwe, S., Fauser, M., Sattlegger, D., Steger, C.: Improving unsupervised defect segmentation by applying structural similarity to autoencoders. In: Proceedings of the 14th International Joint Conference on Computer Vision, Imaging and Computer Graphics Theory and Applications (VISIGRAPP 2019) - Volume 5: VISAPP, pp. 372–380. INSTICC, SciTePress (2019). https://doi.org/10.5220/0007364503720380

9. Chen, X., He, K.: Exploring simple Siamese representation learning. In: 2021 IEEE/CVF Conference on Computer Vision and Pattern Recognition (CVPR), pp. 15745–15753 (2021). https://doi.org/10.1109/CVPR46437.2021.01549

10. Cimpoi, M., Maji, S., Kokkinos, I., Mohamed, S., , Vedaldi, A.: Describing textures in the wild. In: Proceedings of the IEEE Conf. on Computer Vision and Pattern Recognition (CVPR) (2014)

11. Johnson, J., Alahi, A., Fei-Fei, L.: Perceptual losses for real-time style transfer and super-resolution. In: Leibe, B., Matas, J., Sebe, N., Welling, M. (eds.) ECCV 2016. LNCS, vol. 9906, pp. 694–711. Springer, Cham (2016). https://doi.org/10.1007/978-3-319-46475-6_43

12. Kascenas, A., Pugeault, N., O'Neil, A.Q.: Denoising autoencoders for unsupervised anomaly detection in brain MRI. In: Konukoglu, E., Menze, B., Venkataraman, A., Baumgartner, C., Dou, Q., Albarqouni, S. (eds.) Proceedings of The 5th International Conference on Medical Imaging with Deep Learning. Proceedings of Machine Learning Research, 06–08 Jul, vol. 172, pp. 653–664. PMLR (2022)

13. Kingma, D.P., Ba, J.: Adam: A method for stochastic optimization (2017). https://arxiv.org/abs/1412.6980

14. Kumar, D., Verma, C., Illes, Z., Mittal, A., Bakariya, B., Goyal, S.: Anomaly detection in chest X-Ray images using variational autoencoder. In: 2023 6th International Conference on Contemporary Computing and Informatics (IC3I), vol. 6, pp. 216–221 (2023). https://doi.org/10.1109/IC3I59117.2023.10397595

15. Lang, O., et al.: Using generative AI to investigate medical imagery models and datasets. EBioMedicine **102**(105075), 105075 (2024)

16. Li, C.L., Sohn, K., Yoon, J., Pfister, T.: Cutpaste: self-supervised learning for anomaly detection and localization. In: Proceedings of the IEEE/CVF Conference on Computer Vision and Pattern Recognition (CVPR), pp. 9664–9674 (June 2021)

17. Liu, S., Deng, W.: Very deep convolutional neural network based image classification using small training sample size. In: 2015 3rd IAPR Asian Conference on Pattern Recognition (ACPR), pp. 730–734 (2015).https://doi.org/10.1109/ACPR.2015.7486599

18. Pachade, S., et al.: Retinal fundus multi-disease image dataset (rfmid) (2020). https://doi.org/10.21227/s3g7-st65

19. Perlin, K.: An image synthesizer. In: Proceedings of the 12th Annual Conference on Computer Graphics and Interactive Techniques, SIGGRAPH 1985, pp. 287–296. Association for Computing Machinery, New York(1985). https://doi.org/10.1145/325334.325247

20. Shvetsova, N., Bakker, B., Fedulova, I., Schulz, H., Dylov, D.V.: Anomaly detection in medical imaging with deep perceptual autoencoders. IEEE Access 9, 118571–118583 (2021). https://doi.org/10.1109/ACCESS.2021.3107163

21. Tan, J., Hou, B., Day, T., Simpson, J., Rueckert, D., Kainz, B.: Detecting outliers with poisson image interpolation. In: de Bruijne, M., et al. (eds.) MICCAI 2021. LNCS, vol. 12905, pp. 581–591. Springer, Cham (2021). https://doi.org/10.1007/978-3-030-87240-3_56

22. Wang, Z., Simoncelli, E., Bovik, A.: Multiscale structural similarity for image quality assessment. In: The Thrity-Seventh Asilomar Conference on Signals, Systems & Computers 2003, vol. 2, pp. 1398–1402 (2003). https://doi.org/10.1109/ACSSC.2003.1292216

23. Wang, Z., Bovik, A., Sheikh, H., Simoncelli, E.: Image quality assessment: from error visibility to structural similarity. IEEE Trans. Image Process. 13(4), 600–612 (2004). https://doi.org/10.1109/TIP.2003.819861

24. Xu, Z., et al.: Artificial intelligence for anterior segment diseases: a review of potential developments and clinical applications. Ophthalmol. Ther. 12(3), 1439–1455 (2023)

25. Zavrtanik, V., Kristan, M., Skocaj, D.: DRÆM – a discriminatively trained reconstruction embedding for surface anomaly detection . In: 2021 IEEE/CVF International Conference on Computer Vision (ICCV), pp. 8310–8319. IEEE Computer Society, Los Alamitos, CA, USA (Oct 2021)

26. Zhang, R., Isola, P., Efros, A.A., Shechtman, E., Wang, O.: The unreasonable effectiveness of deep features as a perceptual metric. In: CVPR (2018)

27. Zhou, K., et al.: Encoding structure-texture relation with P-Net for anomaly detection in retinal images. In: ECCV (2020)

Generalized Visual Field Pattern Discovery Using Archetypal Analysis

Viska Mutiawani[1,3]($\boxtimes$) , Naeha Sharif[1] , Nigel Morlet[2],
Siobhan Manners[2] , and Ghulam Mubashar Hassan[1]

[1] Department of Computer Science and Software Engineering, The University of
Western Australia, Perth, Australia
[2] School of Population and Global Health, The University of Western Australia,
Perth, Australia
[3] Department of Informatics, Syiah Kuala University, Banda Aceh, Indonesia
`viska.mutiawani@research.uwa.edu.au`

Abstract. Visual field (VF) testing is an important diagnostic tool for
ophthalmologists to assess the extent of vision loss and the affected
regions. VF loss often follows distinctive spatial patterns that are indica-
tive of specific ocular and neurological conditions. Accurate identification
and characterization of these patterns is critical for disease classification and progression monitoring. However, existing VF datasets typically lack annotated labels for these patterns, and manual labelling is
resource-intensive. Moreover, there remains a lack of research focused on
benchmarking generalizable archetypes across different datasets. Therefore, this research proposes a methodology grounded in an unsupervised
learning approach, specifically Archetypal Analysis, to identify representative patterns of visual field loss. The proposed method is evaluated
using two datasets: UWHVF and eFOVID. The resulting generalized VF
patterns are found to be consistent across both datasets. Furthermore,
the identified patterns are reviewed by ophthalmologists and found them
as clinically relevant.

Keywords: Visual Field · Archetypal Analysis · Unsupervised learning

1 Introduction

Visual field (VF) refers to the extent of the area seen while the eye is focused
on a single point. It can be assessed through a VF test, which is a standard
method for measuring a patient's visual sensitivity. Ophthalmologists use VF
testing to monitor the progression of eye diseases, particularly glaucoma [5]. This
enables early detection of vision loss and allows for timely treatment to slow the
progression of visual deterioration. To support such timely intervention, accurate
interpretation of VF patterns is essential.

Machine learning (ML) models capable of automatically and reliably classifying VF patterns have the potential to serve as powerful clinical decision support tools [6]. However, the development of such models is significantly hindered

H. Fang et al. (Eds.): OMIA 2025, LNCS 16209, pp. 54–64, 2026.
https://doi.org/10.1007/978-3-032-10351-2_6

by the scarcity of annotated datasets. Most of the existing VF datasets lack labeled pattern information, making manual interpretation both labor-intensive and prone to variability among clinicians [19].

In the absence of labeled datasets, researchers often turn to unsupervised learning methods to uncover latent structures in the data. K-means is the most common unsupervised clustering technique that partitions the data based on proximity to centroids, identifying representative patterns as the centers of these clusters [1]. Principal Component Analysis (PCA) reduces dimensionality by capturing the directions of highest variance [23], while Archetypal Analysis (AA) identifies representative extreme patterns located at the boundaries of the VF dataset. Mørup and Hansen [15] applied these methods to facial images and found that AA produced more distinctive and interpretable facial patterns. Figure 1a shows a comparison of K-means, AA, and PCA. Unlike K-means or PCA, AA identifies distinctive patterns of VF loss.

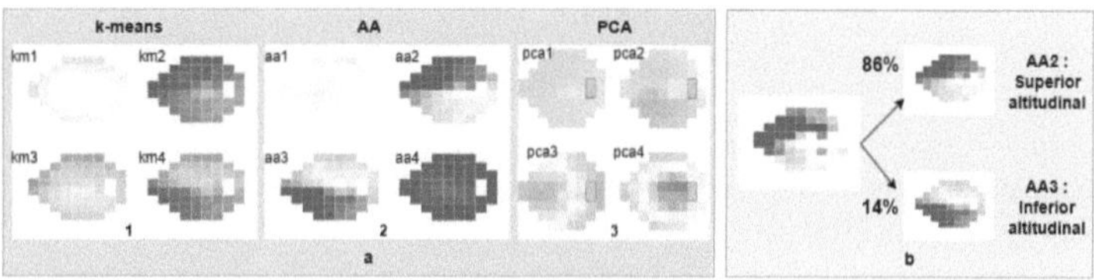

Fig. 1. (a) K-means, AA comparison using sample data from UWHVF [14] with $k = 4$. The PCA image is taken from [8]. (b) Sample VF archetypal decomposition based on Fig. 1a-2.

Extreme patterns in VF, such as nasal step, arcuate, and altitudinal, serve as the "pure" patterns of visual defects. AA can express each patient's VF as a weighted sum of these few extremes to simplify thousands of test points into clear and clinically meaningful profiles [6,8]. For example, describing a patient's VF as 86% like the superior-altitudinal-defect archetype and 14% like the inferior-altitudinal archetype rather than raw sensitivity readings [6] as shown in Fig. 1b. Aside from interpretable results, AA can help detect disease progression [21]. For instance, in the case of glaucoma, patients' worsening vision tends to shift toward one of these extreme patterns, allowing for earlier detection of vision deterioration. Extreme patterns can also act like well-defined labels, letting algorithms group patients by their dominant archetype.

Various AA variants have been proposed to uncover patterns in high-dimensional biomedical data, and some studies have applied different AA techniques to identify clinically meaningful VF archetypes [4,8,24]. However, one major issue that persists across these efforts is the inconsistency of the resulting archetypes, often attributed to differences in datasets and, notably, the initialization strategies employed. In a comprehensive survey by Alcacer et al. [2], it is emphasized that AA is particularly sensitive to initialization and a poor choice can lead to redundant or clinically irrelevant archetypes and convergence to suboptimal local minima. Although various initialization methods have been proposed in the literature [7,10,12,15,20], but their effectiveness in identifying clinically relevant patterns in VF datasets remains largely unexplored.

In this work, we propose a hybrid ensemble framework that integrates multiple initialization methods to generate clinically consistent and generalizable archetypes. We tested this framework on two datasets: UWHVF which contains 28,943 VFs [14], and eFOVID which contains 606,230 VFs [13]. We found that the resulting generalized VF patterns were highly consistent across both datasets. The identified patterns were reviewed and validated by ophthalmologists as clinically relevant.

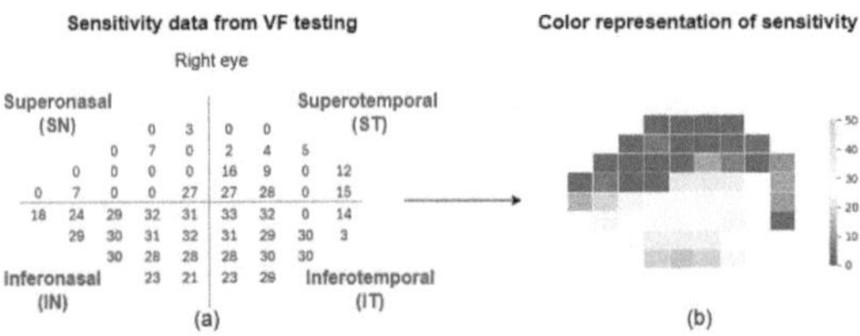

Fig. 2. Example of sensitivity value from right eye VF taken from eFOVID [13]. (a) SN: Upper inner quadrant (toward the nose). ST: Upper outer quadrant. IN: Lower inner quadrant (toward the nose). IT: Lower outer quadrant. (b) Each square represents a sensitivity value, with values ranging from 0 to 50 decibels (dB), in a color gradient of red, white, and light blue. (Color figure online)

2   Visual Field

The visual field (VF) refers to the area visible to a fixated eye and is crucial for detecting the progression of visual disorders. Changes in VF can be presented as localized or widespread vision loss [18]. VF testing is typically performed using the Humphrey Field Analyzer (HFA), which offers several testing protocols (e.g., 30-2, 24-2, 10-2). The HFA measures retinal light sensitivity in decibels (dB), with values typically ranging from 0 (brightest stimulus) to 50 (dimmest). In healthy individuals, average sensitivity is around 30 dB [18]. The inability to detect the brightest light indicates total vision loss at that location [18]. The example of sensitivity value in the VF testing result is presented in Fig. 2. There are four quadrants in a VF: superonasal (SN), superotemporal (ST), inferonasal (IN), and inferotemporal (IT). Comparing corresponding quadrants across the horizontal and vertical meridians helps characterize VF defects, indicating underlying ocular or neurological conditions [17].

3   Archetypal Analysis

Archetypal Analysis (AA) is a technique used to identify extreme points (representative patterns) within the convex hull of a dataset, referred to as archetypes

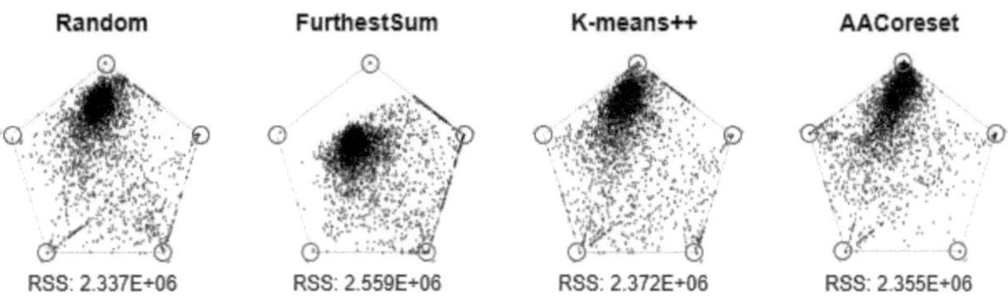

Fig. 3. Comparison of the outcomes of four different initialization methods for AA, for K = V5 (i.e., five archetypes). Each black dot represents a data point expressed as a weighted combination of archetypes, while archetypes are marked with small red circles. The Residual Sum of Squares (RSS) is used to evaluate performance; a lower RSS indicates quantitatively higher-quality archetypes. (Color figure online)

[7]. The core idea of AA is to represent each data point in the dataset as a convex combination of archetypes. Let $\mathbf{X} \in \mathbb{R}^{n \times m}$ be a data matrix representing a multivariate dataset with n observations (data points) and m attributes (features). For a given number of archetypes k, AA aims to determine a matrix $\mathbf{Z} \in \mathbb{R}^{k \times m}$ of k archetypes such that two key principles are satisfied:

1. Each observation $\mathbf{x}_i$ in $\mathbf{X}$ can be approximated as a convex combination of the archetypes:

$$\mathbf{x}_i \approx \sum_{j=1}^{k} \alpha_{ij} \mathbf{z}_j, \qquad where \sum_{j=1}^{k} \alpha_{ij} = 1, \quad \alpha_{ij} \geq 0$$

2. Each archetype $\mathbf{z}_j$ itself must be a convex combination of the data points in $\mathbf{X}$:

$$\mathbf{z}_j = \sum_{i=1}^{n} \beta_{ji} \mathbf{x}_i, \qquad where \sum_{i=1}^{n} \beta_{ji} = 1, \quad \beta_{ji} \geq 0$$

Thus, the objective is to find α, β (and hence $\mathbf{Z}$) such that the Residual Sum of Square (RSS) or

$$\|\mathbf{X} - \mathbf{Z}\alpha\|^2$$

is minimized, subject to the convexity constraints.

3.1 Initialization Methods

The AA process begins with an initialization step, where a set of initial archetypes is selected to start the process [7]. Proper initialization is crucial for ensuring fast convergence and obtaining reliable archetypes. [2]. Initialization methods for AA can be categorized based on their selection strategies. The simplest is randomized initialization, which selects archetypes uniformly at random (as applied by [7,8]). While simple, this approach often results in slow convergence. In contrast, deterministic distance-based methods such as FurthestFirst

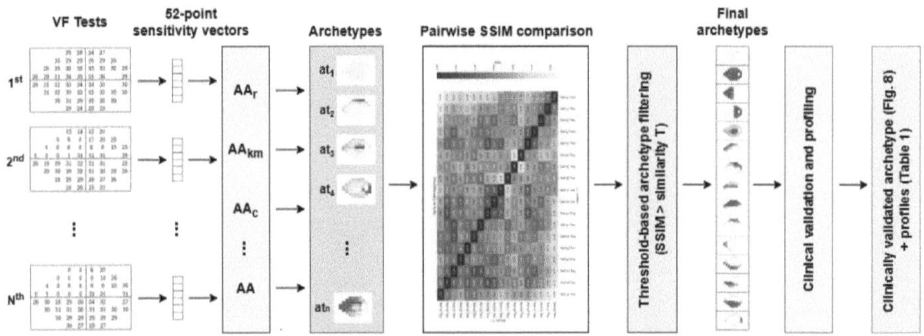

Fig. 4. Overview of the proposed hybrid ensemble framework integrating results from multiple AA variants. AA_r: AA with random initialization. AA_{km}: AA with k-means++ initialization. AA_c: AA with AACoreset initialization. at_1 to at_n: a set of archetypes visualized as images

[10] and FurthestSum [15] select points based on their distance from previously chosen archetypes, aiming to enhance diversity and spatial coverage. However, our experimental results show that for $k > 10$, FurthestSum tends to produce less distinct and more similar archetypes, while FurthestFirst may result in suboptimal selections.

Other initialization methods that aim to address the limitations of distance-based approaches include k-means++ [20] and AA++ [12], both of which are probabilistic distance-aware strategies. Inspired by the success of k-means++ in clustering, Mair [12] introduced AA++, where the first archetype is selected randomly, and subsequent archetypes are chosen based on a probability distribution $P(n)$ proportional to the distance between data points and the convex hull of the already selected archetypes. Aside from the methods mentioned above, another approach is *AACoreset*, introduced by Mair and Brefeld [11]. It selects a small, strategically chosen subset of the data that closely approximates the full dataset. Although *AACoreset* is not a traditional initialization method, it has been effectively used for initializing AA, as demonstrated by Black [3].

While a comprehensive comparison of various initialization approaches is detailed in [12], Fig. 3 offers a focused comparison of four initialization methods applied to Archetypal Analysis. The plots in Fig. 3 illustrate the distribution of data points based on their weights relative to each archetype. A higher concentration of points near an archetype indicates that most data points have dominant weights associated with that specific archetype. The Residual Sum of Squares (RSS) is reported for each method, and while the differences in RSS across methods are relatively minor, this metric alone is insufficient to capture the quality of the resulting archetypes. For example, FurthestSum tends to produce less distinct archetypes, as indicated by dense clustering near overlapping regions. In contrast, AACoreset, K-means++, and Random yield archetypes that are more distinct (i.e., less similar to one another), while still achieving competitive RSS.

A detailed comparison of the initialization methods can be found on the GitHub repository (https://github.com/vvusk/aavf).

4   Proposed Methodology

The proposed methodology, illustrated in Fig. 4, aims to identify VF patterns that are generalizable across different datasets, with the goal of capturing the most prevalent types of visual defects. Furthermore, the identified patterns should also demonstrate clear clinical relevance. In this study we evaluated several AA variants, each utilizing a different initialization strategy, and selected *random*, *k-means++*, and *AAcoreset* for inclusion in our framework. These methods were chosen based on empirical analysis, specifically as the top three performers in terms of RSS and qualitative assessments of the resulting archetypes.

AA generates a set of archetypes determined by the hyperparameter k, which defines the number of archetypes. In our case, each archetype consists of 52 values corresponding to VF sensitivity measurements, representing extreme patterns in the dataset. These archetypes were visualized using a red-white-light blue color gradient Fig. 2b., and the resulting images were saved in PNG format.

To capture a wider spectrum of archetypal patterns and mitigate the effects of initialization sensitivity, each AA variant was run five times. All resulting archetype images were compiled, and pairwise comparisons were performed using the Structural Similarity Index Measure (SSIM) [22], which assesses image similarity based on luminance, contrast, and structural features. SSIM values range from 0 (completely dissimilar) to 1 (identical).

As illustrated in Fig. 4, we used these SSIM comparisons to identify generalized VF patterns. A similarity threshold of $T = 0.93$ was chosen based on empirical observations. A more detailed comparison of the threshold is available in the accompanying GitHub repository (https://github.com/vvusk/aavf). If three or more archetype images exceeded this threshold in pairwise similarity, they were considered to represent the same underlying pattern, and one image was selected as the representative. This process was repeated until all images had been analyzed. The resulting set of representative archetypes was defined as generalized visual field (VF) patterns and was reviewed by two domain experts for clinical validation and profiling: *NM*, a Senior Consultant Ophthalmologist with over 20 years of clinical experience, and *SM*, a licensed optical dispenser. These validated patterns can serve as benchmark references for applying AA to VF data.

5   Experiments

This section describes the datasets used in this research, outlines the implementation details, and discusses the results of this study.

5.1 Datasets

This study utilizes two datasets: UWHVF [14] and eFOVID [13]. UWHVF is the largest publicly available visual field (VF) dataset and comprises 28,943 VF records. eFOVID, the largest known VF dataset in Australia, contains 606,230 VF records. For consistency, only tests conducted using the Humphrey Field Analyzer (HFA) 24-2 protocol were included, totaling 547,713 VFs. A preprocessing step was applied to filter out unreliable tests, excluding any visual field with false positive (FP), false negative (FN), or fixation loss (FL) rates greater than 33%. After this filtering, 427,175 VFs from the eFOVID dataset remained for analysis.

This study focuses exclusively on the sensitivity values derived from VF data as suggested by our domain experts to be more clinically relevant. The original HFA 24-2 test provides 54 sensitivity measurements, but the two blind spot locations were excluded in both datasets used for this study, resulting in 52 sensitivity values per test. To ensure consistency in spatial layout, the sensitivity data for left eyes in the eFOVID dataset [13] were flipped to match the right-eye format, as was done in UWHVF [14]. As a result, both datasets were processed using a consistent right-eye layout.

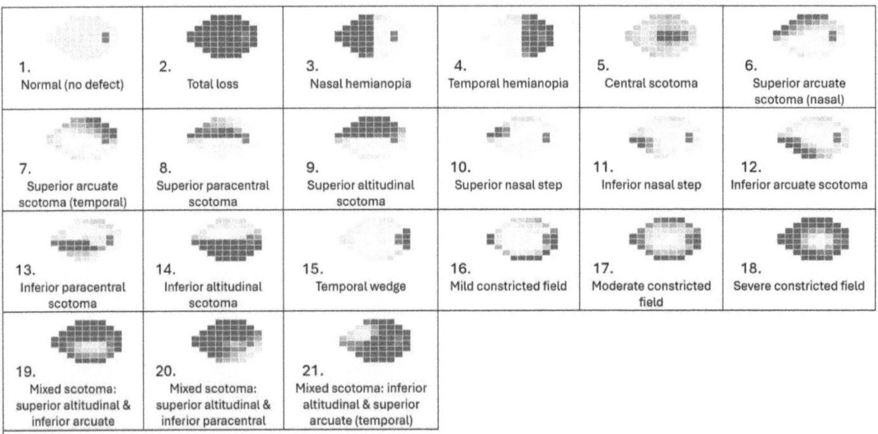

Fig. 5. Generalized VF patterns as the outcome of the hybrid ensemble framework.

5.2 Implementation Details

We implemented the proposed methodology using Python on a system equipped with an Intel i7 CPU (20 cores, 5.4 GHz) and 32 GB of RAM. We performed the experiments using the Python package by Motevalli [16], with initialization methods adapted from [12], and the coreset strategy from [11].

AA requires specifying a value for k, which represents the number of archetypes to be generated. To determine an appropriate value of k, we plotted the RSS for $k = 2$ to $k = 30$ for UWHVF, as can be seen in the GitHub repository (https://github.com/vvusk/aavf). The elbow method was then applied to these plots to identify the optimal number of archetypes. Typically, increasing k results in a lower RSS, but beyond a certain point, the decrease becomes flat: this flattened-out point is known as the elbow [9]. From the candidate k values, we further did qualitative analysis by visually inspecting the archetypes. Based on this combined assessment, we selected $k = 19$ for the whole dataset.

We applied the same approach to select an appropriate value of k for the eFOVID. However, due to computational constraints associated with running AA on the full eFOVID dataset, we utilized the AACoreset [11] algorithm to select a representative sample. This representative sample enables learning algorithms to perform similarly to when trained on the complete data but with significantly improved efficiency [11]. We used 15% of the eFOVID data, resulting in a subset of 64,076 VFs that could be processed within the available computational resources.

5.3   Results and Discussion

Experiments with the UWHVF dataset yielded 18 distinct VF patterns, labeled 1–18 and presented in Fig. 5. When applying the same methodology to the eFOVID dataset, these 18 patterns were also consistently identified. In addition, we identified three additional patterns in the eFOVID dataset, which are numbered 19–21 in Fig. 5. These additional patterns appear to be composite or mixed scotomas, formed by the combination of fundamental patterns from the original set. Specifically, Pattern 19 is a combination of Patterns 9 and 12, Pattern 20 combines Patterns 9 and 13, and Pattern 21 results from Patterns 7 and 14. These findings suggest that the original 18 patterns serve as building blocks for more complex visual field defects.

Two ophthalmologists (NM & SM) have verified and profiled all patterns shown in Fig. 5 as clinically relevant. Several of these patterns also appear in the archetypes identified by Elze [8] and Yousefi [24]. However, we identified some differences. Compared to Elze's findings [8], additional patterns are identified, which are patterns number 6, 16, 18, 19, 20, and 21. Similarly, in Yousefi's study [24], patterns 3, 4, 6, 8, 13, 16, 18, 19, 20, and 21 were absent. These differences may be attributed to variations in the underlying datasets used across studies, as well as methodologies used to extract archetypes (differing initialization strategies). Notably, the datasets used in prior studies were not publicly available, limiting reproducibility and direct comparison. While this study may not have captured the full spectrum of VF defects, the resulting archetypes consistently reflect the most prevalent and clinically meaningful patterns, as validated by experts.

The analysis of generalized VF patterns utilizes four VF quadrants, as shown in Fig. 2. Table 1 summarizes the generalized VF patterns and their corresponding quadrant analysis. Table 1 explains the VF patterns from a normal visual

Table 1. Generalized VF patterns and their effects on different quadrants. SN: Super-onasal, ST: super-otemporal, IN: Infer-onasal, IT: Infer-otemporal.

No	Description	SN	ST	IN	IT
1	Visual field is within normal limits	normal	normal	normal	normal
2	Complete vision loss across entire VF	loss	loss	loss	loss
3	Vision loss in nasal half	affected	normal	affected	normal
4	Vision loss in temporal half	normal	affected	normal	affected
5	Isolated vision loss in central VF	center affected	center affected	center affected	center affected
6	Curved band visual loss in superior nasal field	affected	mostly normal	normal	normal
7	Curved band visual loss in the superior temporal field	mildly affected	affected	normal	normal
8	Focal loss near the center of superior field	paracentral affected	paracentral affected	normal	normal
9	Complete vision loss of the superior half of VF	affected	affected	normal	normal
10	Step-like defect at the superior nasal field	affected	mostly normal	mostly normal	mostly normal
11	Step-like defect at the inferior nasal field	mostly normal	mostly normal	affected	mostly normal
12	Curved band visual loss in inferior field	normal	normal	affected	mildly affected
13	Focal loss near the center of inferior field	normal	normal	paracentral affected	paracentral affected
14	Complete vision loss of the inferior half	normal	normal	affected	affected
15	Increased size of physiological blind spot	normal	temporal affected	normal	temporal affected
16	Slight reduction of peripheral vision with central field largely preserved	mildly affected	mildly affected	mildly affected	mildly affected
17	Moderate peripheral VF loss but central VF still present	moderately affected	moderately affected	moderately affected	moderately affected
18	Marked reduction of peripheral vision, resulting in "tunnel vision"	severely affected	severely affected	severely affected	severely affected
19	Combined loss in superior half and inferior arcuate region	affected	affected	mildly affected	mildly affected
20	Combined superior altitudinal loss with inferior paracentral defect	affected	affected	paracentral affected	paracentral affected
21	Combined inferior half loss with a superior temporal arcuate defect	normal	affected (arcuate)	affected	affected

field to a pattern with a complete loss of sensitivity across the entire VF. Defects can be localized, such as nasal or temporal hemianopia, central scotoma, arcuate or paracentral scotomas, and altitudinal loss affecting the upper or lower half of the field. Other patterns include nasal steps, enlarged blind spots, and constricted fields ranging from mild peripheral narrowing to severe "tunnel vision." These patterns are often linked to specific ocular or neurological conditions.

6 Conclusion

This study proposed a methodology to identify generalized VF patterns using AA across multiple initialization methods. By applying this approach to two datasets (UWHVF and eFOVID), we demonstrated that consistent and clinically relevant VF patterns can be extracted by aggregating archetypes and pairwise SSIM-based comparisons. Ophthalmologists validated our findings and showed overlap with known patterns from prior research while revealing additional clinically meaningful patterns not previously reported. This generalized VF pattern provides a reliable benchmark for future AA applications in VF modeling, classification, and progression analysis.

References

1. Agarwal, P.K., Mustafa, N.H.: K-means projective clustering. In: Proceedings of the Twenty-Third ACM SIGMOD-SIGACT-SIGART Symposium on Principles of Database Systems, pp. 155–165 (2004)
2. Alcacer, A., Epifanio, I., Mair, S., Mørup, M.: A survey on archetypal analysis. arXiv preprint arXiv:2504.12392 (2025)
3. Black, A.S., et al.: Archetypal analysis of geophysical data illustrated by sea surface temperature. Artif. Intell. Earth Syst. **1**(3), e210007 (2022)
4. Branco, J., et al.: Archetypal analysis of longitudinal visual fields for idiopathic intracranial hypertension patients presenting in a clinic setting. PLOS Dig. Health **2**(5), e0000240 (2023)
5. Broadway, D.C.: Visual field testing for glaucoma-a practical guide. Commun. Eye Health **25**(79–80), 66 (2012)
6. Cai, S., Elze, T., Bex, P.J., Wiggs, J.L., Pasquale, L.R., Shen, L.Q.: Clinical correlates of computationally derived visual field defect archetypes in patients from a glaucoma clinic. Curr. Eye Res. **42**(4), 568–574 (2017)
7. Cutler, A., Breiman, L.: Archetypal analysis. Technometrics **36**(4), 338–347 (1994)
8. Elze, T., Pasquale, L.R., Shen, L.Q., Chen, T.C., Wiggs, J.L., Bex, P.J.: Patterns of functional vision loss in glaucoma determined with archetypal analysis. J. R. Soc. Interface **12**(103), 20141118 (2015)
9. Eugster, M., Leisch, F.: From spider-man to hero-archetypal analysis in r (2009)
10. Hochbaum, D.S., Shmoys, D.B.: A best possible heuristic for the k-center problem. Math. Oper. Res. **10**(2), 180–184 (1985)
11. Mair, S., Brefeld, U.: Coresets for archetypal analysis. Adv. Neural Inf. Process. Syst. **32** (2019)
12. Mair, S., Sjölund, J.: Archetypal analysis++: rethinking the initialization strategy. Trans. Mach. Learn. Res. (2024)
13. Manners, S., et al.: Epidemiology of field of vision disorders (efovid) study, Western Australia, 1988–2022. Report 1: data collection and aggregation protocol. Clin. Exp. Ophthalmol. **52**(8), 819–832 (2024)

14. Montesano, G., Chen, A., Lu, R., Lee, C.S., Lee, A.Y.: UWHVF: a real-world, open source dataset of perimetry tests from the humphrey field analyzer at the university of washington. Transl. Vision Sci. Technol. **11**(1), 2–2 (2022)
15. Mørup, M., Hansen, L.K.: Archetypal analysis for machine learning and data mining. Neurocomputing **80**, 54–63 (2012)
16. Motevalli Soumehsaraei, B., Barnard, A.: Archetypal analysis package (2019). https://doi.org/10.25919/5d3958889f7ff. cSIRO. v1. Software
17. Pereira, M.L.M., Kim, C.S., Zimmerman, M.B., Alward, W.L., Hayreh, S.S., Kwon, Y.H.: Rate and pattern of visual field decline in primary open-angle glaucoma. Ophthalmology **109**(12), 2232–2240 (2002)
18. Reddy, G.: Practical Guide to Interpret Visual Fields. Jaypee Brothers Medical Publishers (2020)
19. Tanna, A.P., et al.: Interobserver agreement and intraobserver reproducibility of the subjective determination of glaucomatous visual field progression. Ophthalmology **118**(1), 60–65 (2011)
20. Vassilvitskii, S., Arthur, D.: k-means++: the advantages of careful seeding. In: Proceedings of the Eighteenth Annual ACM-SIAM Symposium on Discrete Algorithms, pp. 1027–1035 (2006)
21. Wang, M., et al.: An artificial intelligence approach to detect visual field progression in glaucoma based on spatial pattern analysis. Invest. Pphthalmol. Visual Sci. **60**(1), 365–375 (2019)
22. Wang, Z., Bovik, A.C., Sheikh, H.R., Simoncelli, E.P.: Image quality assessment: from error visibility to structural similarity. IEEE Trans. Image Process. **13**(4), 600–612 (2004)
23. Wold, S., Esbensen, K., Geladi, P.: Principal component analysis. Chemom. Intell. Lab. Syst. **2**(1–3), 37–52 (1987)
24. Yousefi, S., Pasquale, L.R., Boland, M.V., Johnson, C.A.: Machine-identified patterns of visual field loss and an association with rapid progression in the ocular hypertension treatment study. Ophthalmology **129**(12), 1402–1411 (2022)

Uncertainty-Aware Multimodal Fusion for Reliable Fundus Disease Classification Using a Vision-Language Foundation Model

Meng Wang[1,2], Tian Lin[3], Aidi Lin[3], Ke Zou[1,2], Ting Xu[1,2], Yanda Meng[4], Dianbo Liu[1,2], Yih Chung Tham[1,2,5,6], Haoyu Chen[3(✉)], and Huazhu Fu[7(✉)]

[1] Centre for Innovation and Precision Eye Health, Yong Loo Lin School of Medicine, National University of Singapore, Singapore 117549, Singapore
[2] Department of Ophthalmology, Yong Loo Lin School of Medicine, National University of Singapore, Singapore 117549, Singapore
[3] Joint Shantou International Eye Center, Shantou University and the Chinese University of Hong Kong, Shantou 515041, Guangdong, China
drchenhaoyu@gmail.com
[4] Department of Computer Science, University of Exeter, Exeter EX4 4RN, UK
[5] Singapore Eye Research Institute, Singapore National Eye Centre, Singapore, Republic of Singapore
[6] Ophthalmology and Visual Sciences Academic Clinical Program (EYE ACP), Duke-NUS Medical School, Singapore, Singapore
[7] Institute of High Performance Computing (IHPC), Agency for Science, Technology and Research (A*STAR), 1 Fusionopolis Way, #16-16 Connexis, Singapore 138632, Singapore
hzfu@ieee.org

Abstract. Accurate and trustworthy diagnosis of fundus diseases is essential for the safe clinical deployment of artificial intelligence (AI) systems. In this study, we present a novel multimodal diagnostic framework that enhances both classification performance and uncertainty quantification. Our method leverages a pre-trained vision-language foundation model to extract visual features from fundus images and semantic embeddings from disease label texts. Two predictive pathways, supervised classification and imagetext similarity, are independently modeled, and their outputs are transformed into belief masses and uncertainty scores using Dirichlet-based evidential modeling. These modality-specific predictions are then integrated using a DempsterShafer-inspired uncertainty-aware fusion strategy, which dynamically calibrates trust based on the reliability of each modality. Experimental results on a multi-class fundus disease dataset and two out-of-distribution (OOD) benchmarks show that our method outperforms state-of-the-art baselines in fundus disease diagnosis, achieves over 80% accuracy in OOD detection, and supports uncertainty-guided triaging. These results demonstrate the effectiveness and reliability of our framework for real-world AI-assisted ophthalmic screening.

M. Wang and T. Lin—Contributed equally.

© The Author(s), under exclusive license to Springer Nature Switzerland AG 2026
H. Fang et al. (Eds.): OMIA 2025, LNCS 16209, pp. 65–74, 2026.
https://doi.org/10.1007/978-3-032-10351-2_7

Keywords: Uncertainty modeling · Vision-language model · Multimodal fusion · Fundus image diagnosis

1   Introduction

Blindness and visual impairment pose a major global health burden, affecting hundreds of millions of people worldwide [1,4,10]. Early detection and timely treatment of retinal diseases are critical to preventing irreversible vision loss [5,7]. However, large-scale screening remains challenging, especially in low-resource settings, due to the shortage of trained ophthalmologists and diagnostic infrastructure [10,15]. Additionally, fundus image characteristics can vary significantly across diseases, imaging devices, and populations, complicating the development of robust and generalizable diagnostic models [2,8]. This challenge is further amplified in open-set scenarios, where previously unseen diseases may emerge, posing risks to the reliability of AI-based systems. The advent of large foundation models (LFMs) trained on diverse ophthalmic datasets has greatly advanced the field of AI-assisted retinal diagnosis. These models provide strong visual representation capabilities, capturing structural and semantic features from fundus images. When fine-tuned on specific tasks, LFMs have demonstrated impressive accuracy in fundus disease classification [3,12,16]. However, most existing approaches focus solely on visual cues and often lack mechanisms for modeling uncertainty or recognizing OOD samples-capabilities that are crucial for building trustworthy AI systems in clinical deployment.

To address these limitations, we propose a reliable multimodal diagnostic framework that integrates complementary information from both visual and semantic modalities. Inspired by prior work on evidence-based uncertainty modeling and multi-view fusion [6,13,14], our method leverages a vision-language foundation model (RetiZero) to extract visual features from fundus images and semantic embeddings from disease labels. Two predictive pathways are constructed: a supervised classification pathway and an imagetext similarity pathway. For each modality, we apply a Dirichlet-based evidential modeling technique to estimate class-wise belief masses and epistemic uncertainty. These outputs are then fused using a DempsterShafer-inspired uncertainty-aware combination rule, which adaptively calibrates the trust in each modality and yields robust and reliable predictions. In summary, our main contributions are as follows:

1) We propose a multimodal diagnostic framework that combines visual and semantic representations to improve both classification performance and prediction trustworthiness in fundus disease diagnosis.
2) We introduce a principled evidential modeling and uncertainty-aware fusion strategy that enables dynamic trust calibration across modalities, enhancing model robustness in both in-distribution and open-set conditions.

3) We conduct comprehensive experiments across multiple fundus disease datasets, demonstrating that our approach achieves state-of-the-art diagnostic accuracy, well-calibrated uncertainty estimates, and strong OOD detection performance, supporting its practical utility in safe and scalable ophthalmic screening.

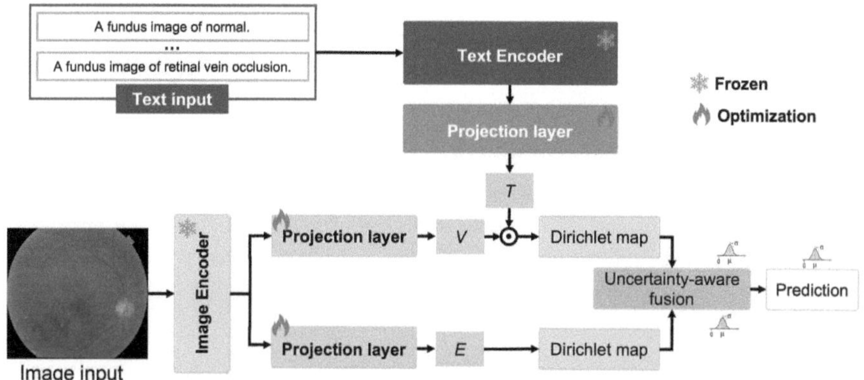

Fig. 1. Overview of our proposed method.

2   Methodology

2.1   Overall Architecture

As illustrated in Fig. 1, the proposed uncertainty-aware multimodal fusion framework is composed of three key components: (1) a vision-language feature extraction module based on the pre-trained foundation model, (2) dual predictive pathways that generate independent modality-specific predictions, and (3) an evidential uncertainty-based dynamic fusion module. During model training, the image encoder of a pre-trained vision-language foundation model (RetiZero) is used to extract high-dimensional visual features from fundus images, while disease category names are embedded via a corresponding text encoder to provide semantic context. The visual features are used for supervised disease classification, whereas the similarity between image and text embeddings provides an auxiliary semantic-guided prediction. Both predictive pathways are equipped with evidential modeling to estimate belief masses and uncertainty scores. These outputs are then dynamically integrated through an uncertainty-aware fusion strategy, which adaptively integrates each modality according to its confidence. This design enables the model to generate reliable predictions with well-calibrated uncertainty, thereby enhancing the trustworthiness of AI-assisted fundus disease diagnosis. The technical details of each component will be presented in the following sections.

2.2   Vision-Language Feature Extraction

We leverage a pre-trained vision-language foundation model, RetiZero, to extract both visual and semantic representations for fundus disease classification. The model consists of two encoders: an image encoder f_{img} that maps fundus photographs to high-dimensional visual embeddings, and a text encoder f_{text} that converts disease category names into semantic feature vectors. Given an input fundus image x, we use a frozen image encoder to extract its visual feature $v = f_{\mathrm{img}}(x) \in \mathbb{R}^d$. For each disease class label c_i, its name is tokenized and passed through a text encoder to obtain the corresponding text embedding $t_i = f_{\mathrm{text}}(c_i) \in \mathbb{R}^d$, where d denotes the shared embedding dimension across modalities. As illustrated in Fig. 1, two separate projection layers are applied to the visual feature. One projects it into a visual embedding $V \in \mathbb{R}^d$ that aligns with the text embeddings for imagetext similarity computation, while the other transforms it into an evidence vector E for image-based classification. Both the similarity scores and classification logits are passed through Dirichlet-based uncertainty modeling. A dynamic fusion module then adaptively combines the predictions based on their respective uncertainty scores.

The projected visual embedding V and the text embeddings t_i are aligned in a shared latent space to enable semantic predictions. Specifically, we compute the cosine similarity between V and each disease label embedding t_i, followed by a softmax normalization:

$$s_i = \frac{V^\top t_i}{\|V\|\|t_i\|}, \quad p_i = \frac{\exp(s_i/\tau)}{\sum_j \exp(s_j/\tau)}, \tag{1}$$

where τ is a temperature scaling parameter, and p_i denotes the semantic prediction score for class c_i.

These semantic predictions provide an additional modality that complements the supervised classification pathway based on the evidence vector E. By leveraging both visual features and class-level textual semantics, this dual-path design enables the model to benefit from global structural cues and contextual priors, thereby improving discrimination, particularly for visually ambiguous or under-represented disease patterns.

2.3   Evidential Modeling

To improve the reliability of model predictions, we incorporate evidential uncertainty modeling into both the imagetext similarity and the supervised classification pathways. Instead of directly outputting point estimates of class probabilities, we model the predictive distribution using a Dirichlet distribution, parameterized by non-negative evidence values. This formulation allows the model to capture both class-specific belief and overall epistemic uncertainty.

Given the visual embedding for similarity-based prediction and the evidence vector from the classification head, we apply a `Softplus` activation to obtain non-negative evidence scores $\mathbf{e} = [e_1, e_2, \ldots, e_K]$ for K disease classes. The Dirichlet parameters are then defined as:

$$\boldsymbol{\alpha} = \mathbf{e} + 1. \tag{2}$$

From this, the belief mass b_i for each class and the overall uncertainty u are computed as:

$$b_i = \frac{e_i}{S}, \quad u = \frac{K}{S}, \quad S = \sum_{i=1}^{K} \alpha_i, \tag{3}$$

where b_i represents the proportion of belief assigned to class i, and u reflects the epistemic uncertainty due to limited evidence. A higher u indicates lower model confidence in its prediction.

To train the model, we adopt an evidential loss function $\mathcal{L}_{\text{Evi}}$ that encourages high confidence for correct predictions while maintaining calibrated uncertainty. It consists of a modified cross-entropy loss $\mathcal{L}_{\text{Ice}}$ derived from the Dirichlet distribution, and a regularization term $\mathcal{L}_{\text{KL}}$ that penalizes unjustified certainty:

$$\mathcal{L}_{\text{Evi}} = \mathcal{L}_{\text{Ice}} + \lambda \cdot \mathcal{L}_{\text{KL}}, \tag{4}$$

where λ is a weighting factor annealed from 0 to 1 over training to avoid early over-regularization.

The modified cross-entropy loss is defined as:

$$\mathcal{L}_{\text{Ice}} = \sum_{k=1}^{K} y_k \left(\Phi(S) - \Phi(\alpha_k) \right), \tag{5}$$

where y_k is the one-hot ground truth label, $\Phi(\cdot)$ denotes the digamma function, and $S = \sum_{i=1}^{K} \alpha_i$ is the Dirichlet strength.

The KL divergence term $\mathcal{L}_{\text{KL}}$ measures the divergence between the predicted Dirichlet distribution and a flat prior:

$$\begin{aligned}
\mathcal{L}_{\text{KL}} = \log &\left(\frac{\Gamma\left(\sum_{k=1}^{K} \tilde{\alpha}_k\right)}{\Gamma(K) \cdot \prod_{k=1}^{K} \Gamma(\tilde{\alpha}_k)} \right) \\
&+ \sum_{k=1}^{K} (\tilde{\alpha}_k - 1) \left[\Phi(\tilde{\alpha}_k) - \Phi\left(\sum_{i=1}^{K} \tilde{\alpha}_i\right) \right],
\end{aligned} \tag{6}$$

where $\Gamma(\cdot)$ is the gamma function, and $\tilde{\alpha} = y + (1 - y) \odot \alpha$ is used to avoid penalizing the ground-truth class.

To further stabilize training and reinforce discriminative learning, we introduce an auxiliary cross-entropy loss directly over the normalized evidence scores:

$$\mathcal{L}_{\text{ce}} = - \sum_{i=1}^{K} y_i \log(e_i). \tag{7}$$

The final loss function combines both components using a curriculum strategy:

$$\mathcal{L} = \mathcal{L}_{\text{ce}} + \alpha \cdot \mathcal{L}_{\text{Evi}}, \tag{8}$$

where α is a scaling factor gradually increased from 0 to 0.1 during training. This prevents over-penalization from the Dirichlet regularization in the early stages, ensuring more stable convergence and better-calibrated predictions.

2.4 Uncertainty-Aware Fusion Strategy

To integrate the predictions from the imagetext similarity and supervised classification pathways in a principled and interpretable manner, we adopt a DempsterShafer-based fusion strategy. This method combines belief masses and uncertainty scores derived from Dirichlet distributions using Dempster's rule of combination, enabling adaptive and conflict-aware decision fusion.

Let $\mathcal{M}_1 = \{\mathbf{b}^{\text{cls}}, u^{\text{cls}}\}$ and $\mathcal{M}_2 = \{\mathbf{b}^{\text{sim}}, u^{\text{sim}}\}$ represent the belief and uncertainty mass functions from the classification and similarity pathways, respectively, where $\mathbf{b} = [b_1, \ldots, b_K]$ are class-wise belief masses and u is the total uncertainty. The fused opinion $\mathcal{M} = \mathcal{M}_1 \oplus \mathcal{M}_2 = \{\mathbf{b}^{\text{fused}}, u^{\text{fused}}\}$ is computed as:

$$b_k^{\text{fused}} = \frac{1}{1-C}\left(b_k^{\text{cls}}b_k^{\text{sim}} + b_k^{\text{cls}}u^{\text{sim}} + b_k^{\text{sim}}u^{\text{cls}}\right), \quad u^{\text{fused}} = \frac{1}{1-C}u^{\text{cls}}u^{\text{sim}}, \tag{9}$$

where the conflict mass C is defined as:

$$C = \sum_{i=1}^{K} \sum_{j=1, j\neq i}^{K} b_i^{\text{cls}}b_j^{\text{sim}}. \tag{10}$$

The fusion operator naturally promotes consensus and down-weights conflicting evidence. When both modalities agree with low uncertainty, the combined belief becomes sharper; when there is high disagreement, the uncertainty mass u^{fused} increases to reflect model hesitation. Finally, the predicted class is determined by selecting the class with the highest fused belief:

$$\hat{y} = \arg\max_k b_k^{\text{fused}}. \tag{11}$$

This approach enables robust multimodal fusion under both in-distribution and out-of-distribution scenarios by prioritizing reliable sources and modeling sample-specific view quality.

3 Dataset and Experiments Settings

To evaluate the performance of the proposed method, we collected a dataset of 3,289 fundus images from multiple ophthalmic clinics with complex feature distributions, including 8 types of fundus diseases and one normal condition. We

Table 1. F1 score of different methods in the task of opthalmic disease diagnosis. AMD: Age-related Macular Degeneration; CSCR: Central Serous Chorioretinopathy; DR: Diabetic Retinopathy; ERM: Epiretinal Membrane; PM: Pathologic Myoia; RD: Retinal Detachment; RVO: Retinal Vein Occlusion.

Category	FLAIR	RETFound	FMUE	RetiZero	RetiZeroUn	**Proposed**	**Proposed_T**
Normal	0.922	0.972	0.962	0.973	0.973	**0.983**	**0.996**
AMD	0.761	0.615	0.922	0.895	0.891	**0.921**	**0.942**
CSCR	0.605	0.642	0.747	0.696	0.711	**0.861**	**0.885**
DR	0.835	0.720	0.855	0.852	0.850	**0.907**	**0.946**
ERM	0.471	0.412	0.400	0.653	0.612	**0.800**	**0.923**
Glaucoma	0.797	0.667	0.786	0.884	0.884	**0.912**	**0.989**
PM	0.867	0.833	0.955	0.989	0.989	**1.000**	**1.000**
RD	0.759	0.758	0.905	0.864	0.864	**0.934**	**0.969**
RVO	0.765	0.567	0.902	0.831	0.875	**0.920**	**0.986**
Average	0.753	0.687	0.826	0.848	0.850	**0.915**	**0.960**

divided it into training (1,970), validation (658), and testing (661) sets for model training, selection, and performance evaluation. RetiZero is a vision-language foundation model tailored for ophthalmic applications, trained on over 340,000 fundus imagetext pairs encompassing more than 400 retinal conditions [12]. By jointly learning visual and semantic representations in a shared embedding space, RetiZero enables robust alignment between fundus images and disease labels. Therefore, in this work, we leverage the frozen image and text encoders of RetiZero to provide high-quality multimodal features for reliable disease diagnosis and uncertainty modeling. We conducted experiments on the public platform PyTorch and RTXA6000 GPU (48G). Adam optimizer was adopted to guide the model optimization with a batch size of 64 and maximum training epochs of 20.

4   Experimental Results

4.1   Experimental Results and Analysis

Table 1 presents the F1 scores of different methods across nine ophthalmic diseases. Overall, the proposed method consistently outperforms state-of-the-art baselines, including FLAIR [11], RETFound [16], and FMUE [9], across all categories. It achieves an average F1 score of 0.915, notably higher than RetiZero (0.848) and its uncertainty-aware variant RetiZeroUn (0.850), which integrates the uncertainty modeling technique from UIOS [13]. These results highlight the effectiveness of our enhanced architecture and uncertainty-aware fusion strategy.

For challenging categories like central serous chorioretinopathy (CSCR) and epiretinal membrane (ERM), both which typically exhibit subtle and heterogeneous manifestations, our model shows significant performance gains (ERM: 0.800 vs. 0.653 by RetiZero; CSCR: 0.861 vs. 0.711 by RetiZeroUn), demonstrating improved capability in recognizing difficult-to-diagnose conditions. Furthermore, when incorporating the uncertainty thresholding mechanism (**Proposed_T**), which refers high-uncertainty cases for clinician review and reports results on only high-confidence predictions, the performance further improves to an average F1 of 0.960. This highlights the potential of uncertainty-aware triaging in real-world deployment scenarios, allowing the model to prioritize reliability over aggressive automation. The strong performance on both prevalent diseases like diabetic retinopathy (DR: 0.946) and age-related macular degeneration (AMD: 0.942), and more complex conditions such as retinal detachment (RD: 0.969) and retinal vein occlusion (RVO: 0.986), underscores the robustness and generalizability of our approach. These results validate the clinical utility of the proposed framework in enhancing diagnostic accuracy while enabling interpretable and risk-aware AI-assisted decision-making.

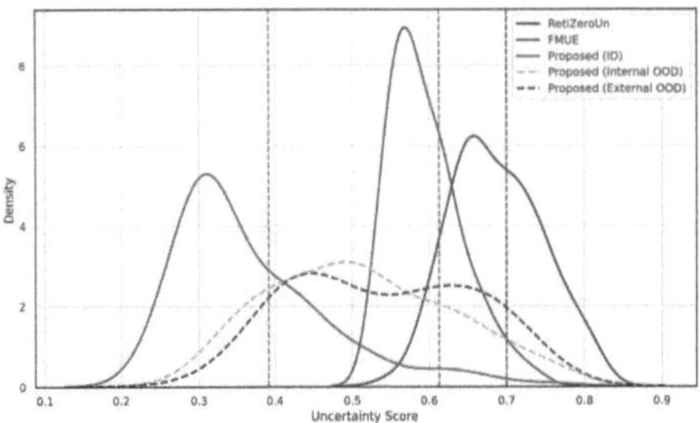

Fig. 2. Distribution of uncertainty scores across different methods and datasets.

4.2   Uncertainty Score Distribution Analysis

Figure 2 illustrates the distribution of uncertainty scores predicted by three methods: RetiZeroUn, FMUE [9], and our Proposed method. Each curve represents the density of uncertainty estimates across all samples, with vertical dashed lines indicating the optimal thresholds computed using Youden's Index (0.70 for RetiZeroUn, 0.613 for FMUE, and 0.392 for Proposed) as follows.

$$J(u) = \text{Sensitivity}(u) + \text{Specificity}(u) - 1, \tag{12}$$

where, Sensitivity(u) denotes the true positive rate, and Specificity(u) denotes the true negative rate, both evaluated on predictions considered reliable at the uncertainty score u. The optimal threshold θ^* is computed as: $\theta^* = \arg\max_u J(u)$. The proposed method demonstrates a noticeably left-skewed distribution, with a higher concentration of samples exhibiting low uncertainty scores (<0.4), suggesting a stronger confidence in its predictions. In contrast, RetiZeroUn and FMUE display broader distributions centered around mid-range uncertainty values, indicating greater ambiguity in their assessments. We further apply the threshold $\theta^* = 0.392$ on the proposed method's uncertainty scores to quantify its OOD detection performance, which is critical for real-world deployment. The Internal OOD dataset, collected from the same institution as the training data but comprising unseen disease categories, yielded an OOD detection rate of 81.9%. In contrast, the external OOD dataset, consisting of unseen diseases from a different medical institution, achieved a detection rate of 94.1%. These results are consistent with the uncertainty score distributions (orange and purple dashed lines), where both OOD datasets exhibit a significant rightward shift relative to the in-distribution curve, reflecting higher model uncertainty when encountering unfamiliar samples. These results demonstrate that the proposed method not only improves confidence calibration on in-distribution (ID) samples but also reliably elevates uncertainty on both internal and external OOD inputs.

5 Conclusion

In this study, we present a novel uncertainty-aware multimodal diagnostic framework for fundus disease classification, which integrates visual and semantic representations via the vision-language foundation model RetiZero. The proposed framework combines supervised classification and imagetext similarity pathways, each modeled using Dirichlet-based evidential learning to estimate belief masses and uncertainty. A DempsterShafer-inspired fusion strategy adaptively integrates the two modalities based on their confidence. Experiments on multi-disease fundus datasets and OOD benchmarks show that our method outperforms state-of-the-art baselines in diagnostic performance, provides well-calibrated uncertainty estimates, and enables effective risk-aware triaging. These results highlight our proposed method's potential for improving both diagnostic performance and trustworthiness in real-world ophthalmic screening.

Acknowledgements. This work is supported by the National Medical Research Council (NMRC) grant, Singapore (MOH-001792-04 and MOH-CSASI22jul-0001), Shantou Science and Technology Program (190917085269835), 2020 Li Ka Shing Foundation Cross-Disciplinary Research Grant (2020LKSFG14B).

References

1. Burton, M.J., et al.: The lancet global health commission on global eye health: vision beyond 2020. Lancet Glob. Health **9**(4), e489–e551 (2021)
2. Chen, C., Liu, Q., Jin, Y., Dou, Q., Heng, P.-A.: Source-free domain adaptive fundus image segmentation with denoised pseudo-labeling. In: de Bruijne, M., et al. (eds.) MICCAI 2021. LNCS, vol. 12905, pp. 225–235. Springer, Cham (2021). https://doi.org/10.1007/978-3-030-87240-3_22
3. Chen, X., et al.: Eyegpt: ophthalmic assistant with large language models. arXiv preprint arXiv:2403.00840 (2024)

4. Dai, L., et al.: A deep learning system for detecting diabetic retinopathy across the disease spectrum. Nat. Commun. **12**(1), 3242 (2021)
5. Försch, S., Klauschen, F., Hufnagl, P., Roth, W.: Artificial intelligence in pathology. Dtsch. Arztebl. Int. **118**(12), 199 (2021)
6. Han, Z., Zhang, C., Fu, H., Zhou, J.T.: Trusted multi-view classification with dynamic evidential fusion. IEEE Trans. Pattern Anal. Mach. Intell. **45**(2), 2551–2566 (2022)
7. Li, Z., et al.: Artificial intelligence in ophthalmology: the path to the real-world clinic. Cell Rep. Med. **4**(7) (2023)
8. Liu, Q., Chen, C., Qin, J., Dou, Q., Heng, P.A.: Feddg: federated domain generalization on medical image segmentation via episodic learning in continuous frequency space. In: Proceedings of the IEEE/CVF Conference on Computer Vision and Pattern Recognition, pp. 1013–1023 (2021)
9. Peng, Y., et al.: Enhancing AI reliability: a foundation model with uncertainty estimation for optical coherence tomography-based retinal disease diagnosis. Cell Rep. Med. **6**(1) (2025)
10. Peng, Y., et al.: Automatic staging for retinopathy of prematurity with deep feature fusion and ordinal classification strategy. IEEE Trans. Med. Imaging **40**(7), 1750–1762 (2021)
11. Silva-Rodriguez, J., Chakor, H., Kobbi, R., Dolz, J., Ayed, I.B.: A foundation language-image model of the retina (flair): encoding expert knowledge in text supervision. Med. Image Anal. **99**, 103357 (2025)
12. Wang, M., et al.: Enhancing diagnostic accuracy in rare and common fundus diseases with a knowledge-rich vision-language model. Nat. Commun. **16**(1), 5528 (2025)
13. Wang, M., et al.: Uncertainty-inspired open set learning for retinal anomaly identification. Nat. Commun. **14**(1), 6757 (2023)
14. Wang, M., et al.: Reliable federated disentangling network for non-iid domain feature. IEEE Trans. Big Data (2024)
15. Yan, Q., et al.: Deep-learning-based prediction of late age-related macular degeneration progression. Nat. Mach. Intell. **2**(2), 141–150 (2020)
16. Zhou, Y., et al.: A foundation model for generalizable disease detection from retinal images. Nature **622**(7981), 156–163 (2023)

RetBench: Which Ophthalmic Foundation Model Performs Best and Why?

Ke Zou[1,2], Jocelyn Hui Lin Goh[1,2,3], Yukun Zhou[5], Samantha Min Er Yew[1,2], Meng Wang[1,2], Huazhu Fu[6], Ching-Yu Cheng[1,2,3,4], and Yih Chung Tham[1,2,3,4(✉)]

[1] Department of Ophthalmology, Yong Loo Lin School of Medicine, National University of Singapore, Singapore, Singapore
[2] Centre for Innovation and Precision Eye Health, Yong Loo Lin School of Medicine, National University of Singapore, Singapore, Singapore
[3] Singapore Eye Research Institute, Singapore National Eye Centre, Singapore, Singapore
[4] Ophthalmology and Visual Science Academic Clinical Program, Duke-NUS Medical School, Singapore, Singapore
thamyc@nus.edu.sg
[5] Centre for Medical Image Computing, University College London, London, UK
[6] Institute of High Performance Computing, A*STAR, Singapore, Singapore

Abstract. Foundation models (FMs) have shown great promise in medical image analysis by improving generalization across diverse downstream tasks. In ophthalmology, several FMs have recently emerged, but there is still no clear answer to a fundamental question: *Which FM performs the best? Are they equally good across different tasks?* The lack of standardized benchmarks makes it difficult to fairly compare these models. To address this gap, we propose RetBench, a comprehensive evaluation suite covering both ophthalmic disease detection (glaucoma, diabetic retinopathy, and age-related macular degeneration) and systemic disease prediction (diabetes and hypertension) based on retinal imaging. We benchmarked four state-of-the-art FMs (RETFound, VisionFM, RetiZero, and DINORET) using standardized datasets from multiple countries and evaluated their performance comprehensive metrics. Our results show that DINORET, RetiZero, and RETFound perform similarly across most tasks. We recommend using DINORET as the base model for glaucoma detection. For instance, RetiZero achieved an average AUC of 0.92 on external validation datasets for systemic disease prediction, compared to 0.88 by the next best model, and showed particularly strong generalization in diabetes prediction. These findings provide an evidence-based answer to the above questions and highlight future directions for improving the clinical applicability of ophthalmic foundation models.

Keywords: Foundation model · Ophthalmology · Benchmarking

H. Fang et al. (Eds.): OMIA 2025, LNCS 16209, pp. 75–84, 2026.
https://doi.org/10.1007/978-3-032-10351-2_8

1 Introduction

Foundation models (FMs) leverage large-scale datasets and pretraining strategies to build versatile models capable of generalizing across a wide range of downstream tasks. In recent years, medical foundation models have achieved significant success across various imaging domains, including radiology [1,7], pathology [13,16], oncology [15], and dermatology [17], demonstrating improved accuracy and generalization on diverse clinical tasks.

Compared to these fields, ophthalmology presents unique opportunities for FM development. Ocular images, such as fundus photographs and optical coherence tomography (OCT) scans, capture rich biomarkers not only for eye diseases but also for systemic conditions, making them a valuable modality for developing generalizable medical foundation models. With the growing availability of ophthalmic imaging data and advancements in model architectures, several ophthalmic FMs [2,6,9–12,14,19,21] have recently emerged, highlighting the potential of foundation models to support a broad range of clinical applications in eye care and beyond. In the following, we provide an overview of four representative FMs in ophthalmology, each characterized by distinct model architectures and pretraining strategies. First, the pioneering retinal foundation model RETFound [19] learns generalizable representations from large-scale unlabeled retinal images, providing a strong foundation for adapting to various ophthalmic applications. Then, VisionFM [10] leverages pretraining across diverse ophthalmic modalities and imaging devices to establish a strong foundation for disease screening and diagnosis, prognosis prediction, disease phenotyping and subtyping tasks. Furthermore, RetiZero [12] trains a knowledge-enriched vision-language foundation model using public datasets, ophthalmology literature, and online resources, enabling zero-shot disease recognition, image-to-image retrieval, AI-assisted clinical diagnosis, few-shot fine-tuning, and both in-domain and cross-domain disease identification. More recently, DINORET [21] employs DINOv2 [8] vision transformers for self-supervised learning on retinal image classification tasks and addresses the issue of catastrophic forgetting during foundation model fine-tuning. While these models have demonstrated strong potential across a range of clinical applications, systematic benchmarking and comparative analysis remain scarce. Yew et al. [18] evaluated RETFound against traditional CNN-based approaches, but direct, head-to-head comparisons among modern foundation models are still lacking. Zhou et al. [20] investigated the composition of pretraining datasets across various FMs, highlighting substantial differences in data sources and scales. However, a comprehensive and systematic comparison of these models under unified evaluation settings remains absent. This issue is further exacerbated by the fact that existing FMs are often pretrained on disparate datasets with heterogeneous data curation pipelines and varying annotation quality. In addition, the lack of a standardized benchmarking framework and consistent evaluation protocols makes it challenging to fairly assess and compare model performance across different ophthalmic and systemic disease tasks.

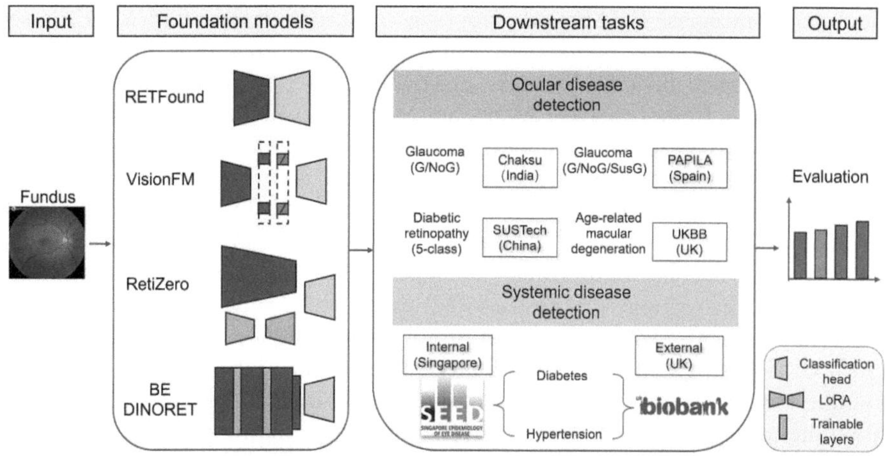

Fig. 1. Overview framework of RetBench.

To address these limitations, we propose **RetBench**, a comprehensive benchmarking suite that covers key tasks in both ocular disease detection and systemic disease prediction from color fundus photographs. Specifically, we curate and organize datasets collected from both public and private sources for core ophthalmic disease detection tasks, including glaucoma, diabetic retinopathy (DR), and age-related macular degeneration (AMD). These datasets have not been previously used for pretraining in existing foundation models. In addition, we construct new datasets for systemic disease prediction tasks, such as diabetes and hypertension, where relevant biomarkers can be inferred from ocular images. To ensure fair comparisons across different foundation models, RetBench employs widely used evaluation metrics to assess model performance across a broad range of disease categories and tasks. Our results show that while most current eye foundation models achieve comparable performance on ocular disease detection tasks, models such as RetiZero and RETFound demonstrate superior performance in systemic disease prediction.

2   RetBench Design

As shown in the Fig. 1 illustrates the overall framework of the proposed RetBench. The core design follows a frozen backbone strategy, where only the classification head is trained for downstream tasks. The benchmark covers both ophthalmic disease detection and systemic disease prediction, with model performance evaluated through comprehensive metrics.

2.1   Foundation Models for Ophthalmology

Four representative ophthalmic foundation models were employed for comparison on this benchmark, each pre-trained with different corpora, image modalities, and strategies. RETFound adopts a masked autoencoder (MAE)-based self-supervised learning framework using large-scale unlabeled retinal fundus and OCT images. Specifically, it is pre-trained on 1.64 million images across two modalities from the EyePACS and MEH-MIDAS datasets. VisionFM is built upon an iBOT-based architecture, employing self-supervised learning with image-token reconstruction and self-distillation. It is pre-trained on 3.4 million images spanning eight ophthalmic modalities, collected from various public and private datasets. The model adopts separate encoders for each modality and incorporates task-specific decoders to support a wide range of clinical applications. RetiZero employs a multimodal architecture that combines a masked autoencoder (MAE) with Low-Rank Adaptation (LoRA) for the image encoder and a CLIP-based text encoder enhanced with uncertainty estimation. Its pre-training corpus consists of approximately 340K paired image-text samples from 30 public ophthalmology datasets, covering two imaging modalities. DINORET leverages a block expansion strategy to adapt pre-trained DINOv2 vision transformers to the ophthalmic domain. It is trained using more than 202K color fundus images sourced from four public datasets. The model inserts identity-initialized duplicate transformer blocks into DINOv2 and fine-tunes only these newly added blocks using contrastive self-supervised learning, thereby retaining general visual representations while adapting to ophthalmic-specific characteristics. For consistency, all four foundation models adopt a data augmentation pipeline similar to that of RETFound.

2.2   Settings and Data Sources

1) Problem Formulation. To ensure a fair comparison across different foundation models, we adopt a unified experimental setting. For each model, we load its pre-trained backbone weights $f(w_i)$, where w_i denotes the frozen parameters of the i-th foundation model. We then train only a lightweight task-specific classification head, denoted as $f_i^c(\cdot)$, as illustrated in Fig. 1. Given an input fundus image x, the prediction for a target task (either ophthalmic disease detection or systemic disease prediction) is defined as:

$$\hat{y} = f_i^c\big(f(w_i)(x)\big) \tag{1}$$

Here, $\hat{y} \in \mathbb{R}^K$ denotes the predicted logits or probabilities for K classes in the given task. Only the classification head f_i^c is optimized during training, while the backbone $f(w_i)$ remains frozen. This unified setup allows us to evaluate the representational quality of different foundation models under identical conditions on two types of tasks. In the following sections, we introduce the detailed task settings and the corresponding datasets used for each task. These include both publicly available and private datasets, covering diverse populations and imaging devices to ensure robustness and generalizability in evaluation.

2) Task 1: Ocular Diseases. Glaucoma, DR, and AMD are among the most common and clinically significant ophthalmic diseases worldwide. These conditions are major causes of visual impairment and blindness, posing a substantial global health and socioeconomic burden. Given their high prevalence, well-established diagnostic criteria, and the availability of annotated datasets, these diseases serve as essential benchmark tasks for evaluating the effectiveness and generalizability of ophthalmic foundation models. Therefore, RetBench includes glaucoma, DR, and AMD as representative tasks for standardized assessment of model performance in this domain.

For glaucoma detection, we utilize the publicly available Chaksu [4] and PAPILA [3] datasets. The Chaksu dataset was developed as an Indian ethnicity fundus image database for glaucoma prescreening. It contains a total of 1,345 color fundus images acquired using three different brands of commercially available fundus cameras. For each image, experts provided binary glaucomatous or non-glaucomatous labels, determined through majority voting to ensure a single consensus label per image. The dataset includes 188 glaucomatous and 1,157 non-glaucomatous images. The PAPILA dataset was curated at the Department of Ophthalmology, Hospital General Universitario Reina Sofía (HGURS), Murcia, Spain, with data collected between 2018 and 2020. It includes records from 244 patients, comprising a total of 488 fundus images in JPEG format, corresponding to both the right and left eyes. All images are categorized into three classes: healthy (333 images), glaucoma (68 images), and glaucoma suspect (87 images). For the DR task, we adopt the SUSTech-SYSU dataset [5], which contains 1,219 fundus images collected from DR patients and healthy controls at Gaoyao People's Hospital and Zhongshan Ophthalmic Center, Sun Yat-sen University. The dataset includes 631 normal images and 588 DR images annotated across five severity levels: mild non-proliferative DR (24 images), moderate non-proliferative DR (365 images), severe non-proliferative DR (73 images), proliferative DR (58 images), and DR with laser spots or scars (68 images). For the AMD task, we use the accessible UK Biobank (UKBB) dataset, which is categorized into two classes: AMD and others, with approximately 680 and 9.3K cases respectively. For all aboved tasks, the corresponding datasets were split into training, validation, and test sets with a ratio of 7:1:2.

3) Task 2: Systematic Diseases. Diabetes and hypertension are among the most common systemic diseases globally, contributing substantially to morbidity and mortality. Both conditions exhibit well-characterized ocular manifestations that can be captured through retinal imaging, a field often referred to as oculomics. Early detection of these diseases via retinal biomarkers enables timely intervention and improved patient outcomes. The Singapore Eye Epidemiology (SEED) cohort is a multi-ethnic longitudinal population study designed to investigate the morbidity, prevalence, risk factors, and novel biomarkers of age-related eye diseases among Malay, Indian, and Chinese populations in Singapore. SEED provides a valuable resource for evaluating ethnic differences in the incidence and progression of ocular and systemic diseases. Similarly, the UKBB is a large-scale multi-ethnic longitudinal population study that includes extensive phenotypic and genetic labels for a wide range of systemic diseases. In this study, we selected diabetes and hypertension from SEED for internal validation, and the same disease labels from UKBB for external validation. The UKBB dataset includes approximately 5K diabetes cases and 12K controls, and approximately 7K hypertension cases and 11K controls.

2.3 Evaluation Protocol and Training Details

In addition to the commonly used area under the receiver operating characteristic curve (AUC), which has been adopted by RETFound, VisionFM, and RetiZero, we also included accuracy (ACC) as the evaluation metric, following the practice of DINORET. This allows for a more comprehensive assessment of the performance of all four foundation models on both ophthalmic disease detection and systemic disease prediction tasks.

To ensure a fair comparison across all foundation models, we adopted a unified training loss function for all experiments. Specifically, all foundation models were trained using the label smoothing Cross entropy loss, which mitigates overconfidence in predictions and promotes better generalization. The loss function is defined as:

$$\mathcal{L} = -(1 - \epsilon) \log(p_y) - \frac{\epsilon}{K} \sum_{i=1}^{K} \log(p_i) \tag{2}$$

where p_y is the predicted probability of the ground-truth class, K is the total number of classes, and ϵ is the smoothing parameter. In all experiments, we set the label smoothing parameter ϵ to 0.1 following RETFound [19], which helps prevent overfitting and promotes better generalization.

3   Experiments

3.1 Implementation Details

All experiments were conducted on the PyTorch platform using an NVIDIA A6000 GPU with 48 GB of memory. We adopted a layer-wise learning rate decay strategy when constructing the optimizer, grouping model parameters with different decay rates based on their depth within the network. All models were optimized using the AdamW optimizer with an initial learning rate of 0.0001. The maximum number of training iterations was set to 100, and the batch size was fixed at 16. During training, different random seeds were used, and the checkpoint with the best AUC on the validation set was saved for all baselines. All experiments employed a bootstrap method with 1,000 sampling iterations to obtain 95% confidence intervals (CIs). All images are resized to 224 × 224 during fine-tuning.

3.2 Experimental Results

Figs. 2 and 3 summarize the performance of the four foundation models on ophthalmic and systemic disease detection tasks across different datasets, using ACC and AUC as evaluation metrics. The experimental results are further elaborated and analyzed in the following sections.

Results of Ocular Diseases. As shown in Fig. 2, we present the performance of different foundation models on three ophthalmic diseases across four datasets from different countries. In terms of AUC with 95% CIs, for glaucoma detection on the Chaksu and PAPILA datasets, DINORET and RetiZero achieved comparable performance, both outperforming VisionFM. On the PAPILA dataset, DINORET also outperformed the other FMs. For DR detection (SUSTech dataset) and AMD detection (UKBB dataset), a similar pattern was observed: RETFound and RetiZero again achieved comparable performance and outperformed VisionFM. In terms of ACC with 95% CIs, the four foundation models demonstrated comparable performance for glaucoma (Chaksu dataset) and AMD (UKBB dataset) detection. On the PAPILA dataset, DINORET, RetiZero and RETFound again achieved litter better performance over VisionFM, with VisionFM outperforming DINORET. For DR detection (SUSTech dataset), RetiZero was significantly better than VisionFM. Overall, these results suggest that RETFound, RetiZero and DINORET tend to outperform VisionFM in ophthalmic disease detection tasks. One possible reason is that VisionFM is based on a ViT-base architecture, whereas RETFound and RetiZero are both built on ViT-large backbones. In addition, DINORET may benefit from the diversity of its pretraining dataset, which includes different ophthalmic datasets, as well as the strong DINOv2 backbone architecture.

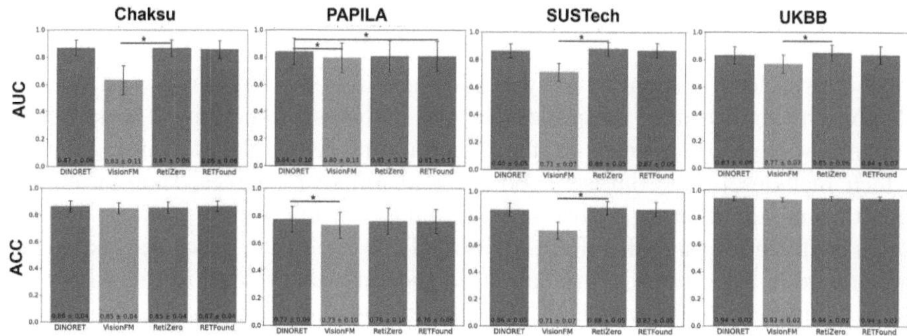

Fig. 2. Performance of the four FMs on ocular disease detection tasks across various datasets. The blue lines with asterisks indicate a p-value < 0.001. (Color figure online)

Results of Systematic Diseases. As shown in Fig. 3, we compare the performance of different foundation models on two systemic disease prediction tasks using datasets from two countries. Based on AUC and ACC with 95% confidence intervals, for diabetes prediction on the SEED internal dataset, DINORET, RetiZero, and RETFound performed comparably, all outperforming VisionFM. On the external validation dataset (UKBB; 2nd column), RetiZero achieved the best performance in both AUC and ACC. For hypertension prediction on the SEED dataset, DINORET, RetiZero, and RETFound again showed similar performance, all surpassing VisionFM. On the external UKBB dataset (4th column), the models exhibited relatively similar AUCs, with DINORET showing a slight advantage in ACC over VisionFM. Overall, performance was lower on the external dataset compared to the internal one, highlighting the challenge of hypertension prediction in external cohorts.

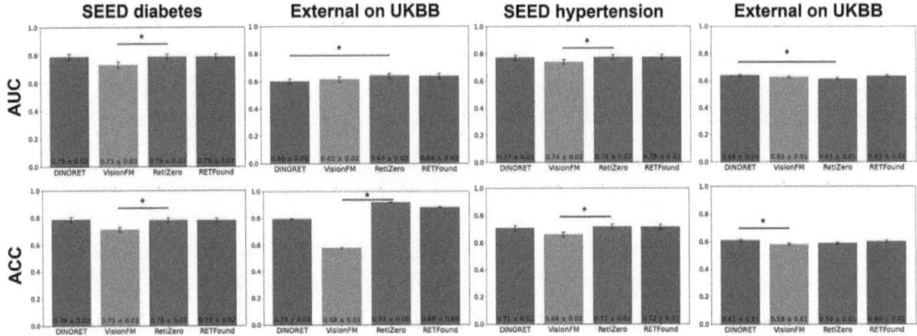

Fig. 3. Performance (AUC and ACC) of the four foundation models on ocular disease detection tasks across various datasets.

Overall, these results suggest that DINORET, RetiZero, and RETFound generally outperform VisionFM in systemic disease prediction tasks, with RetiZero demonstrating stronger generalizability in diabetes prediction. A possible reason is that RetiZero benefits from a richer and more diverse pretraining dataset, which includes public datasets, books, and online resources, thereby enhancing its generalization capabilities. Additionally, its fine-tuning strategy incorporates both Retfound and LoRA. DINORET, on the other hand, showed a slight advantage in hypertension prediction on the external validation set, which may be attributed to the powerful DINOv2 backbone and pretraining on ophthalmic datasets. Nonetheless, all models struggled with hypertension prediction on the external dataset, highlighting an area that warrants further investigation. In summary, our findings indicate that DINORET and RetiZero perform comparably to RETFound on internal datasets for both ophthalmic disease detection and systemic disease prediction tasks, while offering potentially better generalization on external datasets.

4   Conclusions

In this study, we introduced RetBench, a comprehensive benchmark designed to standardize the evaluation of foundation models in ophthalmology. Through extensive experiments across multiple datasets and tasks, we demonstrated that RETFound and RetiZero consistently achieved superior performance compared to DINORET and VisionFM in both ophthalmic disease detection and systemic disease prediction. RetiZero, in particular, exhibited stronger generalization on external datasets, highlighting the importance of diverse pretraining data and effective fine-tuning strategies. DINORET also demonstrates strong potential for both ophthalmic disease detection and systemic disease prediction. We also observed that systemic disease prediction, especially hypertension detection on external cohorts, remains a challenging problem for current FMs. In future work, we will further analyze the model architectures and their efficiency to enhance the transparency of each foundation model. Additionally, we advocate for broader clinical application and deployment of foundation models to strengthen their real-world impact.

References

1. Bluethgen, C., et al.: A vision–language foundation model for the generation of realistic chest x-ray images. Nat. Biomed. Eng. 1–13 (2024)
2. Da Soh, Z., et al.: An integrated language-vision foundation model for conversational diagnostics and triaging in primary eye care. arXiv preprint arXiv:2505.08414 (2025)
3. Kovalyk, O., Morales-Sánchez, J., Verdú-Monedero, R., Sellés-Navarro, I., Palazón-Cabanes, A., Sancho-Gómez, J.L.: Papila: dataset with fundus images and clinical data of both eyes of the same patient for glaucoma assessment. Sci. Data **9**(1), 291 (2022)
4. Kumar, J.H., et al.: Chákṣu: a glaucoma specific fundus image database. Sci. Data **10**(1), 70 (2023)
5. Lin, L., et al.: The sustech-sysu dataset for automated exudate detection and diabetic retinopathy grading. Sci. Data **7**(1), 409 (2020)
6. Liu, Z., et al.: Octcube: a 3d foundation model for optical coherence tomography that improves cross-dataset, cross-disease, cross-device and cross-modality analysis. arXiv preprint arXiv:2408.11227 (2024)
7. Ma, D., Pang, J., Gotway, M.B., Liang, J.: A fully open AI foundation model applied to chest radiography. Nature 1–11 (2025)
8. Oquab, M., et al.: Dinov2: learning robust visual features without supervision. arXiv preprint arXiv:2304.07193 (2023)
9. Peng, Y., et al.: Enhancing AI reliability: a foundation model with uncertainty estimation for optical coherence tomography-based retinal disease diagnosis. Cell Rep. Med. **6**(1) (2025)
10. Qiu, J., et al.: Visionfm: a multi-modal multi-task vision foundation model for generalist ophthalmic artificial intelligence. arXiv preprint arXiv:2310.04992 (2023)
11. Shi, D., et al.: Eyefound: a multimodal generalist foundation model for ophthalmic imaging. arXiv preprint arXiv:2405.11338 (2024)
12. Wang, M., et al.: Common and rare fundus diseases identification using vision-language foundation model with knowledge of over 400 diseases. arXiv preprint arXiv:2406.09317 (2024)
13. Wang, X., et al.: A pathology foundation model for cancer diagnosis and prognosis prediction. Nature **634**(8035), 970–978 (2024)
14. Wong, T.Y., et al.: Eyefm: a multi-modal vision-language copilot foundation model for eyecare (2025)

15. Xiang, J., et al.: A vision–language foundation model for precision oncology. Nature 1–10 (2025)
16. Xu, H., et al.: A whole-slide foundation model for digital pathology from real-world data. Nature **630**(8015), 181–188 (2024)
17. Yan, S., et al.: A multimodal vision foundation model for clinical dermatology. Nat. Med. 1–12 (2025)
18. Yew, S.M.E., et al.: Are traditional deep learning model approaches as effective as a retinal-specific foundation model for ocular and systemic disease detection? arXiv preprint arXiv:2501.12016 (2025)
19. Zhou, Y., et al.: A foundation model for generalizable disease detection from retinal images. Nature **622**(7981), 156–163 (2023)
20. Zhou, Y., et al.: Revealing the impact of pre-training data on medical foundation models (2025)
21. Zoellin, J., et al.: Block expanded dinoret: adapting natural domain foundation models for retinal imaging without catastrophic forgetting. arXiv preprint arXiv:2409.17332 (2024)

On the Limits of Uncertainty-Aware Fine-Tuning for Robust Diabetic Retinopathy Screening

Ting Xu[1,2]($\boxtimes$), Jie Zhang[3], Meng Wang[1,2], Hongyu He[1,2], and Xinbao Zou[4]

[1] Centre for Innovation and Precision Eye Health, Yong Loo Lin School of Medicine, National University of Singapore, Singapore, Singapore
[2] Department of Ophthalmology, Yong Loo Lin School of Medicine, National University of Singapore, Singapore, Singapore
`xuting@nus.edu.sg`
[3] CFAR and IHPC, Agency for Science, Technology and Research (A*STAR), Singapore, Singapore
[4] School of Information Science and Technology, Guangdong University of Foreign Studies, Guangzhou, China

Abstract. Pre-trained foundation models have advanced automated diabetic retinopathy (DR) screening by achieving high diagnostic accuracy from fundus images. To promote safe clinical deployment, uncertainty estimation is often integrated during fine-tuning to measure model confidence and detect out-of-distribution (OOD) inputs. Among challenging OOD cases, adversarial examples represent a subtle form of boundary OOD, where perturbations remain visually plausible but induce confident misclassifications. In this study, we systematically examine how uncertainty-aware fine-tuning (Uncertain-FT) affects model robustness against boundary OOD attacks on DR grading using the APTOS2019 benchmark. Adversarial examples are generated using Projected Gradient Descent (PGD) and Carlini & Wagner (C&W) attacks under both white-box and transfer scenarios, and evaluated on two representative pre-trained models, RetFound and RetiZero. Results show that Uncertain-FT offers limited improvements in adversarial robustness, with attack success rates remaining high under both PGD and C&W attacks. Moreover, many adversarial examples still yield low uncertainty scores, escaping detection, whereas human experts remain unaffected. These findings reveal critical limitations in current uncertainty quantification for detecting boundary OOD threats in DR screening and underscore the need for more robust and trustworthy uncertainty modeling in ophthalmic AI.

Keywords: Uncertainty Estimation · Adversarial Examples · Diabetic Retinopathy Screening

1   Introduction

Deep learning has greatly advanced automated ophthalmic image analysis, enabling accurate screening for diseases such as diabetic retinopathy (DR) and glaucoma [6, 14]. Recently, large-scale foundation models like RetFound [17] and RetiZero [15] have further boosted diagnostic performance by leveraging extensive pre-training on massive unlabeled fundus image datasets. To ensure trustworthiness and safety in clinical practice, uncertainty estimation [3, 10] is widely integrated into downstream fine-tuning to quantify model confidence and to flag abnormal or out-of-distribution (OOD) inputs [4, 5, 8].

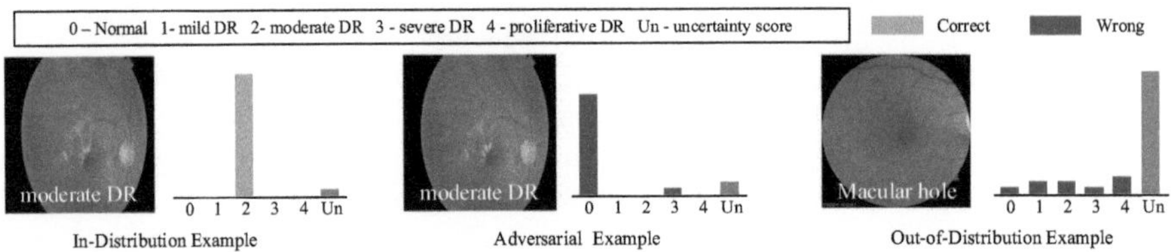

Fig. 1. Illustration of **in-distribution**, **adversarial**, and **OOD** examples in the DR classification task. The adversarial image looks identical to the in-distribution case but is misclassified with low uncertainty, while the OOD image shows high uncertainty.

However, not all OOD threats are equally detectable by existing uncertainty mechanisms. As illustrated in Fig. 1, while conventional OOD samples (e.g., a macular hole image) typically induce high uncertainty, more subtle threats such as adversarial examples—inputs that appear visually identical to in-distribution cases yet are intentionally perturbed—can cause confident misclassifications with low uncertainty. This type of boundary OOD example lies near decision boundaries and exploits blind spots in model calibration, posing a unique risk to safety-critical applications like ophthalmic diagnosis. Although uncertainty-aware training has shown promise for improving model calibration under normal conditions [13], its effectiveness in defending against boundary OOD threats remains underexplored in ophthalmic AI. This gap calls for a deeper investigation into how uncertainty estimation behaves under deliberate adversarial manipulation [7].

In this work, we systematically assess whether uncertainty-aware fine-tuning (Uncertain-FT) can enhance robustness against boundary OOD attacks in DR classification. We generate adversarial examples using Projected Gradient Descent (PGD) [9] and Carlini & Wagner (C&W) [1, 2] attacks under both white-box and transfer settings, and evaluate them on state-of-the-art foundation models RetFound and RetiZero. Our results show that while Uncertain-FT increases attack difficulty, a significant portion of adversarial examples still evade detection, producing low uncertainty despite incorrect predictions—whereas human experts remain unaffected. These findings highlight critical limitations in current uncertainty quantification for handling boundary OOD threats and underscore the need for more robust uncertainty estimation strategies to ensure trustworthy deployment of foundation models in real-world ophthalmic applications.

2   Method

2.1   Preliminaries

Uncertainty Estimation. Reliable uncertainty estimation is crucial for safe AI deployment in medical imaging. Here, we adopt an evidential deep learning framework inspired by Sensoy et al. [11] and further extended by the UIOS model [16]. The classifier predicts non-negative evidence $E = [e_1, \ldots, e_K]$ for each of the K classes using a Soft-plus activation. The Dirichlet parameters are given by:

$$\alpha_k = e_k + 1, \quad S = \sum_{k=1}^{K} \alpha_k. \tag{1}$$

The class probability is computed as $p_k = \alpha_k/S$, while the total uncertainty is quantified as:

$$u = \frac{K}{S}. \tag{2}$$

A lower total evidence S implies higher uncertainty. During inference, predictions with uncertainty u exceeding a threshold θ are flagged for manual review to reduce open-set errors.

Adversarial Examples. Adversarial examples are carefully crafted perturbations added to legitimate inputs to mislead deep neural networks [12]. To assess the robustness of our model and uncertainty estimation methods, we generate adversarial examples using two widely adopted attacks: Projected Gradient Descent (PGD) [9] and the Carlini & Wagner (C&W) attack [1,2].

PGD Attack. Given an input x and true label y, the PGD adversarial example is iteratively computed as:

$$x_{\text{adv}}^{t+1} = \Pi_{\mathcal{B}_\epsilon(x)}\left(x_{\text{adv}}^t + \alpha \frac{\nabla_x \mathcal{L}(f(x_{\text{adv}}^t), y)}{\|\nabla_x \mathcal{L}(f(x_{\text{adv}}^t), y)\|_2}\right), \tag{3}$$

where $\Pi_{\mathcal{B}_\epsilon(x)}$ denotes the projection onto the L_2 ϵ-ball around x, α is the step size, and $\mathcal{L}$ is the cross-entropy loss.

C&W Attack. The C&W attack formulates the adversarial perturbation as the solution to the following constrained optimization:

$$\min_{\delta} \|\delta\|_2^2 + c \cdot \mathcal{L}_{\text{C\&W}}(x + \delta, y), \quad \text{s.t. } x + \delta \in [0, 1]^n, \tag{4}$$

where $\mathcal{L}_{\text{C\&W}}$ is a hinge-like loss encouraging misclassification, and c is a balancing constant.

By applying both attacks, we evaluate how well the uncertainty estimators detect suspicious predictions when the input is deliberately perturbed.

2.2   Robustness Assessment

To determine whether uncertainty-aware fine-tuning (Uncertain-FT) is able to 1) resist adversarial perturbations and 2) emit reliable uncertainty alarms, we design the three-stage framework as follows:

Stage One: Fine-tuning (FT) Strategies. Standard FT is obtained by minimizing only the cross-entropy loss $\mathcal{L}_{\mathrm{CE}}$, while Uncertainty-Aware Fine-Tuning (Uncertain-FT) follows the UIOS framework [16] and optimizes a composite loss that encourages both confident correct predictions and calibrated uncertainty:

$$\mathcal{L}_{\mathrm{UFT}} = \mathcal{L}_{\mathrm{UN\text{-}CE}} + \lambda \cdot \mathcal{L}_{\mathrm{KL}}, \tag{5}$$

$\mathcal{L}_{\mathrm{UN\text{-}CE}}$ is the evidential cross-entropy loss defined as:

$$
\begin{aligned}
L_{UN-CE} &= \int \left[\sum_{k=1}^{K} -y_k \log\left(p_k\right) \right] \frac{1}{B\left(\boldsymbol{\alpha}_i\right)} \prod_{k=1}^{K} p_k^{\alpha_k - 1} dp_k \\
&= \sum_{k=1}^{K} y_k \left(\psi\left(S_k\right) - \psi\left(\alpha_k\right) \right),
\end{aligned}
\tag{6}
$$

where ψ denotes the digamma function, and $B()$ refers to the multinomial beta function associated with the concentration parameter α. $\mathcal{L}_{\mathrm{KL}}$ is defined as:

$$\mathcal{L}_{\mathrm{KL}} = \log\left(\frac{\Gamma\left(\sum_{k=1}^{K} \hat{\alpha}_k\right)}{\Gamma(K) \prod_{k=1}^{K} \Gamma(\hat{\alpha}_k)} \right) + \sum_{k=1}^{K} (\hat{\alpha}_k - 1) \left[\psi(\hat{\alpha}_k) - \psi \sum_{k=1}^{K} \hat{\alpha}_k \right], \tag{7}$$

where $\hat{\alpha} = y + (1-y) \odot \alpha$ is the adjusted parameter of the Dirichlet distribution which could avoid penalizing the evidence of the ground-truth class to 0, and $\Gamma(\cdot)$ is the gamma function. The weighting factor λ is introduced to balance classification accuracy and uncertainty calibration.

Stage Two: Adversarial Example Generation. The two gradient-based attacks presented in Sect. 2.1 are applied under the threat settings (**S1** and **S2**) as follows:

- **PGD.** Adversarial examples are generated by iterating Eq. (3) while keeping the perturbation inside the ℓ_2 ball of radius ϵ.
- **C&W.** Perturbations are obtained by solving the optimisation problem in Eq. (4).

For every perturbed input (x, y) we store the model's prediction $\hat{y}$, the attack-success flag $\mathbf{1}_{\{\hat{y} \neq y\}}$, and the corresponding uncertainty value.

Stage Three: Untargeted Robustness Evaluation. An *untargeted* adversarial attack seeks *any* label change $\hat{y} \neq y$ rather than a specific target class. For each crafted example we record two quantities: (i) the **prediction outcome**

(correct or incorrect) and (ii) the associated **uncertainty score** —Dirichlet evidence u for UIOS. Robustness is judged desirable when attack success is low *or* high-uncertainty warnings are raised whenever misclassification occurs. Untargeted attacks are executed under two complementary settings:

- **S1: The baseline white-box testing.** Gradients of the Uncertain-FT model are used to maximise the cross-entropy loss $\mathcal{L}_{CE}$.
- **S2: Transfer testing.** Adversarial perturbations are first crafted on a Standard-FT source model using $\mathcal{L}_{CE}$ only, and then applied to the Uncertain-FT target, probing cross-model transferability when model parameters are hidden.

3 Experiments

3.1 Settings

<u>Pre-trained Backbones.</u> We adopt two publicly released ophthalmic foundation models: **RetFound** [17] and **RetiZero** [15]. Both are vision transformers trained self-supervised on ~1.6 M unlabelled fundus photographs. All our fine-tuning and attacks are carried out independently on both backbones; results are reported per model.

<u>Down-Stream Dataset.</u> The APTOS 2019 blindness-detection challenge dataset[1] contains 3 662 colour fundus images graded on a five-level DR scale (0–4). We stratify images patient-wise into 70/15/15% train/validation/test splits, keeping the test partition frozen for all attacks.

<u>Fine-tuning Strategies.</u> Unless otherwise stated, we resize images to 224×224 and apply random flips. For both models, we adopt the same hyperparameters as reported in the original papers. For **Standard FT** the loss is the standard cross-entropy $\mathcal{L}_{CE}$; for **Uncertain FT** we use Eq. (5).

<u>Attack Implementation.</u> For every clean test image we generate a single adversarial counterpart under each setting (S1, S2) and attack type (PGD, C&W):

- **PGD:** ℓ_2 radius $\epsilon = 5$, step size $\alpha = 0.5$, $t = 40$ steps.
- **C&W:** ℓ_2 attack with confidence parameter $c = 1$ and 400 Adam iterations; binary search over 5 scales of c.

<u>Evaluation Metrics.</u> *Accuracy* (ACC) and *F1-score* (F1) are measured on the clean test set and adversarial samples respectively. For adversarial settings, we report: (i) *Attack Success Rate* (ASR): the proportion of test samples for which the prediction is incorrect, (ii) *Uncertainty Score* (UN-SCORE): the average model uncertainty for the given input condition. We adopt Dirichlet evidence u (UIOS) as the uncertainty value. A robust model should yield low ASR and high UN-SCORE on adversarial inputs.

Table 1. Unified DR grading performance and robustness under Standard FT and Uncertain FT across different scenarios. S1: white-box attacks; S2: transfer attacks.

Scenario	Model	FT Method	Attack	Acc	F1	ASR	Un-Score
Clean	RetFound	Standard	—	0.847	0.675	—	—
	RetFound	Uncertain	—	0.8415	0.6851	—	0.1457
	RetiZero	Standard	—	0.8415	0.6658	—	—
	RetiZero	Uncertain	—	0.8552	0.6813	—	0.2223
S1	RetFound	Uncertain	PGD	0.5765	0.2246	0.4235	0.1024
	RetFound	Uncertain	C&W	0.0109	0.0087	0.9891	0.3187
	RetiZero	Uncertain	PGD	0.3087	0.1228	0.6913	0.1845
	RetiZero	Uncertain	C&W	0.0164	0.0174	0.9836	0.3906
S2	RetFound	Standard	PGD	0	0	1	0.1858
	RetFound	Standard	C&W	0.6475	0.5144	0.3525	0.2064
	RetiZero	Standard	PGD	0	0	1	0.2766
	RetiZero	Standard	C&W	0.5027	0.3733	0.4973	0.3237

3.2   Performance and Robustness Analysis

Table 1 summarizes the DR grading performance and robustness of RetFound and RetiZero under Standard Fine-Tuning (Standard FT) and Uncertainty-Aware Fine-Tuning (Uncertain FT) across three scenarios: clean, white-box attacks (S1), and transfer attacks (S2). On the clean APTOS2019 test set, both models achieve consistent accuracy and F1 score under both fine-tuning strategies, indicating reliable baseline grading performance. Uncertain FT slightly increases the classfication performance for clean samples.

In the white-box setting (S1), adversarial examples are generated directly against the Uncertain-FT models by maximizing the prediction loss while the uncertainty estimation acts as an additional branch. This uncertainty head can act like gradient masking, partially hindering the attack from finding the most effective perturbation directions. As a result, attack success rates for PGD achieve around 42.4% (RetFound) and 69.1% (RetiZero), and for C&W are high due to its more complex attack strategy. The uncertainty scores for successful attacks increase but still cannot fully distinguish adversarial inputs.

In the transfer setting (S2), adversarial examples crafted on the Standard-FT models are directly applied to the Uncertain-FT models. Since these perturbations are not constrained by the uncertainty head during generation, they better exploit vulnerabilities in the prediction branch. Consequently, the transfer attacks achieve higher success rates: PGD achieves 100%. However, C&W drops to 35.25% and 49.73%, respectively. We explain that there is some kind of overfitting to Standard-FT models.

---

[1] https://www.kaggle.com/datasets/mariaherrerot/aptos2019.

Overall, these results reveal that Uncertainty-Aware Fine-Tuning can partially defend against white-box attacks like PGD, because it introduces more complex loss landscape. However, it remains vulnerable to more advanced attacks like C&W and transfer attacks, both of which even bypass the uncertainty mechanism. This highlights the need for more robust uncertainty modeling for DR screening.

3.3   Uncertainty Distributions Analysis

To further understand how uncertainty estimation responds to adversarial perturbations, we analyze the uncertainty score distributions for correctly and incorrectly classified samples. Figure 2 shows the distributions for clean and adversarial samples, using Uncertain-FT RetFound under C&W attack in the S1 (white-box) setting as an example.

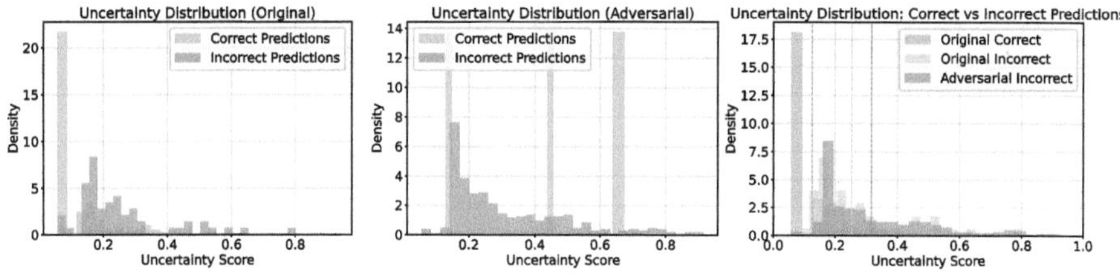

Fig. 2. Uncertainty score distributions for clean and adversarial samples. **Left**: Clean predictions on Uncertain-FT RetFound; **Middle**: S1 white-box C&W attack on Uncertain-FT RetFound; **Right**: Overlap shows that many misclassified adversarial samples still have low uncertainty, indicating limited discriminative power.

The left panel depicts the original (clean) data: correctly predicted samples tend to have low uncertainty scores, while misclassified samples exhibit slightly higher uncertainty on average. The middle panel shows the distribution for adversarial examples: although the attack forces misclassification, many adversarial samples still produce low uncertainty scores similar to correct predictions. This is further highlighted in the right panel, which overlays the distributions and reveals substantial overlap between clean correct, clean incorrect, and adversarial incorrect samples. These results indicate that adversarial perturbations not only mislead the classifier but also bypass the uncertainty estimation, producing low uncertainty even for wrong predictions. Notably, in some settings, the mean uncertainty value of adversarial examples is very near to the one of correctly classified samples. Please refer to the Supplementary Material.

Figure 3 further analyzes the per-class uncertainty score distributions for clean and adversarial samples under the S1 white-box C&W attack on Uncertain-FT RetFound. While some classes (e.g., Class 0) show an obvious increase in uncertainty for adversarial samples, other classes exhibit distributions similar to those of clean data. This suggests that the effect of adversarial perturbations

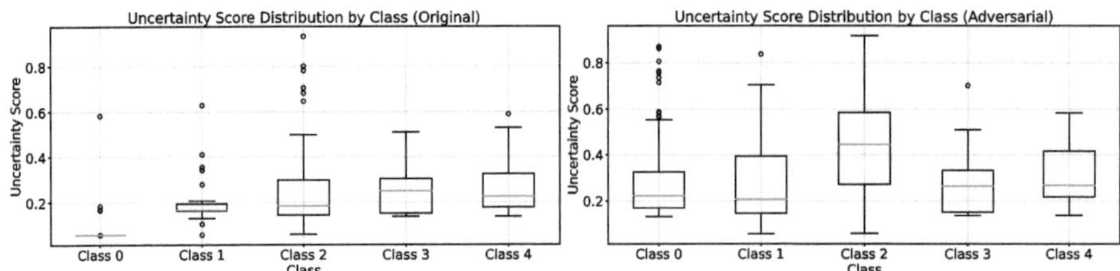

Fig. 3. Per-class uncertainty score distributions for clean (**left**) and adversarial (**right**) samples under S1 white-box C&W attack on Uncertain-FT RetFound. While some classes show noticeable increases in uncertainty for adversarial samples, others have similar distributions to clean samples, indicating that the impact of adversarial perturbations on uncertainty varies across classes.

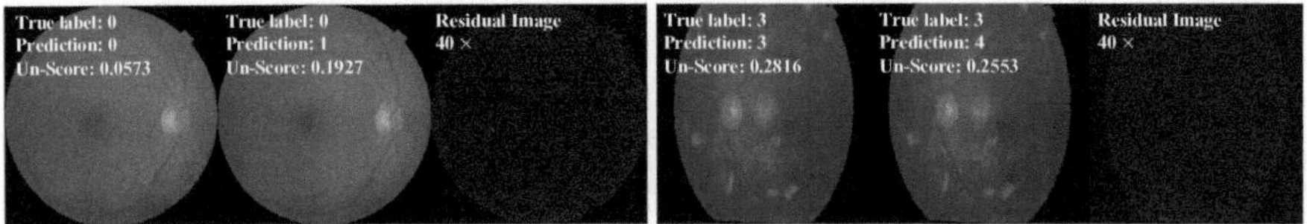

Fig. 4. Visual examples of adversarial samples under the S1 white-box C&W attack on the Uncertain-FT RetiFound model. For each pair: the clean image (**left**), the adversarial image (**middle**) which remains visually identical but fools the model with low uncertainty, and the residual perturbation magnified 40× (**right**). These examples illustrate that imperceptible attacks can mislead predictions and bypass existing uncertainty measures.

on uncertainty is class-dependent: for certain DR grades, the uncertainty mechanism responds more sensitively to attacks, whereas for others, it remains less informative. These observations highlight the need for class-aware uncertainty modeling to better detect boundary OOD threats in ophthalmic AI. More visualization results for other settings are provided in the Supplementary Material.

3.4   Adversarial Visualization and Human Perceptibility

Figure 4 shows example adversarial samples generated under the S1 white-box C&W attack on the Uncertain-FT RetFound model. For each pair, the left image depicts the original clean fundus image with correct prediction and low uncertainty, while the middle image shows the corresponding adversarial version, which remains visually indistinguishable to human observers but causes a misclassification with only slightly higher uncertainty. The right image presents the residual perturbation magnified 40× for better visibility. These qualitative examples demonstrate that subtle adversarial perturbations can evade both human inspection and current uncertainty estimation, underscoring the need for more robust uncertainty modeling to detect boundary OOD threats. More visualization results for different settings are provided in the Supplementary Material.

4   Conclusion

In this work, we systematically evaluated the impact of uncertainty-aware fine-tuning on the adversarial robustness of foundation models for diabetic retinopathy screening. Our results show that while uncertainty estimation slightly improves model calibration and reduces attack success rates under PGD attacks, it remains insufficient to defend against stronger boundary attacks such as C&W. Moreover, many adversarial examples still produce low uncertainty scores, revealing blind spots in current uncertainty quantification.

In future work, we plan to extend our evaluation to other ophthalmic and systemic diseases, explore diverse uncertainty estimation strategies, and design more adaptive adversarial attacks to better stress-test model reliability. Developing more robust and trustworthy uncertainty mechanisms remains crucial for the safe deployment of AI systems in real-world clinical settings.

Acknowledgements. This work is supported by the National Medical Research Council (NMRC) grant, Singapore (MOH-001792-04 and MOH-CSASI22jul-0001)

References

1. Carlini, N., Wagner, D.: Adversarial examples are not easily detected: bypassing ten detection methods. In: Proceedings of the 10th ACM Workshop on Artificial Intelligence and Security, pp. 3–14 (2017)
2. Carlini, N., Wagner, D.: Towards evaluating the robustness of neural networks. In: 2017 IEEE Symposium on Security and Privacy (SP), pp. 39–57. IEEE (2017)
3. Chen, J., et al.: A survey on deep learning in medical image registration: new technologies, uncertainty, evaluation metrics, and beyond. Med. Image Anal. **100**, 103385 (2025)
4. DeVries, T., Taylor, G.W.: Learning confidence for out-of-distribution detection in neural networks. arXiv preprint arXiv:1802.04865 (2018)
5. Gal, Y., et al.: Uncertainty in deep learning (2016)
6. Gulshan, V., et al.: Development and validation of a deep learning algorithm for detection of diabetic retinopathy in retinal fundus photographs. JAMA **316**(22), 2402–2410 (2016)
7. Karunanayake, N., Gunawardena, R., Seneviratne, S., Chawla, S.: Out-of-distribution data: an acquaintance of adversarial examples-a survey. ACM Comput. Surv. **57**(8), 1–40 (2025)
8. Kendall, A., Gal, Y.: What uncertainties do we need in bayesian deep learning for computer vision? Adv. Neural Inf. Process. Syst. **30** (2017)
9. Madry, A., Makelov, A., Schmidt, L., Tsipras, D., Vladu, A.: Towards deep learning models resistant to adversarial attacks. arXiv preprint arXiv:1706.06083 (2017)
10. Ojha, J., Presacan, O., Lind, P.G., Monteiro, E., Yazidi, A.: Navigating uncertainty: a user-perspective survey of trustworthiness of AI in healthcare. ACM Trans. Comput. Healthc. **6**(3), 1–32 (2025)
11. Sensoy, M., Kaplan, L., Kandemir, M.: Evidential deep learning to quantify classification uncertainty. Adv. Neural Inf. Process. Syst. **31** (2018)

12. Szegedy, C., et al.: Intriguing properties of neural networks. arXiv preprint arXiv:1312.6199 (2013)
13. Teye, M., Azizpour, H., Smith, K.: Bayesian uncertainty estimation for batch normalized deep networks. In: International Conference on Machine Learning, pp. 4907–4916. PMLR (2018)
14. Ting, D.S.W., et al.: Artificial intelligence and deep learning in ophthalmology. Br. J. Ophthalmol. **103**(2), 167–175 (2019)
15. Wang, M., et al.: Common and rare fundus diseases identification using vision-language foundation model with knowledge of over 400 diseases. arXiv preprint arXiv:2406.09317 (2024)
16. Wang, M., et al.: Uncertainty-inspired open set learning for retinal anomaly identification. Nat. Commun. **14**(1), 6757 (2023)
17. Zhou, Y., et al.: A foundation model for generalizable disease detection from retinal images. Nature **622**(7981), 156–163 (2023)

Semi-automated Retinal Microsurgery Video Annotation with SAM2: Comparative Analysis of Prompt Strategies

Adriana Namour[1]([✉]), Oluwatosin Alabi[1], Minghan Zhao[1], Charalampos Komninos[1], Tom Vercauteren[1], Lyndon da Cruz[1,2,3], Sebastien Ourselin[1], and Christos Bergeles[1]

[1] School of Biomedical Engineering and Imaging Sciences, King's College London, London SE1 7EU, UK
{adriana.namour,firstname.lastname}@kcl.ac.uk, lyndon.dacruz1@nhs.net
[2] Moorfields Eye Hospital, London EC1V 2PD, UK
[3] Institute of Ophthalmology, University College London, London EC1V 9EL, UK

Abstract. Time-consuming annotation of surgical video frames for pixel-level semantic segmentation hinders the development of intraoperative guidance systems for retinal microsurgery. This study evaluates prompting strategies within the Segment Anything Model 2 (SAM2) framework for generating dense segmentation masks. Three datasets were derived from videos of phantom retinal surgery, namely internal limiting membrane (ILM) peeling, by prompting SAM2 with either single-point prompts, bounding boxes, or manually annotated masks per object. Each dataset was used to train supervised segmentation models, namely U-Net, DeepLabV3+, TransUNet, and nnU-Net, under identical architectural and training settings. Performance was assessed using mean Intersection-over-Union and compared with manually annotated ground truth. Results indicate that bounding box prompts yield acceptable segmentation quality with minimal manual effort, whereas manually annotated mask prompts deliver superior pixel-level accuracy and consistency across sequences. Single-point prompts did not produce datasets that could assist with capturing fine instrument details. These findings support the use of SAM2 as a semi-automated annotation tool and offer comparative insight into prompting strategies for generating high-quality training labels in ophthalmic surgical video segmentation.

Keywords: Retinal microsurgery · Semi-automated annotation · Prompt-based segmentation

1 Introduction

Retinal microsurgery demands pixel-accurate segmentation of instruments and anatomy under microscope view to enable real-time guidance and automation

H. Fang et al. (Eds.): OMIA 2025, LNCS 16209, pp. 95–104, 2026.
https://doi.org/10.1007/978-3-032-10351-2_10

[12]. Supervised learning for this task relies on dense, frame-level annotations, yet manually labelling high-resolution surgical video is prohibitively time-consuming and does not scale [9].

Internal limiting membrane (ILM) peeling involves removing a transparent, submicron-thin layer from the central macula, under low-contrast biomicroscopy visualization and carries a high risk of complications such as retinal tears or detachment if the tool-tissue distance is not precisely controlled [14]. Real-time segmentation of ILM boundaries and instrument tips can help reduce iatrogenic injury and support future AI-driven interventions, including the integration of robotics in vitreoretinal surgery [7].

Several supervised methods have achieved real-time segmentation of instruments and retinal anatomy in vitreoretinal surgery, e.g. [12,15], but these rely on dense, manually annotated masks that are costly to produce [9]. To reduce this burden, approaches such as weak or sparse supervision, temporal label propagation, and transfer learning have been proposed. Domain adaptation techniques have also been applied in medical imaging [5,6], yet suitable source datasets for retinal microsurgery remain unavailable, and simpler propagation methods (e.g. optical flow or point tracking) often fail to capture the fine-scale changes in tool tips and tissue boundaries. Prompt-based models such as the Segment Anything Model 2 (SAM2) can produce high-quality masks from minimal input [10,11], but their real-time use in the operating room is not possible due to the prompt-generation overhead and per-frame latency, which is on the order of seconds.

We investigate leveraging SAM2 as a semi-automatic label generator for retinal microsurgery. By seeding points, boxes, or masks as prompts across a phantom ILM-peel video, SAM2 generates dense pseudo-labels that train lightweight segmentation networks. While recent work has evaluated SAM2 prompting in robotic endoscopic surgery [18], our study is the first to systematically compare mask, box, and point prompts in retinal surgery. Situated in the context of vitreoretinal (VR) surgery, our contributions are twofold: an evaluation of these prompting strategies for dense pseudo-label generation and an exploration of training robust, lightweight segmentation models on the resulting labels to achieve the real-time performance required for surgical guidance.

2   Related Work

Rapid, accurate annotation and real-time inference both pose bottlenecks for deploying surgical video segmentation. Below, we first review annotation-efficient methods, then examine how foundation models can ease label creation, and finally survey lightweight architectures for live guidance.

2.1   Annotation-Efficient Learning

High-quality masks are costly to produce, motivating methods that reduce manual effort. Semi-supervised approaches exploit consistency or pseudo-labels on unannotated frames [16]. Video propagation techniques extend sparse labels via optical flow or template matching [17]. Integrating propagation methods with foundation models via interactive prompts can bootstrap dense annotations across entire sequences [1]. However, these methods often struggle with fine tool tips and low-contrast anatomy.

2.2 Foundation Models in Medical Imaging

Promptable segmentation models can bootstrap dense masks from minimal inputs. The original Segment Anything Model (SAM) accepts points or boxes to outline objects [10], and SAM2 adds streaming memory and mask-propagation for videos [11]. In retinal imaging, self-supervised pretraining (e.g., RETFound) has likewise improved disease-detection accuracy [20], and surveys highlight both promise and challenges of foundation models for medical analysis [19].

2.3 Lightweight Segmentation for Real-Time Deployment

Surgical guidance requires models that run at ≥ 25 fps on limited hardware. U-Net variants [13], DeepLabV3+ [4], and nnU-Net's automated pipeline [8] balance speed and accuracy, while hybrids like TransUNet capture long-range context with moderate cost [3]. However, all demand large, high-quality training sets.

Gap. No prior work systematically compares point, box, and mask prompts as mechanisms for generating surgical video segmentation training data in retinal microsurgery. We address this by evaluating these strategies on phantom ILM-peel videos and quantifying their impact on annotation effort and downstream performance.

3 Methodology and Experiments

3.1 Data

For this study, we recorded high-fidelity phantom ILM-peel procedures to closely mimic clinical microsurgery. An expert consultant vitreoretinal surgeon performed all simulations on a Bioniko retinal phantom under standard OR conditions, using a Zeiss surgical microscope for high-resolution video capture, authentic 25-gauge vitreoretinal instruments, and standard intraocular illumination via a light probe. Video was captured through the microscope's optical output at 1280×720 px and 25 fps. Eleven such sequences were recorded.

We manually annotated 166 keyframes with pixel-wise semantic masks across five classes (retina, ILM coat, light torch, forceps, and scissors). From eight of these sequences, we selected 53 keyframes (one every 50 frames) as prompts for SAM2, generating dense, pixel-wise segmentation masks for all 2,333 frames in those videos. The remaining 113 annotated keyframes from the last three sequences were held out to be part of the test set.

3.2　SAM2 Prompting Strategies

The Segment Anything Model 2 (SAM2) was employed to generate dense segmentation masks by propagating prompts over entire video sequences. Three prompting strategies were evaluated, yielding three datasets:

- D_2 (Manual mask prompts): full manually-annotated semantic segmentation masks used as prompts (53 keyframes)
- D_1 (Box prompts): Bounding boxes automatically extracted from the D_2 masks by taking the minimum and maximum x and y coordinates for each object.
- D_3 (Single-point prompts): Object centroids computed from the D_2 keyframes.

Examples of sample prompts and their propagated pseudo-masks for each strategy are shown in Fig. 1.

For each keyframe in every sequence, per-object prompts were inserted into SAM2's memory mechanism, then SAM2-generated masks were propagated to all frames via the default `propagate_in_video()` API. Outputs were saved as integer PNGs (labels 0–5), matched to the original spatial resolution and filenames.

3.3　Annotation Time Estimation

Due to the nature of the task, which requires exhaustive, pixel-level correctness, manual semantic mask annotation was performed at full resolution and averaged 15 min per keyframe (a total of 13.25 h for 53 frames). In contrast, once the D_2 masks were available, box and point prompts were generated automatically.

3.4　Model Architectures

The performance of four segmentation networks when trained using the D_1 - D_3 datasets was compared. The networks are:

- U-Net (ResNet-34 encoder)
- DeepLabV3+ (ResNet-50 encoder)
- TransUNet
- nnU-Net V2 (automated configuration)

All mentions of "nnU-Net" in this paper denote the V2 implementation.

Each architecture was trained separately on each dataset, resulting in three independent training runs per model (e.g., three U-Nets, one for each of D_1, D_2, and D_3). All models produced six-class outputs corresponding to the annotated semantic labels.

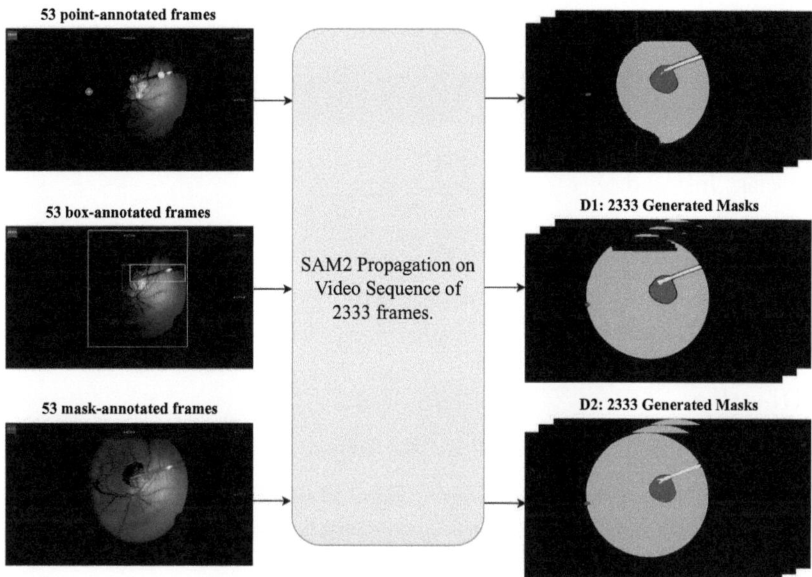

Fig. 1. Overview of SAM2 prompt propagation. Each row corresponds to one prompting strategy–single-point (D_3), bounding-box (D_1), and semantic mask (D_2). In each row, the left image is a representative annotated keyframe (from the set of 53) with the respective prompt; the center panel illustrates propagation across the full 2,333-frame sequence; and the right panel shows the resulting stack of dense pseudo-masks generated by SAM2.

3.5 Training Setup

For U-Net, DeepLabV3+, and TransUNet, networks were trained for 30 epochs using a batch size of 8, AdamW optimizer (learning rate 1e−4, weight decay $1e − 5$), and a StepLR scheduler (decay factor 0.5 every 10 epochs). Two loss functions were independently evaluated for each model-dataset pair:

– Combo Loss: 0.5×Cross-Entropy + 0.5×Dice
– Lovász-Softmax: surrogate soft Jaccard loss [2]

For nnU-Net, default training configurations were used without hyperparameter tuning. The model was trained for 1000 epochs using its automated preprocessing, augmentation, and loss scheduling pipeline. Unlike the default five-fold cross-validation used in nnU-Net, only fold 0 was used, with the same fixed train/val/test split applied across all other models to enable consistent comparison.

All training and evaluation used the same split: 53 manually annotated keyframes reserved for testing, with the remainder split into train and validation subsets. Final evaluation was conducted on the full set of 166 manually annotated keyframes (the 53 prompt frames and 113 held-out frames from three unused sequences) to evaluate generalisation performance.

3.6 Evaluation Metrics

The following segmentation metrics were computed on the test set and averaged across all semantic classes:

– Mean Intersection-over-Union (mIoU)
– Per-class IoU and Dice

Both global and per-object results were calculated. To better assess clinically relevant differences, metrics were also calculated excluding background labels. Inference time per image (forward pass only) was measured across all model-dataset combinations to assess deployment feasibility.

4 Results

4.1 Quantitative Segmentation Performance

All model-dataset combinations were evaluated on the 166-frame test set using mean Intersection-over-Union (mIoU), computed per class and averaged across semantic categories. Full results are reported in Table 1. Across all architectures and loss functions, models trained on D_2 (manual mask prompts + SAM2 propagation) consistently outperformed those trained on D_1 (bounding boxes) and D_3 (centroid points).

For example, U-Net (ResNet-34) trained on D_2 achieved mIoU $= 0.713$, compared to 0.683 on D_1 and 0.630 on D_3. TransUNet (Combo loss) followed a similar pattern (0.699 on D_2 vs 0.667, and 0.638 on D_1 and D_3, respectively), as did nnU-Net (0.685 on D_2 vs 0.659 and 0.592).

These results indicate that SAM2 prompting with full-mask supervision (D_2) yields stronger training signals than point- or box-based prompting. D_2's structure-preserving propagation appears particularly important for capturing thin tool boundaries and illumination artefacts common in retinal surgery video.

Table 1. Mean IoU (mIoU) of all models trained on each SAM2-prompted dataset. Best value per row is shown in bold.

Model/Loss	D_1	D_2	D_3
U-Net (Combo)	0.683	**0.713**	0.630
U-Net (Lovasz)	**0.684**	0.668	0.642
DeepLabV3+ (Combo)	0.671	**0.698**	0.621
DeepLabV3+ (Lovasz)	0.683	**0.700**	0.638
TransUNet (Combo)	0.667	**0.699**	0.638
TransUNet (Lovasz)	0.664	**0.692**	0.640
nnU-Net	0.659	**0.685**	0.592

Across the seven model-loss configurations, D_2-trained models achieved an average mIoU increase of $+0.021$ (±0.016) over D_1 and $+0.065$ (±0.021) over

D_3. Paired Wilcoxon signed-rank tests on the per-image mIoU distributions confirmed that D_2's advantage over D_1 is significant in every configuration ($p < 0.01$) and over D_3 in six of seven configurations ($p < 0.01$; the U-Net (Lovász) comparison against D_3 produced $p = 0.057$, indicating a strong trend) (Table 2).

Table 2. Per-class IoU for the best D_2 model (U-Net ResNet-34, Combo loss).

Class	D_1	D_2	D_3	$\Delta(D_2\text{-}D_1)$	$\Delta(D_2\text{-}D_3)$
Forceps	0.347	0.376	0.297	+0.029	+0.078
Light Torch	0.763	0.834	0.741	+0.071	+0.093
Vertical Scissors	0.244	0.252	0.224	+0.008	+0.028

For the leading D_2-trained model, instrument-level IoU rose from $0.347 \rightarrow 0.376$ for forceps, $0.763 \rightarrow 0.834$ for light torch, and $0.244 \rightarrow 0.252$ for vertical scissors–gains of $+0.029$, $+0.071$, and $+0.008$ over D_1 and $+0.078$, $+0.093$, and $+0.028$ over D_3, respectively. These improvements underscore D_2's superior ability to capture fine tool tips and thin boundaries.

4.2 Inference Latency and Annotation Efficiency

To support real-time deployment of lightweight segmentation networks in ophthalmic surgery, we benchmarked inference runtimes on $1280 \times 720\,\text{px}$ frames. U-Net and DeepLabV3+ averaged 28 ms-38 ms per frame, TransUNet 20 ms, and nnU-Net 29 ms, all meeting the 25 fps threshold for clinical guidance.

Manual mask annotation of the 53 keyframes for D_2 required 13.25 h (15 min per keyframe), while automatic derivation of box (D_1) and point (D_3) prompts and full SAM2 propagation across eight videos completed in minutes (see Sec. 3.3). Importantly, models trained on D_2 pseudo-labels achieved superior segmentation accuracy, demonstrating that the upfront investment in full-mask annotation is offset by its value in producing high-fidelity, real-time-ready models.

4.3 Qualitative Analysis

We visually inspected representative test frames by overlaying predictions from nnU-Nets trained on datasets D_1 (generated via box prompts), D_2 (generated via mask prompts), and D_3 (generated via point prompts). Figure 2 presents these overlaid segmentation outputs on the same test frame: the D_2-trained model delivers the sharpest delineation of the instrument tip and thin ILM boundaries, whereas the D_1 and D_3 models occasionally mis-segment specular highlights, occluded regions, or fine edges.

Supplementary Videos 1 and 2 (submitted separately) display continuous segmentation outputs and per-frame inference times for the D_2- and D_3-trained models, respectively–confirming real-time performance (≥ 25 fps) and illustrating how prompt choice affects segmentation fidelity in deployment.

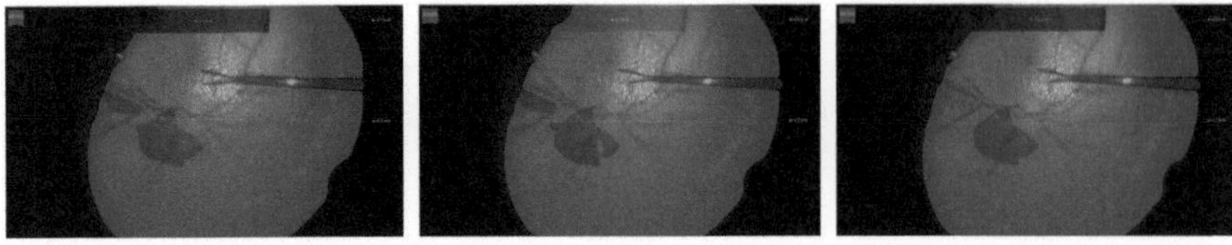

Fig. 2. nnU-Net predictions on the same frame. From left: models trained on D_1, D_2, and D_3. The D_2-trained model yields the most precise delineation of the instrument tip.

5 Discussion

Our experiments demonstrate that full-mask prompts (D_2) achieve the best balance between manual effort and segmentation performance. Although single-point (D_3) and bounding-box (D_1) prompts reduce annotation time, they yield weaker training signals, especially for thin instrument tips and fine tissue boundaries. By contrast, structured mask prompts preserve spatial detail and support higher-quality pseudo-labels for lightweight models.

Bounding-box prompts provide only coarse spatial guidance, which cannot capture narrow tools or subtle anatomical features. Single-point prompts lack information on object extent, leading to fragmented or incomplete masks. The observed mIoU gains of D_2 over D_1 are supported by statistical tests but remain moderate in magnitude. Future work could investigate whether augmenting bounding-box prompts with targeted mask refinements around instrument tips, or increasing the number of annotated keyframes, can narrow this gap–potentially reducing the reliance on full-mask annotation without sacrificing segmentation fidelity.

Direct SAM2 inference in the operating room remains impractical; prompt generation adds overhead and its per-frame latency of several seconds far exceeds the 40 ms budget required for 25 fps operation. Instead, our pipeline uses SAM2 as a semi-automatic data annotator, producing high-quality pseudo-labels that train compact networks capable of full-resolution inference at 25 fps. These findings highlight that data-centric design–selecting the right prompt strategy–governs deployment feasibility for lightweight models.

Full-mask prompts (D_2) demonstrate that, in practice, only a small subset of frames needs manual annotation to train high-quality segmentation models for entire video sequences. Our aim is to evaluate how foundation-model-generated pseudo-labels can enable lightweight segmentation networks, rather than to benchmark increasingly complex backbone architectures.

This study has limitations. The phantom dataset represents a single procedure under controlled conditions and may not capture clinical variability. We did not integrate SAM2 prompting into a live inference loop, nor did we explore temporal or advanced attention mechanisms in the segmentation networks. Future work should validate generalization on clinical videos, include temporal consistency constraints, and automate prompt selection to further reduce manual input.

6   Conclusion

This study evaluated semi-automatic annotation of ILM-peel videos using SAM2 prompts and assessed the impact of point, box, and mask input strategies on pseudo-label quality and model performance. Mask-based prompts (D_2) yielded the most accurate labels relative to manual effort, and lightweight networks trained on these pseudo-labels achieved full-resolution segmentation at 25 fps.

By restricting SAM2 to offline pseudo-label generation rather than real-time inference, our pipeline produces training datasets that enable the development of lightweight segmentation models for real-time guidance in vitreoretinal surgeries, ready for clinical deployment and supportive of semi-automated ophthalmic image-analysis workflows.

Acknowledgements. The authors would like to acknowledge funding from the EPSRC Centre for Doctoral Training in Smart Medical Imaging (EP/S022104/1) and from the King's-China Scholarship Council PhD Scholarship programme (K-CSC).

References

1. Alabi, O., et al.: CholecinstanceSeg: a tool instance segmentation dataset for laparoscopic surgery. Sci. Data **12**(1), 1–12 (2025)
2. Berman, M., Triki, A.R., Blaschko, M.B.: The lovász-softmax loss: a tractable surrogate for the optimization of the intersection-over-union measure in neural networks. In: Proceedings of the IEEE Conference on Computer Vision and Pattern Recognition, pp. 4413–4421 (2018)
3. Wang, Y., et al.: TransUNet: rethinking the U-Net architecture design for medical image segmentation through the lens of transformers. Med. Image Anal. **97**, 103280 (2024)
4. Chen, L.C., Zhu, Y., Papandreou, G., Schroff, F., Adam, H.: Encoder-decoder with atrous separable convolution for semantic image segmentation. In: Proceedings of the European Conference on Computer Vision (ECCV), pp. 801–818 (2018)
5. Dou, Q., Ouyang, C., Chen, C., Chen, H., Heng, P.A.: Unsupervised cross-modality domain adaptation of convnets for biomedical image segmentations with adversarial loss. arXiv preprint arXiv:1804.10916 (2018)
6. Ganin, Y., Lempitsky, V.: Unsupervised domain adaptation by backpropagation. In: International Conference on Machine Learning, pp. 1180–1189. PMLR (2015)
7. Gijbels, A., Wouters, N., Stalmans, P., Van Brussel, H., Reynaerts, D., Vander Poorten, E.: Design and realisation of a novel robotic manipulator for retinal surgery. In: 2013 IEEE/RSJ International Conference on Intelligent Robots and Systems, pp. 3598–3603. IEEE (2013)
8. Isensee, F., Jaeger, P.F., Kohl, S.A., Petersen, J., Maier-Hein, K.H.: NNU-Net: a self-configuring method for deep learning-based biomedical image segmentation. Nat. Methods **18**(2), 203–211 (2021)

9. Kamtam, D.N., et al.: Deep learning approaches to surgical video segmentation and object detection: a scoping review. Comput. Biol. Med. **194**, 110482 (2025)

10. Kirillov, A., et al.: Segment anything. In: Proceedings of the IEEE/CVF International Conference on Computer Vision, pp. 4015–4026 (2023)

11. Ravi, N., et al.: Sam 2: segment anything in images and videos. arXiv preprint arXiv:2408.00714 (2024)

12. Rieke, N., et al.: Real-time localization of articulated surgical instruments in retinal microsurgery. Med. Image Anal. **34**, 82–100 (2016)

13. Ronneberger, O., Fischer, P., Brox, T.: U-Net: convolutional networks for biomedical image segmentation. In: Navab, N., Hornegger, J., Wells, W.M., Frangi, A.F. (eds.) MICCAI 2015. LNCS, vol. 9351, pp. 234–241. Springer, Cham (2015). https://doi.org/10.1007/978-3-319-24574-4_28

14. Semeraro, F., Morescalchi, F., Duse, S., Gambicorti, E., Russo, A., Costagliola, C.: Current trends about inner limiting membrane peeling in surgery for epiretinal membranes. J. Ophthalmol. **2015**(1), 671905 (2015)

15. Sommersperger, M., Weiss, J., Ali Nasseri, M., Gehlbach, P., Iordachita, I., Navab, N.: Real-time tool to layer distance estimation for robotic subretinal injection using intraoperative 4D OCT. Biomed. Opt. Express **12**(2), 1085–1104 (2021)

16. Wei, M., Budd, C., Garcia-Peraza-Herrera, L.C., Dorent, R., Shi, M., Vercauteren, T.: SegMatch: semi-supervised surgical instrument segmentation. Sci. Rep. **15**(1), 14042 (2025)

17. Wu, Z., Schmidt, A., Kazanzides, P., Salcudean, S.E.: Augmenting efficient real-time surgical instrument segmentation in video with point tracking and segment anything. Healthc. Technol. Lett. **12**(1), e12111 (2025)

18. Yu, J., et al.: Sam 2 in robotic surgery: an empirical evaluation for robustness and generalization in surgical video segmentation. arXiv preprint arXiv:2408.04593 (2024)

19. Zhang, S., Metaxas, D.: On the challenges and perspectives of foundation models for medical image analysis. Med. Image Anal. **91**, 102996 (2024)

20. Zhou, Y., Chia, M.A., Wagner, S.K., Ayhan, M.S., Williamson, D.J., Struyven, R.R., Liu, T., Xu, M., Lozano, M.G., Woodward-Court, P., et al.: A foundation model for generalizable disease detection from retinal images. Nature **622**(7981), 156–163 (2023)

Cross Domain Few Shot Learning for Intra-Operative OCT Segmentation

Minghan Zhao[1]([✉]), Gongyu Zhang[1], Adriana Namour[1],
Charalampos Komninos[1], Lyndon da Cruz[1,2,3], Sebastien Ourselin[1],
and Christos Bergeles[1]

[1] School of Biomedical Engineering and Imaging Sciences, King's College London,
London SE1 7EU, UK
{minghan.zhao,Gongyu.Zhang,Adriana.Namour,Charalampos.Komninos,
Sebastien.Ourselin,Christos.Bergeles}@kcl.ac.uk, lyndon.dacruz1@nhs.net
[2] Moorfields Eye Hospital, London EC1V 2PD, UK
[3] Institute of Ophthalmology, University College London, London EC1V 9EL, UK

Abstract. Retinal procedures such as epiretinal membrane (ERM) peeling and macular hole repair demand precise instrument positioning to avoid contact with the retina, as even the smallest forces can cause sight impairment. Intraoperative Optical Coherence Tomography (iOCT) delivers depth details and real-time views of tissue and tool interactions. Accurate segmentation of iOCT images would permit estimation of the distance between surgical instruments and retinal layers, and the incorporation of safety alerts. Although pre-operative OCT (pOCT) segmentation is tractable, iOCT segmentation presents challenges due to the lack of annotation, the presence of instruments, shadows, tissue variations, and low signal-to-noise ratio (SNR). To overcome the problems, we pioneered the application of few-shot segmentation (FSS) frameworks that transfer information from well-annotated pOCT data to iOCT segmentation with only a handful of labeled examples. We discussed four FSS methods and evaluated them on three iOCT datasets collected from different surgical scenarios on real patients.

Keywords: Intra-operative OCT Segmentation · Few Shot Learning · Domain Adaptation

1 Introduction

Vitreoretinal procedures, such as macular hole repair and epiretinal membrane (ERM) peeling, require precise instrument positioning to prevent retinal damage as even the tiniest and borderline perceptible forces can cause sight loss [12]. Intraoperative Optical Coherence Tomography (iOCT) provides real-time, cross-sectional images of the retina and tools, aiding surgical decision-making with regards to membrane approach, subretinal injections, etc. Figure 1c and 1d show iOCT examples captured during macular hole repair and epiretinal membrane

H. Fang et al. (Eds.): OMIA 2025, LNCS 16209, pp. 105–114, 2026.
https://doi.org/10.1007/978-3-032-10351-2_11

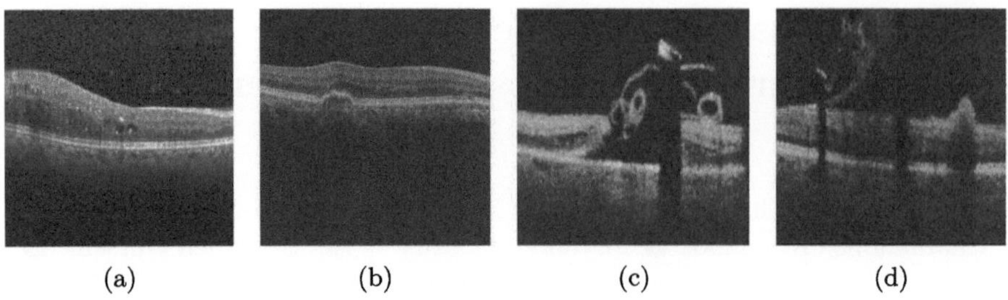

Fig. 1. The imaging doamin gap betwwen pre-operative (pOCT) and intra-operative OCT (iOCT). Panels a and b show pOCT: (a) Duke dataset [4]; (b) AROI dataset [15]. Panels c and d present iOCT: (c) macular-hole surgery; (d) ERM peeling surgery. The pOCT images show clean retinal anatomy, whereas the iOCT scans reveal surgical instrument tools, shadows and noise that characterize the surgical domain gap.

(ERM) peeling. Unlike the en-face view of the surgical microscope, iOCT enables depth-resolved visualization of retinal layers and instrument positioning [5], and can be used to maintain a safe tool-to-retina distance.

Accurate segmentation of retinal layers and surgical instruments is essential for precise tool-to-retina distance estimation and therefore prevention of iatrogenic injury [22]. Besides, segmentation provides a structured representation of retinal layers and instrument boundaries, enabling the development of automated systems that can extract precise spatial relationships for real-time surgical guidance. Supervised deep learning has significantly advanced pOCT segmentation, benefiting from large annotated datasets and stable imaging conditions. In contrast, iOCT segmentation faces three major challenges: data scarcity, scenario variety, and domain shift. First, generating manual annotations for iOCT images is time-consuming, requiring domain expertise to distinguish retinal structures, surgical instruments, artifact-induced distortions, and dynamic tissue interactions [1]. Previous research on iOCT segmentation [2,6,13,17,20] relies on hundreds of annotated iOCT images to train fully supervised segmentation models, and such datasets are not publicly accessible. Second, models trained by traditional fully supervised learning on limited iOCT datasets often fail to generalize across different surgeries, particularly when encountering instruments or tissues not seen during training. Third, models trained on pOCT cannot generalize directly to iOCT due to differences in signal-to-noise-ratio and tool occlusions [1]. Examples of pOCT and iOCT images are shown in Fig 1 to illustrate the differences. Therefore, addressing the annotation scarcity and domain gap requires a novel learning paradigm capable of adapting to new imaging conditions with minimal labeled data in the target domain, motivating the use of Cross-Domain Few-Shot Learning (CD-FSL).

In this paper, we applied four few shot learning (FSL) pipelines to segment iOCTs, in the presence of tools and shadows, and from real surgical cases. Unlike existing iOCT segmentation methods, we trained Few Shot Segmentation (FSS) models on large and well-annotated pOCT datasets but performed inference on iOCT images, to minimize the annotation burden and increase algorithm generalization ability. The pipeline is illustrated in 2. The resulting segmentation can offer surgeons real-time intra-operative feedback, ultimately helping them maintain safe tool positioning and reducing the risk of retinal trauma.

Our contribution can be summarized as follows: Firstly, we collected iOCT videos from different surgical scenarios on real patients, including ERM peeling and macular hole repair, and built three datasets to evaluate the generalization ability of the models across different scenarios and imaging conditions. Secondly, we are the first to apply FSS models on iOCT-assisted retina surgery. Thirdly, we have done an extensive comparison of the state-of-the-art FSS techniques, tailored to our problem.

2   Related Work

This section provides the necessary background literature on iOCT segmentation and FFS (Few Shot Segmentation) methods.

Previous research on iOCT segmentation primarily focuses on fully supervised segmentation models. U-Net [18] style networks are commonly used because of their efficiency with small training sets [19] and the fast inference speed. Park et al. [17] trained a modified U-Net model on iOCT B-scans collected from ex-vivo (enucleated) porcine eyes to segment background, tissue, and needle in anterior iOCT. Some groups [2,6,13,20] trained a U-Net style model with Resnet18 [9] as the backbone on B-scans acquired from ex-vivo porcine eyes to segment the tool and the internal limiting membrane (ILM) and the retinal pigment epithelium (RPE) surface boundaries. Although some iOCT segmentation methods optimized training strategies, such as semi-supervised learning [11] and pre-training [6,20,23], or employed data augmentation techniques [17], they still needed to be trained on hundreds of annotated iOCT B-scans. The large-scale annotation is infeasible for complex scenes, for example, the iOCT B-scans captured during a macular hole surgery and an ERM peeling in Fig. 1. This again highlights the need to develop a method that can train a segmentation model with only a few annotated iOCT images.

FFS has been applied in medical image segmentation to address the scarcity of annotated datasets. By leveraging only a few labeled examples, FSL reduces reliance on large-scale annotations, making it useful for tasks where manual labeling is costly [7]. Existing FFS methods can be categorized into two types according to whether the parameter is learnable or not in the metric phase, namely FSS based on parametric metric learning and non-parametric metric learning. FSS with parametric metric learning, such as PATNet [14] and SSP [7], transforms support images and query images into an embedding space, and then decodes the similarity score between support and query features by metric tools with parameter-learning. FSS with non-parametric metric learning, such as FAMNet [3], employs distance measurement functions as the metric function and classifies query images from the pixel level with the pixel-wise distance between support and query features.

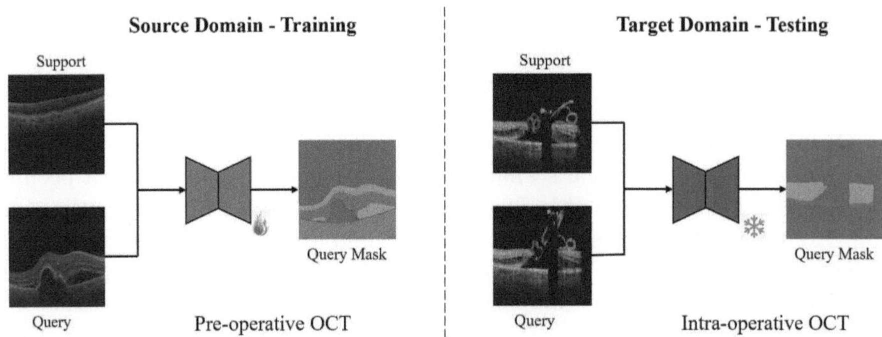

Fig. 2. Cross-domain few-shot segmentation pipeline. Left panel shows source domain (training): a single support B-scan from a well-annotated pre-operative OCT volume guides the network to segment its paired query B-scan, producing a multi-class retinal mask. Right panel shows target domain (inference): the same, now frozen, network receives one labeled intra-operative OCT support slice and segment an unseen query slice despite the domain shift.

CD-FSS, extended from FFS, aims at performing segmentation inference in an unseen target domain. The main challenge of CD-FSS is to overcome the performance degradation caused by domain shifts between the source domain and the target domain. A common solution is to perform domain adaptation by transforming domain-specific features into a domain-agnostic space.

3   Method

3.1   Problem Setting

We formulate a cross-domain few-shot semantic segmentation (CD-FSS) problem for iOCT as follows. The source domain $D_s = (I_S, M_s)$ is high-resolution retinal pOCT images without tools, such as in Fig. 1a and 1b, while the target domain $D_t = (I_t, M_t)$ is iOCT of low quality with shadows, tools, and deformed tissues, such as in Fig. 1c and 1d. I is the input image and M is the label space, where $I_s \neq I_t$ and $M_s \neq M_t$. The few-shot segmentation model trained on large-scale pOCT images in D_s could transfer the knowledge to iOCT in D_t and segment novel classes with only a few annotated iOCT images. Given a N-way K-shot few-shot learning task, both training and testing set consist of episodes, each of which is constructed by support set $S = \{(I_i^s, M_i^s)\}_{i=1}^{N \times K}$ and one query image $Q = (I_i^q, M_i^q)$. Fig 2 visualizes the CD-FSS task for iOCT segmentation.

3.2   Models

This section compares four FSS methods, including PATNet [14], SSP [7], DR-Adapter [21], and FAMNet [3]. PATNet [14], DR-Adapter [21], and FAMNet [3] are tailored for cross domain tasks. SSP [7], DR-Adapter [21], and PATNet

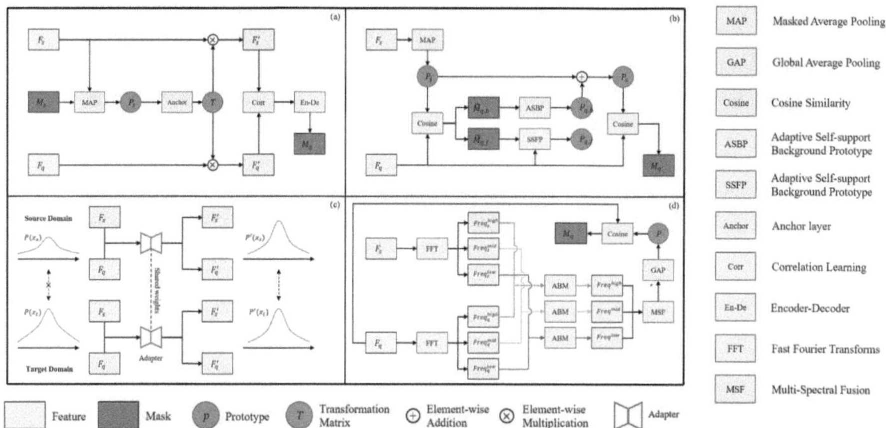

Fig. 3. The overall architecture of four few shot segmentation (FSS) networks, namely (a) PATNet [14], (b) SSP [7], (c) DR-Adapter [21], and (d) FAMNet [3].

[14] perform feature representation and transformation in spacial domain, while FAMNet [3] extract and match features in frequency domain.

To overcome the domain shifts, PATNet [14] and FAMNet [3] applied linear transformations with learnable weights to map the domain-specific features into a domain-agnostic space, which can be formulated as $F' = WF$, where F and F' denote the features before and after transformations. DR-Adapter [21] rectified target domain distributions to the source domain by injecting gaussian noises into source domain statistics. Given a feature map F_o with mean μ_o and variance σ_o, the perturbed feature map F_p is obtained using the Adaptive Instance Normalization formula [10] defined as $F_p = (1 + \beta)F_o + (\alpha - \beta)\mu_o$, where α and β are perturbation factors (Fig. 3).

Spacial Domain Models. PATNet [14] transforms domain-specific features into domain-agnostic ones and learns segmentation in the new metric space. The model first extracts pyramid features and generate the support prototype by Masked Average Pooling (MAP). Then, a transformation matrix is built based on the support prototype with learnable weights to transform both support and query features into a domain-agnostic space. After that, multi-level correlation maps are computed between transformed support and query features and processed by a convolutional encoder-decoder [16] to predict the final query mask.

SSP [7] is a self-support matching strategy based on Gestalt principle, namely pixels belonging to the same object are more similar than those to different objects of same class. Unlike PATNet [14], which perform support-query matching only with support prototypes, SSP [7] generates query prototypes from high-confidence query predictions, and matches query features with query prototypes.

DR-Adapter [21] is an adapter that can align unknown target domain distributions with the source domain distribution, so that the segmentation model

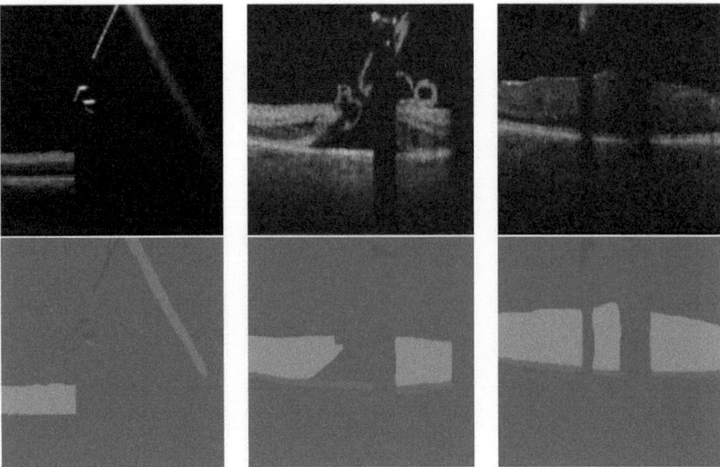

Fig. 4. Representative iOCT B-scans (top) and their pixel-wise ground-truth masks (bottom) taken from the three study datasets: D_{Normal} (left), D_{MHS} (centre, macular-hole surgery), and D_{ERM} (right, epiretinal-membrane surgery), with the corresponding annotation masks on the bottom row: blue represents the background, orange the ILM-RPE region, green the RPE layer, red the tools, purple the artifact introduced by tools, and brown the detached tissue layers.

well-trained in the source domain can process various target domain features. During training, the adapter perturbs the statistics of the source domain features by adding gaussian noises into source domain statistics.

Frequency Domain Models. FAMNet [3] leverages the frequency domain similarity to generalize the knowledge from the source domain to the target domain. The support and query frequency features are divided into three bands, and support-query matching is performed by attention-based matching (ABM) in specific frequency bands. Then, a Multi-spectral Fusion (MSF) module fuses the frequency-decoupled features from different bands.

4   Experiments

4.1   Dataset

We conducted training on two pOCT datasets of different scales, the Duke dataset [4] and the AROI [15] dataset. The Duke dataset consists of 110 high-resolution spectral domain (SD-OCT) scans collected from 10 patients with diabetic macular edema (DME). Annotations include fluid regions and eight retinal layer boundaries. The AROI [15] dataset contains 1136 B-scans from 24 patients suffering from age-related macular degeneration, with the annotations of three retinal layers and three retinal fluids.

Table 1. One-shot performance with Duke-trained models. Entries are mean DICE/IoU (%) on the three test sets for PATNet [14], FAMNet [3], DR-Adapter [21], and SSP [7].

Methods	D_{Normal}		D_{MHS}		D_{ERM}		Average	
	DICE	IoU	DICE	IoU	DICE	IoU	DICE	IoU
PATNet [14]	29.6 ± 0.7	26.8 ± 0.5	23.1 ± 1.0	19.6 ± 0.6	36.7 ± 1.0	31.2 ± 1.0	29.8	25.9
FAMNet [3]	40.3 ± 0.0	36.0 ± 0.0	32.5 ± 0.0	28.4 ± 0.0	45.7 ± 0.0	42.4 ± 0.0	39.5	35.6
DR-Adapter [21]	51.1 ± 0.6	43.4 ± 0.6	45.0 ± 0.6	35.3 ± 0.5	$\mathbf{60.0 \pm 0.7}$	$\mathbf{50.4 \pm 0.4}$	51.9	**43.0**
SSP [7]	$\mathbf{55.2 \pm 0.4}$	$\mathbf{45.6 \pm 0.3}$	$\mathbf{45.9 \pm 0.6}$	$\mathbf{35.5 \pm 0.4}$	55.9 ± 0.7	44.0 ± 0.6	**52.3**	39.8

Table 2. One-shot performance of AROI-trained models. Entries list mean IoU/DICE (%) on the three test sets for PATNet [14], FAMNet [3], DR-Adapter [21], and SSP [7].

Methods	D_{Normal}		D_{MHS}		D_{ERM}		Average	
	DICE	IoU	DICE	IoU	DICE	IoU	DICE	IoU
PATNet [14]	35.2 ± 0.5	31.1 ± 0.4	32.3 ± 0.7	25.9 ± 0.6	38.8 ± 0.8	32.04 ± 0.8	35.4	29.7
FAMNet [3]	43.7 ± 0.7	36.6 ± 0.5	46.4 ± 0.2	37.4 ± 0.2	62.1 ± 0.2	54.0 ± 0.3	50.7	42.6
DR-Adapter [21]	$\mathbf{56.1 \pm 0.8}$	$\mathbf{47.3 \pm 0.6}$	$\mathbf{53.1 \pm 0.2}$	$\mathbf{42.2 \pm 0.2}$	$\mathbf{66.4 \pm 3.1}$	$\mathbf{56.5 \pm 3.3}$	**58.5**	**48.7**
SSP [7]	55.3 ± 0.2	46.3 ± 0.2	46.9 ± 0.8	36.8 ± 0.7	55.8 ± 2.0	45.4 ± 1.7	52.7	42.8

We labeled three private iOCT datasets collected from our partner eye hospital to evaluate the domain adaptation ability of our model[1]. The first dataset, D_{Normal}, contains 84 images from 8 patients, which were collected in the presence of a 25 Gauge vitrector within a scanned region of 6 mm × 6 mm. The vitrector was placed above the retina, and iOCT scans at this target region were recorded. We labeled the ILM-RPE region, i.e. the tissues from the top boundary of ILM to the top boundary of RPE, surgical tools, and the artifacts introduced by these tools. The second dataset, D_{MHS}, contains 25 images, captured during a macular hole surgery. We labeled the ILM-RPE region, the RPE layer, surgical tools, and the detached retina layers. The third dataset, D_{ERM}, contains 15 images, captured during an ERM peeling surgery. We labeled the ILM-RPE region, RPE layers, and surgical tools. All three datasets were captured by Zeiss Rescan 700 and annotated manually under the guidance of experienced surgeons with segment-anything-annotator [8]. Figure 4 shows examples from the three iOCT datasets and their annotations.

4.2   Results

We evaluated four FFS methods illustrated in Sect. 3.2, namely PATNet [14], SSP [7], DR-Adapter [21], and FAMNet [3]. We followed official open-source code provided by the developer and retrained the models on the Duke and AROI dataset separately without changing any training procedure. Some hyperparameters, such as learning rate and epochs, were adjusted to produce the best results

---

[1] Data can be made available through a transfer agreement, upon request.

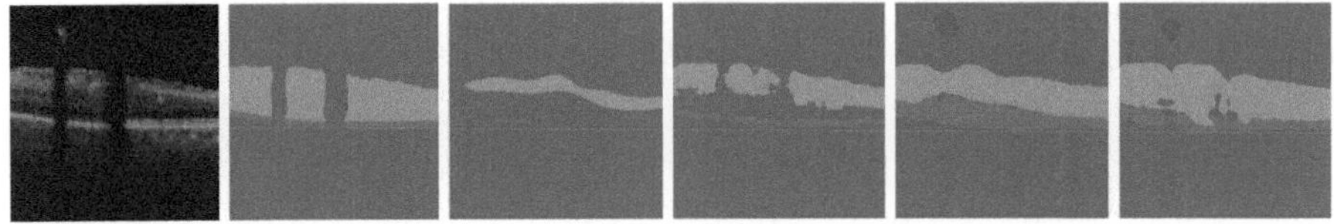

Fig. 5. Qualitative one-shot segmentation on the D_{ERM} test set. From the left to right are the (a) original image, (b) ground truth mask and visualized 1-shot segmentation results predicted by (c) PATNet, (d) FAMNet, (e) SSP, (f) DR-Adapter.

on our dataset. We reported the standard Dice coefficient (DICE) and Mean intersection over-union (IoU) as the evaluation metric for our CD-FSS task. For each class, DICE and IoU were calculated by $DICE = \frac{2TP}{2TP+FP+FN}$ and $IoU = \frac{TP}{TP+FP+FN}$, where TP, FP, and FN are true positive, false positive, and false negative of the segmentation prediction. We averaged $DICE$ and IoU for all classes to find the final results. Table 1 and Table 2 shows DICE and mIoU on three iOCT testing datasets produced by the four FFS methods trained on the Duke and AROI dataset, respectively. Figure 5 visualizes the query masks predicted by the four methods.

Among all models trained on a dataset with a smaller sample size (Duke) shown in Table 1, SSP [7] achieves the best average DICE. However, when the training is on a larger source domain dataset (AROI) as shown in Table 2, DR-Adapter [21] performs the best on both DICE and IoU. Additionally, after switching to a larger training set, performance improvements can be observed in three models, demonstrating the effectiveness of large-scale datasets for FFS. FAMNet [3] achieves the largest performance improvement (25.6% DICE, 28.3% IoU), potentially because of the frequency-domain learning paradigm benefiting more from larger training datasets.

In terms of inference efficiency, the per-frame processing time reveals differences across methods. SSP is the fastest, achieving 0.05 s per frame, followed by PATNet at 0.12 s, FAMNet at 0.16 s, and DR-Adapter being the slowest at 0.36 s. All methods were tested on an NVIDIA GeForce RTX 4060. The frequency-domain operations in FAMNet don't introduce much latency compared to other spatial domain methods. While DR-Adapter produced the best segmentation performance, its relatively slow inference time makes it less suitable for real-time surgical applications. Therefore, methods like SSP and FAMNet may offer a better balance between accuracy and speed in time-sensitive intra-operative scenarios.

5 Conclusion

In this paper, we applied cross-domain few-shot segmentation methods on iOCT segmentation, which can transfer knowledge learned from the high-resolution pOCT domain to the unseen low-resolution iOCT domain with only one pixel-level annotated iOCT image. The models are trained on pOCT data without tools and with clear retina layers, but perform prediction on iOCT data with lower SNR, tools, shadows, and artifacts. We trained the models on two pOCT datasets of different scales, and tested them on three iOCT datasets captured during different surgical scenarios to evaluate the generalization ability. The proposed approach can help overcome the annotation problem faced by iOCT segmentation, narrow the gap between pOCT and iOCT domain, and could potentially generalize to similar domain gaps (e.g. 3T MRI to 0.55T MRI). There are certain limitations to consider, such as limited scales of testing sets, as well as lower performance compared to traditional OCT segmentation tasks. Our future goal is to develop a more robust model, build larger testing sets for model evaluation, and incorporate this work within a computer-assisted iOCT interpretation system that enhances surgical safety through tool/retina proximity detection.

Acknowledgements. The authors would like to acknowledge funding from the King's-China Scholarship Council PhD Scholarship programme (K-CSC) and from the EPSRC Centre for Doctoral Training in Smart Medical Imaging (EP/S022104/1).

References

1. Anderson, M., et al.: Biomedical data annotation: an oct imaging case study. J. Ophthalmol. **2023**(1), 5747010 (2023)
2. Arikan, D., et alI.: Real-time deformation-aware control for autonomous robotic subretinal injection under IOCT guidance. arXiv preprint arXiv:2411.06557 (2024)
3. Bo, Y., Zhu, Y., Li, L., Zhang, H.: Famnet: Frequency-aware matching network for cross-domain few-shot medical image segmentation. In: Proceedings of the AAAI Conference on Artificial Intelligence, vol. 39, pp. 1889–1897 (2025)
4. Chiu, S.J., Allingham, M.J., Mettu, P.S., Cousins, S.W., Izatt, J.A., Farsiu, S.: Kernel regression based segmentation of optical coherence tomography images with diabetic macular edema. Biomed. Opt. Express **6**(4), 1172–1194 (2015)
5. Ciarmatori, N., Pellegrini, M., Nasini, F., Talli, P.M., Sarti, L., Mura, M.: The state of intraoperative oct in vitreoretinal surgery: recent advances and future challenges. Tomography **9**(5), 1649–1659 (2023)
6. Dehghani, S., et al.: Robotic navigation autonomy for subretinal injection via intelligent real-time virtual IOCT volume slicing. In: 2023 IEEE International Conference on Robotics and Automation (ICRA), pp. 4724–4731. IEEE (2023)
7. Fan, Q., Pei, W., Tai, Y.W., Tang, C.K.: Self-support few-shot semantic segmentation. In: Avidan, S., Brostow, G., Cissé, M., Farinella, G.M., Hassner, T. (eds.) European Conference on Computer Vision, pp. 701–719. Springer, Cham (2022). https://doi.org/10.1007/978-3-031-19800-7_41
8. He, H.: Segment anything annotator. https://github.com/haochenheheda/segment-anything-annotator (2023). Accessed 5 June 2025
9. He, K., Zhang, X., Ren, S., Sun, J.: Deep residual learning for image recognition. In: Proceedings of the IEEE Conference on Computer Vision and Pattern Recognition, pp. 770–778 (2016)
10. Huang, X., Belongie, S.: Arbitrary style transfer in real-time with adaptive instance normalization. In: Proceedings of the IEEE International Conference on Computer Vision, pp. 1501–1510 (2017)

11. Huang, Y., Asaria, R., Stoyanov, D., Sarunic, M., Bano, S.: PseudoSegRT: efficient pseudo-labelling for intraoperative OCT segmentation. Int. J. Comput. Assist. Radiol. Surg. **18**(7), 1245–1252 (2023)
12. Jagtap, A.D., Riviere, C.N.: Applied force during vitreoretinal microsurgery with handheld instruments. In: The 26th Annual International Conference of the IEEE Engineering in Medicine and Biology Society, vol. 1, pp. 2771–2773. IEEE (2004)
13. Kim, J.W., et al.: Towards deep learning guided autonomous eye surgery using microscope and IOCT images. arXiv e-prints, pp. arXiv–2306 (2023)
14. Lei, S., Zhang, X., He, J., Chen, F., Du, B., Lu, C.T.: Cross-domain few-shot semantic segmentation. In: Avidan, S., Brostow, G., Cissé, M., Farinella, G.M., Hassner, T. (eds.) European Conference on Computer Vision, pp. 73–90. Springer, Cham (2022). https://doi.org/10.1007/978-3-031-20056-4_5
15. Melinščak, M., Radmilovič, M., Vatavuk, Z., Lončarić, S.: AROI: annotated retinal oct images database. In: 2021 44th International Convention on Information, Communication and Electronic Technology (MIPRO), pp. 371–376. IEEE (2021)
16. Min, J., Kang, D., Cho, M.: Hypercorrelation squeeze for few-shot segmentation. In: Proceedings of the IEEE/CVF International Conference on Computer Vision, pp. 6941–6952 (2021)
17. Park, I., Kim, H.K., Chung, W.K., Kim, K.: Deep learning based real-time oct image segmentation and correction for robotic needle insertion systems. IEEE Robot. Autom. Lett. **5**(3), 4517–4524 (2020)
18. Ronneberger, O., Fischer, P., Brox, T.: U-Net: convolutional networks for biomedical image segmentation. In: Navab, N., Hornegger, J., Wells, W.M., Frangi, A.F. (eds.) MICCAI 2015. LNCS, vol. 9351, pp. 234–241. Springer, Cham (2015). https://doi.org/10.1007/978-3-319-24574-4_28
19. Shah, A., Zhou, L., Abrámoff, M.D., Wu, X.: Multiple surface segmentation using convolution neural nets: application to retinal layer segmentation in oct images. Biomed. Opt. Express **9**(9), 4509–4526 (2018)
20. Sommersperger, M., Weiss, J., Ali Nasseri, M., Gehlbach, P., Iordachita, I., Navab, N.: Real-time tool to layer distance estimation for robotic subretinal injection using intraoperative 4D oct. Biomed. Opt. Express **12**(2), 1085–1104 (2021)
21. Su, J., Fan, Q., Pei, W., Lu, G., Chen, F.: Domain-rectifying adapter for cross-domain few-shot segmentation. In: Proceedings of the IEEE/CVF Conference on Computer Vision and Pattern Recognition, pp. 24036–24045 (2024)
22. Wang, Y., et al.: Retinal oct layer segmentation via joint motion correction and graph-assisted 3D neural network. IEEE Access **11**, 103319–103332 (2023)
23. Weiss, J., Sommersperger, M., Nasseri, A., Eslami, A., Eck, U., Navab, N.: Processing-aware real-time rendering for optimized tissue visualization in intraoperative 4D OCT. In: Martel, A.L., et al. (eds.) MICCAI 2020. LNCS, vol. 12265, pp. 267–276. Springer, Cham (2020). https://doi.org/10.1007/978-3-030-59722-1_26

Reasoning-Enhanced Vision-Language Model for Interpretable Diabetic Retinopathy Detection in Ultra-Wide-Field Fundus Images

Zhenyu Tang[1,2], Lingzhi Chen[1], Lilong Wang[1], Yankai Jiang[1], Jun Li[3], and Xiaosong Wang[1(✉)]

[1] Shanghai AI Laboratory, Shanghai, China
wangxiaosong@pjlab.org.cn
[2] Shanghai Jiao Tong University, Shanghai, China
[3] Qingdao Eye Hospital of Shandong First Medical University, Qingdao, China

Abstract. Ultra-wide-field (UWF) fundus photography provides a comprehensive view of the retina, enabling diabetic retinopathy (DR) detection in peripheral regions often missed in traditional imaging techniques. However, the lack of large-scale public UWF datasets hinders related deep learning-based DR detection research. Moreover, models trained on conventional classification targets frequently lack interpretability in their predictions or produce results that are misaligned with clinical criteria. To address these challenges, we first compile a dataset (UWF-DR) comprising over 5,000 UWF images, each graded for DR and annotated with lesion presence. Utilizing the annotations with clinical guidelines and GPT-4o's vision-language capabilities, we generate reasoning-enhanced image captions that mirror the decision-making processes of ophthalmologists. An instruction dataset is constructed based on these captions and augmented with sub-task instructions. We fine-tune a multi-modal large language model on UWF-DR to generate reasoning for DR detection. Experimental results demonstrate the benefit of reasoning-based enhancement, showcasing superior grading performance and high alignment with clinical criteria. The dataset is available at UWF-DR.

Keywords: Diabetic Retinopathy · Ultra-wide-field Fundus Photography · Reasoning-Enhanced · Vision-Language Model

1 Introduction

Diabetic retinopathy (DR), a major complication of diabetes, is a leading cause of blindness worldwide [2,22]. Regular fundus examinations are critical for screening, diagnosing, and managing DR, as early intervention can significantly reduce the risk of severe visual impairment [7]. Conventional color fundus photography (CFP), typically capturing a 30–60° field of view (FoV), has been the standard

---

Z. Tang, L. Chen and L. Wang—Equal contribution.

© The Author(s), under exclusive license to Springer Nature Switzerland AG 2026
H. Fang et al. (Eds.): OMIA 2025, LNCS 16209, pp. 115–125, 2026.
https://doi.org/10.1007/978-3-032-10351-2_12

for DR assessment. However, its limited scope often fails to detect peripheral retinal lesions, which are now recognized as key indicators of DR progression. Recent advances in imaging technology have introduced ultra-wide-field (UWF) fundus photography, which offers an expansive 200° FoV, allowing for comprehensive visualization of the retina, including its peripheral regions [21,26]. Clinical studies have demonstrated that UWF imaging detects a higher prevalence of DR-related lesions in the retinal periphery, such as hemorrhages, microaneurysms, and neovascularization [19]. These findings underscore the clinical value of UWF imaging in early DR detection and accurate severity assessment [18].

Since the rise of deep learning, extensive studies have utilized deep convolutional neural network (CNN) and transformer-based models for the automated detection of DR [12,23,28]. These applications include early detection of referrable DR, DR severity grading, and identification of DR-related lesions using CFP. The availability of publicly CFP accessible datasets with DR grading and lesion annotations, *e.g.*, Messidor [6], OIA-DDR [13] and IDRID [17], has enabled researchers to train and validate models effectively, accelerating progress in this field. In contrast, research on AI-based DR detection using UWF images remains relatively limited [1,16]. Meanwhile, publicly available datasets of UWF images for DR analysis are also limited and lack fine-grained DR severity grades and lesion annotations [5,9].

Recently, foundation models trained with techniques like self-supervised learning (SSL) or contrastive learning have been increasingly applied to retinal image analysis. For instance, RETFound [29] leverages millions of unlabeled CFP and OCT images for masked autoencoder pretraining. KeepFIT [27] and FLAIR [20] adopt CLIP-like approaches, using paired retinal images and texts to pre-train visual encoders for DR detection tasks. However, these methods often overlook the integration of multimodal data and the interpretability of model decisions when transferring from pre-trained foundation models to specific downstream classification tasks. Concurrently, multimodal large language models (MLLMs) are emerging as more powerful VLMs that combine visual understanding with natural language generation. By embedding medical knowledge and enabling natural language-driven tasks, MLLMs significantly enhance reasoning reliability and interpretability, which have shown promising results in medical image interpretation and diagnosis [3,11,15,24].

In this paper, we introduce a large-scale **UWF** image dataset annotated with **DR** severity levels and related lesions information (UWF-DR). Additionally, we develop a **VLM** with enhanced **R**easoning capabilities (UWF-VLMR) for DR grading and lesion identification. The contribution of this work is three-fold:

1) A large-scale, fine-grained UWF-DR dataset: We collect and curate a dataset of over 5,000 high-quality UWF images. Each image was meticulously annotated by ophthalmologists, including DR severity grading and the presence of seven lesion types closely associated with DR progression. This UWF-DR dataset not only serves as the foundation for our research but will also be publicly released to facilitate future studies on UWF-based DR analysis.

2) Reasoning-enhanced image captions and instructions: Leveraging GPT-4o's [10] advanced visual and reasoning capabilities, we automate the generation

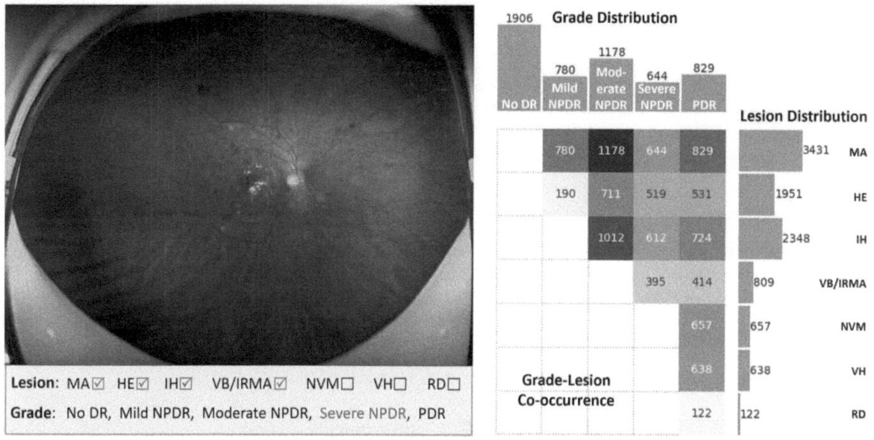

Fig. 1. Illustration of the UWF-DR dataset. On the left is a sample image and corresponding DR grade and lesion annotations. On the right is the distribution of grade, lesion, and their co-occurrence.

of reasoning-enhanced image captions and instructions. By designing prompts embedded with clinical knowledge and guidelines related to DR grading, lesion identification, and their interrelationships, the generated captions and instructions closely mirror the decision-making processes of ophthalmologists.

3) UWF-VLMR with better DR detection performance: We developed UWF-VLMR, a fine-tuned MLLM based on the InternVL [4] framework, using UWF images and the synthesized reasoning-enhanced instructions. Compared to other foundation models, our proposed model demonstrates general improvements in DR grading and lesion identification tasks, achieving superior recognition accuracy, interpretability, and clinical alignment in its outputs.

2   Dataset

The UWF-DR dataset used in this study consists of 5,337 qualified UWF images collected from a large ophthalmic hospital using the Optos UWF^{TM} camera. The DR severity levels are classified based on established clinical guidelines [25] and practical experience, briefly summarized as follows: i) No DR: No apparent DR signs; ii) Mild NPDR: Few microaneurysms (MA), occasionally accompanied by minor dot hard exudates (HE); iii) Moderate NPDR: Increased MAs and presence of HEs or intraretinal hemorrhages (IH); iv) Severe NPDR: Extensive MAs, IHs, HEs, often with venous beading or intraretinal microvascular abnormalities (VB/IRMA); v) PDR: Presence of neovascularization membrane (NVM), vitreous hemorrhage (VH), or retinal detachment (RD). Each image was meticulously annotated by experienced retinal specialists, who assigned DR severity levels and identified the presence or absence of seven DR-related lesions. Figure 1 illustrates a representative example and the distribution of annotations.

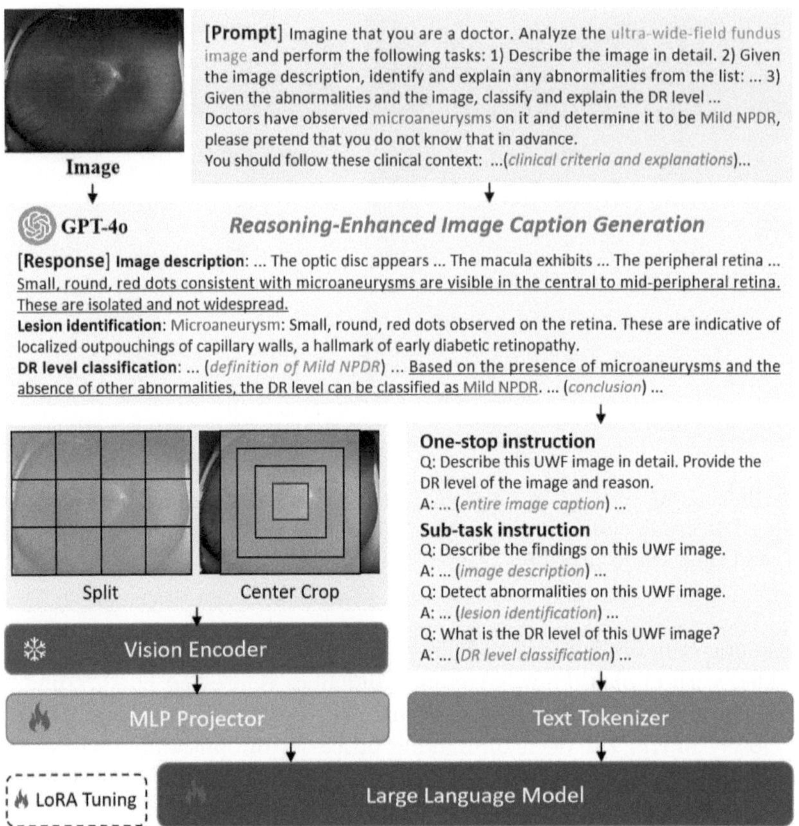

Fig. 2. Overview of UWF-VLMR. Captions are generated by GPT-4o with images, annotations, and necessary clinical contexts for reasoning. One-stop and sub-task instruction data are constructed with the captions. A VLM is trained on UWF-DR using both patch stitched images and mixed instructions.

3   Method

Figure 2 depicts UWF-VLMR, a VLM-training framework with Reasoning-enhanced instruction data on UWF images. The framework involves two stages: 1) reasoning-enhanced instruction data synthesis and 2) vision-language model tuning. The details of both stages are described in the following.

3.1   Reasoning-Enhanced Instruction Data Synthesis

Reasoning-Enhanced Image Caption Generation. To align DR grading with clinical decision-making, we design a reasoning-enhanced caption generation framework, which generates clinically interpretable reports by explicitly emulating the two-step diagnostic process used by ophthalmologists: i) systematic identification of retinal abnormalities and ii) rule-based synthesis of findings into standardized severity grades. As shown in Fig. 2, we prompt GPT-4o with detailed requirements to perform three tasks sequentially in a clinical tone. To ensure accuracy, the prompt template $t(\cdot, \cdot, \cdot)$ is supplemented with raw annotations of grades $g_i \in \{0, 1, 2, 3, 4\}$ and lesions $l_i \in \{0, 1\}^7$ from UWF-DR, clinical contexts c including standards and lesion explanations, for the i-th image u_i. The resultant captions $r_i = \text{GPT4o}(t(c, g_i, l_i), u_i)$ with 364.8 words on average adopt a structured, logic-driven format: the initial descriptive analysis prioritizes the spatial position and appearance of clinically relevant visual features, *e.g.*, MAs and HEs, followed by lesion classification grounded in observational evidence, and concludes with severity grading based on predefined clinical protocols.

One-Stop and Sub-task Instruction Construction. We construct question-answer (QA) pairs (q, r_i) for the i-th image using full captions, where q is the one-stop instruction as in Fig. 2. While language models leverage prior context for incremental predictions, directly training a model to autoregressively generate full captions risks error propagation, as inaccuracies in early lesion detection may disproportionately compromise subsequent grading steps (*e.g.*, misidentifying MAs may lead to misclassification of Mild NPDR). To mitigate this, we split the reasoning-enhanced captions r_i for the i-th image into the three tasks $r_i = r_{i1} \cdot r_{i2} \cdot r_{i3}$, where $\cdot$ is string concatenation. Each task is paired with explicit sub-task instructions to isolate the model's focus, thereby reducing overreliance on prior steps and strengthening its capacity to address inherently challenging sub-tasks independently. The constructed sub-task instruction QA pairs are denoted as $(q_j, r_{ij}), j \in \{1, 2, 3\}$ for the i-th image and j-th subtask. The final reasoning-enhanced instruction data, $\mathcal{D} = \{(q, r_i, u_i) | i \in \mathcal{N}\} \cup \bigcup_{j=1}^{3} \{(q_j, r_{ij}, u_i) | i \in \mathcal{N}\}$, where $\mathcal{N}$ is the set of indices for UWF-DR, is comprised of visual question answering pairs based on both the one-stop and sub-task instructions.

3.2   Vision-Language Model Tuning

Vision-Language Model Architecture. To incorporate multi-modal information, a pre-trained Vision Transformer (ViT) is integrated into the large language model backbone. At each step, we sample a batch of QA pairs with corresponding UWF images from the constructed dataset uniformly, that is, $(x_{\text{text}}, y, x_{\text{image}}) \sim \text{Uniform}(\mathcal{D})$. The model is tuned in a causal language model manner, namely, the instructions, answers and the image tags are structured in a template $f_{\text{template}}(x_{\text{text}}, y)$ as model input x. The ViT encoder f_{ViT} is frozen, and an MLP projector M is utilized to align the visual tokens to the language token space. The instruction tokens z are subsequently obtained by the concatenation of the language tokens z_{text} and the projected visual tokens z_{image}:

$$z = [z_{\text{text}}, M(z_{\text{image}})] = [f_{\text{tok}}(x), M(f_{\text{ViT}}(x_{\text{image}}))], \tag{1}$$

where f_{tok} is the language tokenizer. Ultimately, the tokens are fed into a pre-trained large language model f_{LLM} adapted with LoRA [8]. The tuning process is supervised with cross-entropy loss $f_{\text{CE}}(\cdot, \cdot)$ masked on the answer tokens $(f_{\text{mask}}^y(\cdot))$, frequently used in causal language models:

Table 1. Performance on DR grading and lesion detection. Acc: accuracy. $(\cdot)_{Avg}$: averaged on each class. $F1_{No}$, $F1_{Mild}$, $F1_{Mod}$, $F1_{Sev}$ and $F1_{PDR}$ are F1 scores for No DR, Mild NPDR, Moderate NPDR, Severe NPDR, and PDR respectively. The best and second-best results are bolded and underlined, respectively.

Method	DR Grading								Lesion	
	Acc	κ	$F1_{Avg}$	$F1_{No}$	$F1_{Mild}$	$F1_{Mod}$	$F1_{Sev}$	$F1_{PDR}$	Acc_{Avg}	$F1_{Avg}$
Fundus Image Foundation Models										
RETFound [29]	0.609	0.566	0.609	0.811	0.245	**0.615**	0.479	**0.895**	0.894	**0.781**
KeepFIT [27]	0.648	0.544	0.625	0.780	0.375	0.542	**0.585**	0.844	0.887	0.739
FLAIR [20]	0.661	0.564	0.631	0.845	**0.477**	0.518	<u>0.560</u>	0.755	0.874	0.707
MLLMs										
GPT-4o (zero-shot) [10]	0.355	0.148	0.295	0.537	0.195	0.255	0.041	0.447	0.770	0.343
LLaVA-Med [11]	0.627	0.507	0.571	0.796	0.268	0.546	0.428	0.816	0.884	0.716
InternVL [4]	0.659	0.537	0.576	0.789	0.160	0.580	0.495	0.853	0.896	0.681
UWF-VLMR (sub-task)	**0.694**	**0.595**	<u>0.638</u>	**0.862**	<u>0.447</u>	0.597	0.427	<u>0.859</u>	<u>0.901</u>	0.730
UWF-VLMR (one-stop)	<u>0.687</u>	<u>0.592</u>	**0.641**	<u>0.852</u>	0.400	<u>0.602</u>	0.504	0.845	**0.902**	<u>0.745</u>

$$\mathcal{L} = f_{CE}(y, f^y_{\text{mask}}(f_{\text{LLM}}(z))). \tag{2}$$

Image Processing. To maximize the preservation of detailed information in UWF images while retaining both key regions and global context, we design a hybrid patch stitching strategy. First, following the MLLMs, the original image is evenly split into non-overlapping local images arranged in a 4 × 3 layout. Then, four multi-scale square regions are cropped around the centroid of the image, with side lengths being 1.0, 0.75, 0.5, and 0.25 times the shorter side of the original image. Subsequently, all the 16 patches obtained above are uniformly resized to 448 × 448, stitched together, and fed as inputs into the vision encoder.

4   Experimental Results

Implementation Details. UWF-DR is randomly split into training, validation, and testing sets with a ratio of 7:1:2. Training employed a batch size of 16, the AdamW [14] optimizer with a learning rate of 2e−5, and 4 Nvidia A100 GPUs. InternVL-26B with LoRA rank set to 16 is selected for our VLM backbone.

Metrics. Accuracy, Cohen's Kappa and F1 scores are selected for evaluation. The prediction probabilities of an MLLM required for AUC computation are inherently difficult to obtain (i.e., iterating over $O(V^L)$ conditional probabilities to obtain logits, where $V > 100,000$ is the token vocabulary size, and $L = 1024$ is the maximum number of tokens), as the model outputs conditional probabilities over tokens rather than direct class probabilities for the entire input. To facilitate metrics computation, we attach a formatted conclusion to each caption for automated extraction of lesions or grades.

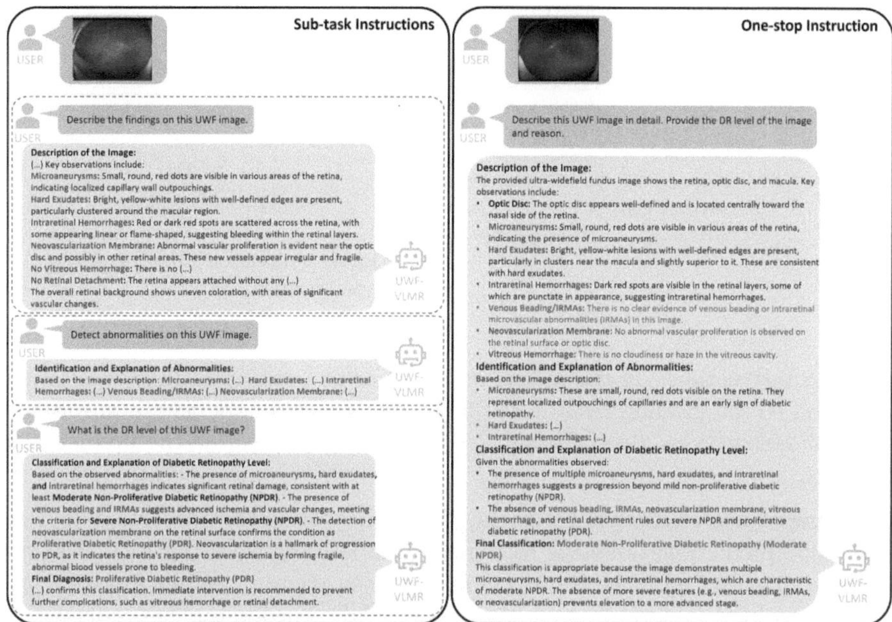

Fig. 3. Qualitative results of UWF-VLMR. The correct grade or lesion predictions are highlighted in green, while the failure cases are in red. Some less informative contents are omitted for better display. (Color figure online)

4.1 Comparison on DR Grading and Lesion Identification

Baselines. We compare UWF-VLMR against both fundus image foundation models and MLLMs. For fundus image foundation models, recent works, i.e., RETFound [29], KeepFIT [27], and FLAIR [20], are fine-tuned for comparison. For MLLMs, we fine-tune LLaVA-Med [11], and InternVL [4] with LoRA on UWF-DR with structured template answers. Zero-shot knowledge of GPT-4o [10] is also evaluated with multi-choice questions. Methods are trained on both grading and lesion detection tasks jointly, except for RETFound [29], where performance degradation is observed when trained jointly.

Classification Performance. Table 1 shows the grading and lesion classification performance on UWF-DR. Generally, fundus image foundation models exhibit strong performance compared with MLLMs, showing the benefit of their knowledge transfer. With our reasoning-enhanced framework, UWF-VLMR outperforms the foundation models on both grading and lesion classification tasks. Notably, the low performance of zero-shot GPT-4o shows its lack of prior knowledge about DR detection on UWF images, and hence the improvement is not inherently from merely distilling the GPT-4o model. The results of inferencing with one-stop and sub-task instructions are also reported (marked in brackets), and the observed difference is not significant. Figure 3 showcases qualitative results with comprehensive details of UWF-VLMR with both one-stop and

Table 2. Ablation studies of UWF-VLMR.

Setting	Option	Acc	κ	F1
Image Processing	Vanilla	0.666	0.566	0.631
	Patch stitching	0.678	0.581	0.643
Instruction	Template	0.630	0.504	0.533
	One-stop only	0.620	0.496	0.560
	Sub-task only	0.668	0.563	0.606
	Mixed	0.678	0.581	0.643

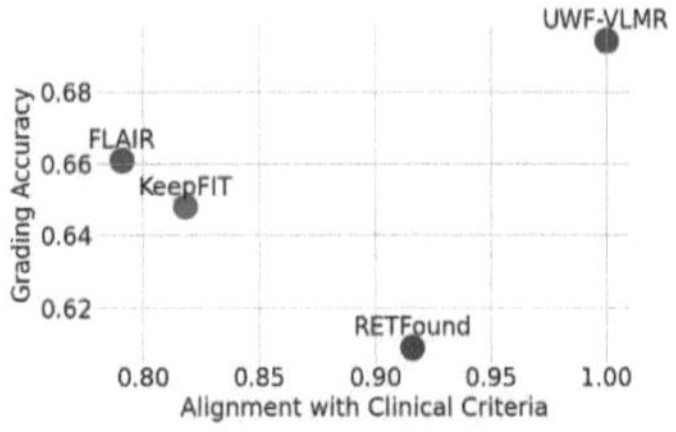

Fig. 4. Prediction alignment with clinical criteria.

sub-task instructions. In the failure case, the error propagates from VB/IRMA detection to the grading results. In the following, we report results in terms of sub-task instructions given the smaller inferencing burden (as the prediction is shorter).

Alignment with Clinical Criteria. We further assess the proportion of grade and lesion predictions adhering to clinical criteria (detailed in Sect. 2), as shown in Fig. 4, together with the corresponding grading accuracy. While fundus image foundation models perform well, they do not fully encode the co-occurrence of lesions and grades, leading to misaligned predictions for 8.4%20.9% of the samples. In contrast, UWF-VLMR, trained with reasoning-enhanced texts, effectively captures these correlations, achieving 100% alignment with clinical criteria across all test samples. This results in superior performance and the highest alignment accuracy among the compared methods.

4.2   Ablation Study

Ablation studies on image processing and instruction design are performed, and the results on DR grading are shown in Table 2. Given the extensive computation consumption, we perform ablation studies on the InternVL-8B backbone. In the context of image processing, experimental results demonstrate that the patch stitching technique improves over vanilla patching strategy of InternVL, indicating the benefit of the introduced image processing strategy. More sophisticated patch stitching methods may be applied and compared in further work. Concerning the instruction design, the results demonstrate that using sub-task instructions alone during training yields better performance than using one-stop instruction alone. This approach effectively mitigates the risk of error propagation in the reasoning process. The mixed strategy of combining sub-task and one-stop instructions further integrates both merits, attaining optimal overall performance, surpassing the simple template answers by 11% in F1 scores.

5   Limitations and Future Work

We performed expert evaluation on $\sim 10\%$ of the GPT-generated data due to the large scale. A more thorough evaluation, involving more clinical assessment on model-generated contents and other UWF imaging systems will be performed in the future.

6   Conclusion

In this paper, we introduce a large-scale, high-quality dataset, UWF-DR, for DR detection, comprising 5,337 UWF images annotated with lesions and grades. To achieve more interpretable DR grading, we construct reasoning-enhanced image captions with clinical contexts. Subsequently, a large vision-language model trained on this dataset, UWF-VLMR, demonstrates superior grading performance and high alignment with clinical criteria. This work may pave the way for developing reliable and interpretable models on UWF images.

Acknowledgments. This work has received support from Shanghai AI Laborary and the Shandong Provincial Medical and Health Science and Technology Project (202407020141, 202507020749).

Disclosure of Interests. The authors have no competing interests to declare that are relevant to the content of this article.

References

1. Bai, Y., et al.: Unsupervised lesion-aware transfer learning for diabetic retinopathy grading in ultra-wide-field fundus photography. In: Wang, L., Dou, Q., Fletcher, P.T., Speidel, S., Li, S. (eds.) International Conference on Medical Image Computing and Computer-Assisted Intervention, pp. 560–570. Springer (2022). https://doi.org/10.1007/978-3-031-16434-7_54
2. Bourne, R., et al.: Causes of vision loss worldwide, 1990–2010: a systematic analysis. Lancet Glob Health **1**(6), e339–49 (2010)
3. Chen, P., et al.: GMAI-MMBENCH: a comprehensive multimodal evaluation benchmark towards general medical AI. arXiv preprint arXiv:2408.03361 (2024)
4. Chen, Z., et al.: InterNVL: scaling up vision foundation models and aligning for generic visual-linguistic tasks. In: Proceedings of the IEEE/CVF Conference on Computer Vision and Pattern Recognition, pp. 24185–24198 (2024)
5. CodaLab Competitions: Ultra-widefield fundus imaging for diabetic retinopathy challenge 2024. https://codalab.lisn.upsaclay.fr/competitions/18605 (2024). Accessed 23 May 2025
6. Decencière, E., et al.: Feedback on a publicly distributed image database: the MESSIDOR database. In: Image Analysis & Stereology, pp. 231–234 (2014)
7. Group, E.T.D.R.S.R., et al.: Grading diabetic retinopathy from stereoscopic color fundus photographs—an extension of the modified airlie house classification: ETDRS report number 10. Ophthalmology **98**(5), 786–806 (1991)
8. Hu, E.J., et al.: LORA: low-rank adaptation of large language models. ICLR **1**(2), 3 (2022)
9. Hu, Y., Wang, C., Song, W., Tiulpin, A., Liu, Q.: A scanning laser ophthalmoscopy image database and trustworthy retinal disease detection method. In: In: Linguraru, M.G., et al. (eds.) International Conference on Medical Image Computing and Computer-Assisted Intervention, pp. 46–56. Springer, Cham (2024). https://doi.org/10.1007/978-3-031-72086-4_5

10. Hurst, A., et al.: GPT-4o system card. arXiv preprint arXiv:2410.21276 (2024)
11. Li, C., et al.: LLAVA-Med: training a large language-and-vision assistant for biomedicine in one day. Adv. Neural. Inf. Process. Syst. **36**, 28541–28564 (2023)
12. Li, J., et al.: Integrated image-based deep learning and language models for primary diabetes care. Nat. Med. **30**(10), 2886–2896 (2024)
13. Li, T., Gao, Y., Wang, K., Guo, S., Liu, H., Kang, H.: Diagnostic assessment of deep learning algorithms for diabetic retinopathy screening. Inf. Sci. **501**, 511–522 (2019)
14. Loshchilov, I., Hutter, F.: Decoupled weight decay regularization. arXiv preprint arXiv:1711.05101 (2017)
15. Lu, M.Y., et al.: A multimodal generative ai copilot for human pathology. Nature **634**(8033), 466–473 (2024)
16. Oh, K., Kang, H.M., Leem, D., Lee, H., Seo, K.Y., Yoon, S.: Early detection of diabetic retinopathy based on deep learning and ultra-wide-field fundus images. Sci. Rep. **11**(1), 1897 (2021)
17. Porwal, P., et al.: Indian diabetic retinopathy image dataset (IDRID): a database for diabetic retinopathy screening research. Data **3**(3), 25 (2018)
18. Price, L.D., Au, S., Chong, N.V.: Optomap ultrawide field imaging identifies additional retinal abnormalities in patients with diabetic retinopathy. Clin. Ophthalmol. **9**, 527–531 (2015)
19. Silva, P.S., et al.: Peripheral lesions identified on ultrawide field imaging predict increased risk of diabetic retinopathy progression over 4 years. Ophthalmology **122**(5), 949–956 (2015)
20. Silva-Rodriguez, J., Chakor, H., Kobbi, R., Dolz, J., Ayed, I.B.: A foundation language-image model of the retina (flair): encoding expert knowledge in text supervision. Med. Image Anal. **99**, 103357 (2025)
21. Singer, M., Sagong, M., van Hemert, J., Kuehlewein, L., Bell, D., Sadda, S.R.: Ultra-widefield imaging of the peripheral retinal vasculature in normal subjects. Ophthalmology **123**(5), 1053–1059 (2016)
22. Ting, D.S.W., Cheung, G.C.M., Wong, T.Y.: Diabetic retinopathy: global prevalence, major risk factors, screening practices and public health challenges: a review. Clin. Exp. Ophthalmol. **44**(4), 260–277 (2016)
23. Wang, H., et al.: Hard exudate detection based on deep model learned information and multi-feature joint representation for diabetic retinopathy screening. Comput. Methods Programs Biomed. **191**, 105398 (2020)
24. Wang, L., Liu, M., Zhang, S., Wang, X.: BrainSCK: brain structure and cognition alignment via knowledge injection and reactivation for diagnosing brain disorders. In: Linguraru, M.G., et al. (eds.) International Conference on Medical Image Computing and Computer-Assisted Intervention, pp. 45–55. Springer (2024). https://doi.org/10.1007/978-3-031-72069-7_5
25. Verdaguer, J.T., et al.: Proposed international clinical diabetic retinopathy and diabetic macular edema disease severity scales. Ophthalmology **110**(9), 1677–1682 (2003)
26. Witmer, M.T., Parlitsis, G., Patel, S., Kiss, S.: Comparison of ultra-widefield fluorescein angiography with the Heidelberg spectralis® noncontact ultra-widefield module versus the optos® optomap®. Clin. Ophthalmol. **7**, 389–394 (2013)
27. Wu, R., Zhang, C., Zhang, J., Zhou, Y., Zhou, T., Fu, H.: Mm-retinal: Knowledge-enhanced foundational pretraining with fundus image-text expertise. In: Linguraru, M.G., et al. (eds.) International Conference on Medical Image Computing and Computer-Assisted Intervention, pp. 722–732. Springer, Cham (2024). https://doi.org/10.1007/978-3-031-72378-0_67

28. Xu, Y., Zhou, Z., Li, X., Zhang, N., Zhang, M., Wei, P.: FFU-Net: feature fusion u-net for lesion segmentation of diabetic retinopathy. Biomed. Res. Int. **2021**(1), 6644071 (2021)
29. Zhou, Y., Chia, M.A., Wagner, S.K., Ayhan, M.S., Williamson, D.J., Struyven, R.R., Liu, T., Xu, M., Lozano, M.G., Woodward-Court, P., et al.: A foundation model for generalizable disease detection from retinal images. Nature **622**(7981), 156–163 (2023)

PASO: A Multipurpose Porcine Anterior Segment Dataset Featuring Spectral and Reconstructed OCT Volume Scans and Surgical Instrument Segmentation Masks

Jonas Nienhaus[1]([envelope]), Rebekka Peter[2,3], Florian Kapeller[1],
Katharina Dettelbacher[1], Ryan Sentosa[1], Eleonora Tagliabue[2],
Hessam Roodaki[4], Wolfgang Drexler[1], Thomas Schlegl[1],
Franziska Mathis-Ullrich[3], Tilman Schmoll[4], and Rainer Leitgeb[1]

[1] Center for Medical Physics and Biomedical Engineering, Medical University of
Vienna, 1090 Vienna, Austria
`jonas.nienhaus@meduniwien.ac.at`
[2] Carl Zeiss AG, Innovation Hub KIT, 76344 Eggenstein-Leopoldshafen, Germany
`rebekka.peter@zeiss.com`
[3] Surgical Planning and Robotic Cognition Lab, Friedrich-Alexander University
Erlangen-Nürnberg, 91054 Erlangen, Germany
[4] Carl Zeiss Meditec AG, 73447 Oberkochen, Germany

Abstract. Intra-surgical optical coherence tomography (OCT) complements surgical microscopes by adding a third spatial dimension to the imaging context during ophthalmic interventions. Recent advancements in OCT technology and artificial intelligence are driving innovations in computer-guided and robotic ophthalmic surgery. However, developing and evaluating models for OCT reconstruction, visualization, and automated scene understanding demands suitable datasets and annotations. For this purpose, we present the porcine anterior segment OCT (PASO) dataset. It contains 141 volume scans acquired from 47 enucleated porcine eyes using a cutting-edge microscope-integrated swept-source OCT prototype with a field of view of 11.8 mm by 11.8 mm and an imaging depth of around 5 mm. The anterior segments, including cornea, iris, and anterior lens surface, were imaged before, during, and after tissue manipulation with 12 microsurgical instruments, resulting in a multi-faceted dataset. The dataset contains raw spectra as well as reconstructed scans averaged from 12 repetitions. Additionally, for 1020 cross-sectional scans extracted from 19 porcine eye volumes, surgical instrument segmentation (SIS) masks are provided, generated using the segmentation foundation model SAM and manually refined. Baseline algorithms are presented for reconstruction and adjustable averaging of scans, and for surgical instrument segmentation. As the first publication of raw and reconstructed OCT scans of ex-vivo porcine eyes during

---

J. Nienhaus and R. Peter—Contributed equally.

instrument-tissue manipulation, our dataset serves as a valuable catalyst for progress in the field of computer- and robot-assisted ophthalmic surgery research.

Keywords: Machine Learning Dataset · Optical Coherence Tomography · Surgical Instrument Segmentation · Image Restoration · Ophthalmic Surgery · Computer-Assisted Surgery

1   Motivation

The demographic shift towards an aging population is leading to an increased demand for ophthalmic interventions, while the number of available surgeons is not keeping pace [19]. This disparity highlights the urgent need for computer-assisted and robot-assisted ophthalmic surgery systems to enhance surgical safety and efficiency, particularly for novice surgeons. Automated scene understanding, such as the localization of surgical instruments, is crucial for the development of computer-assisted and robot-assisted surgery systems. Technologies like virtual instrument-to-tissue sensors rely heavily on accurate scene understanding to function effectively [1,15,20]. Over the past decade, deep learning algorithms have become the state-of-the-art for scene understanding [8–10], yet they face a significant bottleneck: the availability of machine learning datasets and annotations, which are particularly scarce and costly in the surgical domain.

Existing intra-operative datasets for automated scene understanding in anterior segment ophthalmic surgery, such as CaDIS [8] for semantic segmentation of anatomical structures and surgical instruments, Cataract-1K [9] for semantic segmentation, irregularity detection, and phase recognition, and OphNet [10] for workflow understanding, have paved the way for advancements in this field. However, these datasets are from the surgical microscope imaging domain, which offers limited depth perception—a critical drawback for both surgeons and automation techniques. Optical coherence tomography (OCT) emerges as a complementary imaging modality in ophthalmic surgery [6] that provides enhanced depth sensing capabilities and 3D visualization. Despite its potential, there is currently no comprehensive dataset of surgical scans publicly available.

Techniques for image reconstruction from raw spectra and image restoration are vital for optimizing the visualization of OCT-scanned structures, reducing noise levels, and enhancing image clarity. Similar to scene understanding, the trend in image reconstruction and restoration is moving towards data-driven approaches working with reconstructed [3,5] or raw data [12,21,23], necessitating robust and diverse datasets.

In this work, we introduce the PASO dataset which encompasses porcine anterior segment scans, with porcine eyes serving as a valuable model for research in computer-assisted and robot-assisted ophthalmic surgery due to their anatomical similarity to human eyes and availability [18]. Our dataset includes raw interferometry and reconstructed data (Fig. 1), along with surgical instrument segmentation (SIS) masks, thereby advancing research in both OCT restoration and scene understanding. Our contributions include:

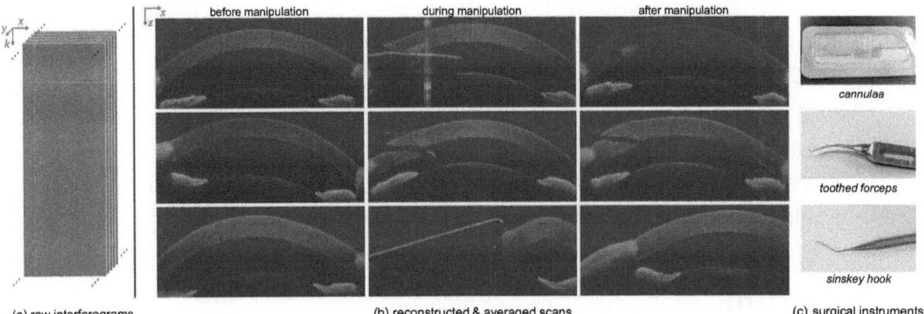

Fig. 1. The PASO dataset contains volumetric OCT scans of ex-vivo porcine eyes as raw spectra and as reconstructed, averaged scans, acquired before, during and after manipulation with different surgical instruments (highlighted in B-scans).

- A diverse OCT dataset of porcine anterior eye segment volume scans before, during, and after tissue manipulation, acquired using a cutting-edge OCT device.
- Complementary data representations in form of interferograms and averaged reconstructed scans together with reconstruction code, opening a large variety of use cases in OCT data reconstruction, processing, and analysis.
- Pixel-wise surgical instrument masks and baseline results for SIS achieved with state-of-the-art (SOTA) SIS models.
- Comprehensive metadata annotations, detailed dataset characteristics, and utility Python code make the dataset suitable for the development and evaluation of (data-based) algorithms for OCT reconstruction and scene understanding.

The PASO dataset is available at [14].

2 Porcine Anterior Segment Optical Coherence Tomography dataset (PASO)

The PASO dataset is made available as interferograms and as averaged reconstructed scans (cf. Figure 1). Acquired in a setting depicted in Fig. 2, it encompasses 141 optical coherence tomography (OCT) volumes of 47 enucleated porcine eyes, partially including surgical instruments in the scene.

2.1 Imaging System and Parameters

The prototype that was used for imaging is a swept-source optical coherence tomography (SS-OCT) system integrated into an ophthalmic surgical microscope (Artevo 800, ZEISS, Jena, Germany) [2]. Its laser, a MEMS-VCSEL (Thorlabs Inc., Newton, NJ, USA), was operated at central wavelength of 1060 nm and a sweep repetition rate of 600 kHz. Laser power on the sample was measured

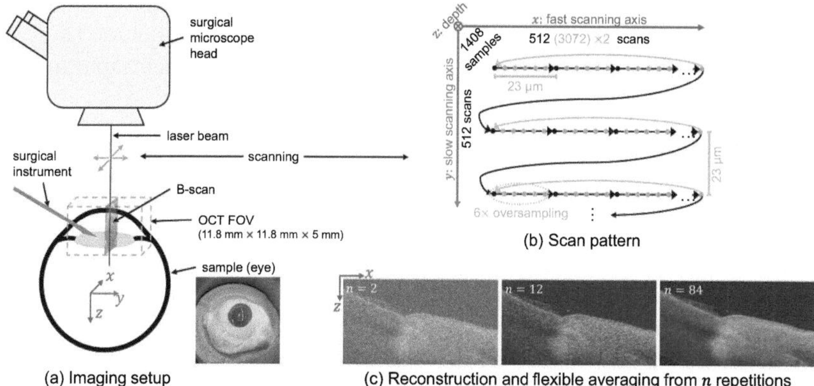

Fig. 2. (a) Overview of the experimental setup and (b) the raster scanning pattern. (c) Using repetitions and oversampling along x, B-scans with flexible averaging can be reconstructed. Not to scale.

as 5.7 mW on the first day of imaging. Scanning was performed along a raster trajectory (see Fig. 2 (b)), in which the fast-scanning axis was oversampled by a factor of 6 with respect to the full spot size. Furthermore, every B-scan was repeated, before moving to the consequent B-scan position. The two repetitions in conjunction with the oversampling along the fast-scanning axis effectively yield 12 repetitions around every sampling location. The resulting laterally isotropic volume then consists of 512 by 512 A-scans, which cover a lateral field of view of 11.8 mm by 11.8 mm and were acquired within approximately 5 s. Raw interferograms, each consisting of 1408 samples and covering a depth of approximately 5 mm in tissue, were stored as two-bit unsigned integers, resulting in a total raw volume size of approximately 8.9 GB, or 1.2 TB in total. Since direct k-clocking [22] was applied, sampling can be assumed to be linear in wavenumber.

2.2 Acquisition Procedure

For the dataset, 47 enucleated porcine eyes from a local butcher shop were imaged. The samples were stored in phosphate buffered saline solution with 20 mL Tween 20 detergent and refrigerated, following [4]. Imaging was performed over the course of two days. With few exceptions which are clearly indicated in the individual volume annotations, each eye was imaged three times: Once before any manipulation, once during a mock manipulation, and once afterwards on the often cut or even destroyed eyes. For this purpose, the samples were put on a holder, which was then placed under the microscope head with the OCT field of view (FOV) centered either on the corneal apex or chamber angle (see Fig. 2 (a)). Zero delay and focus were generally optimized depending on the current FOV, in most cases to cover the anterior segment from the anterior corneal surface to the lens. The mock procedures were performed using a variety of micro-surgical instruments such as forceps, hooks, incision knives and a phacoemulsification tip. Samples were in some cases repositioned between subsequent acquisitions. For each raw volume, basic annotations were created, which include the type of surgical instruments – if any – and whether the sample has been manipulated.

2.3   Reconstruction and Post Processing

Raw OCT scans are reconstructed as usual in SS-OCT. Steps include numerical dispersion compensation [7], Hann windowing, the fast Fourier transform, magnitude calculation, and logarithmic scaling. Facilitating close A-scans from repetitions and lateral oversampling, it is possible to generate averaged, noise-reduced scans. The number of scans used for averaging can be varied (c.f. Fig. 2 (c)). Images averaged from 12 scans – resulting from the two repetitions and 6 times oversampling – are induced directly.

Python implementations for data loading, reconstruction, and adjustable averaging from raw interferograms are provided alongside the dataset.

2.4   Characteristics and Limitations

While we believe the dataset has potential to serve as a valuable basis for a wide array of applications, there are inherent trade-offs, some of which can be addressed using the provided code and data representations. Firstly, the scans averaged from 12 repetitions still exhibit some speckle noise. Due to the availability of all raw interferograms in conjunction with reconstruction code, this may be remedied by including more distant A-scans into averaging, trading off lateral resolution for noise reduction as shown in Fig. 2 (c). Secondly, volume acquisition started and ended at a random B-scan position due to the lack of a volume trigger to the prototype. In case of accumulative sample movement during the duration of one volume acquisition, this led to moderate discontinuities between adjacent B-scans or repetitions in a few cases. Thirdly, while the PASO dataset provides a large and diverse set of volumes, this – in some cases – comes at the cost of unrealistic instrument-tissue interactions, which enhances variability but does not fully imitate procedures such as cataract or cornea surgery. Lastly, while relatively similar in most anatomical dimensions and widely used as a model, enucleated porcine eyes differ slightly from in vivo human eyes [18]. This is further alleviated by the relatively young age of slaughtered pigs, typically resulting in comparably soft and clear lenses.

3   PASO-SIS for Surgical Instrument Segmentation

As a subset of the PASO dataset, PASO-SIS comprises 1020 cross-sectional B-scans featuring surgical instruments during instrument-tissue manipulation, collected from 19 individual ex-vivo porcine eyes from PASO. It includes 6 different surgical instruments (SIs) (chopper, OVD cannula, sinskey, slit knife, stab knife, trocar) commonly used in cataract surgery, with pixel-wise annotation masks provided for precise SI localization. Additionally, the dataset offers 1000 cross-sectional B-scans captured without surgical instruments, taken before and after manipulation. The cross-sectional B-scans are extracted along both spatial dimensions of the OCT volumes. This results in B-scans displaying cross-sections of both the short and long SI axis. In the following, we present the B-scans in their original resolution, which is significantly higher in the axial direction than in the spatial direction. Therefore, the representation is distorted compared to the actual eye and SI geometry.

3.1 Surgical Instrument Segmentation Masks

The dataset includes binary masks for pixel-wise SIS, where black pixels (value = 0) represent the background and white pixels (value = 1) denote SIs. Figure 3 (a) presents pairs of B-scans and annotation masks, including close-ups for enhanced visibility.

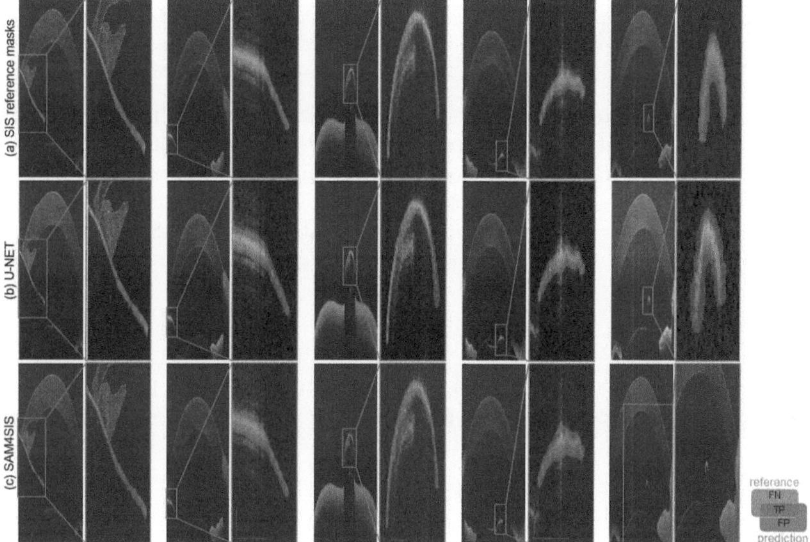

Fig. 3. (a) SIS reference masks visualized as transparent green overlays on B-scans and close-ups. Example 1 and 2 show the long SI axis, example 3–5 the short SI axis. (b) and (c) present the predicted SI masks from U-NET [17] and SAM4SIS [16] as transparent blue overlay. In the close-ups in (b) and (c), reference (green) and prediction (blue) are highlighted, with purple indicating their intersection. Thus, false-negatives (FN) are green, false-positives (FP) blue, and true-positives (TP) purple. Column 5 presents a failure case for the SAM4SIS prediction. (Color figure online)

To localize SIs in the PASO volumes, en-face projections were generated for 19 volumes acquired during tissue manipulation. These projections were created by computing the maximum intensity along the depth axis, followed by thresholding at the 90th percentile to emphasize prominent features. This method facilitates easy manual localization of surgical instruments using axis-aligned bounding boxes. Every fourth cross-sectional B-scan intersecting with this bounding box is extracted along both spatial dimensions (Fig. 4).

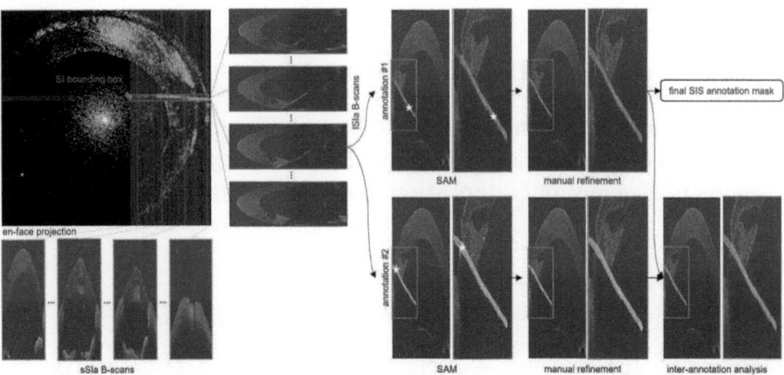

Fig. 4. PASO-SIS annotation pipeline. SIs are localized in en-face projections of OCT volumes, and marked with manual SI bounding boxes (pink). B-scans intersecting with bounding boxes are extracted along both the sSIa and lSIa. SAM segmentation masks are generated based on a manually selected input point prompt (white star). The generated SAM mask is manually refined to generate the final SIS annotation mask. (Color figure online)

Binary SIS masks are generated utilizing the segmentation foundation model *Segment Anything Model (SAM)* [11] through manual point prompting and, if necessary, manual correction of proposed masks.

3.2   Characteristics and Limitations

On average, the instruments occupy 0.18% (SD = 0.0016) of each B-scan, equating to approximately 1,309.5 pixels out of a total B-scan size of 720,896 pixels.

All B-scans were annotated by the same person over a period of several weeks. The average time for annotation per B-scan was approximately 37 s. The inter-annotation variance was determined by the average Hausdorff distance, intersection over union (IoU), and Dice coefficient between two annotations made by the same person on different days for 50 randomly selected B-scans, and is 8.44 pixels, (SD = 6.16), 0.69 (SD = 0.099), and 0.81, (SD = 0.07), respectively.

Due to speckle noise and reflection artifacts, a clear ground truth is generally indefinable, cf. Figure 3 example 2 and 4. The delineation of instrument boundaries was at the discretion of the annotator, taking into account prior knowledge of the instruments' geometry and material, the anatomy of porcine eyes, the imaging principles and artifact formation, as well as spatial consistency between adjacent B-scans. The highly reflective material properties of metallic surgical instruments often result in reflection artifacts appearing as white lines overlaying the instrument contours. The area behind the metallic instruments is shadowed, obscuring the complete cross-sectional geometry and making only the front side visible. Generally, the visual features of surgical instruments in OCT scans lack sufficient detail for reliable instrument type classification.

4 Surgical Instrument Segmentation Baseline

We present results from state-of-the-art SIS models, trained and evaluated on the PASO-SIS dataset. Following the dataset's documentation, we use a split of approximately 76% for training, 12% for validation, and 12% for testing, ensuring that B-scans from the same porcine eye are exclusively assigned to one split. We evaluate two models for SIS.

U-NET [17]: Known for its effectiveness in medical imaging segmentation tasks and a reliable benchmark in various imaging domains.

SAM4SIS [16]: A weakly supervised model for surgical instrument segmentation requiring only image-level annotations (SI present / not present), utilizing the segmentation power of the *Segment Anything Model 2 (SAM2)*.

For both models, we apply the default parameters as specified in their respective references [16,17]. All input B-scans are down-scaled by 50% in the first encoder layer. The B-scans without SIs present are only used for SAM4SIS.

4.1 Metrics

We use established metrics for pixel-wise binary semantic segmentation including mean Intersection over Union (mIoU) and mean Dice score (mDICE). Recognizing the limitations of overlap-based metrics in assessing small structures like the surgical instruments, as discussed by Maier-Hein et al. [13], we complement these with the uncertainty-aware boundary-based normalized surface distance (NSD).

4.2 Results and Discussion

Table 1. Comparison of the supervised learning model UNET and the weakly-supervised model SAM4SIS, with annotation variance as an upper bound reference.

Method	mDICE	mIoU	mNSD	$mNSD_{0.5}$	$mNSD_{0.75}$
Annotation Variance	0.8473	0.7454	0.9858	1.0	1.0
U-NET [17]	0.7125	0.5772	0.9154	0.9528	0.9370
SAM4SIS [16]	0.5986	0.4937	0.7239	0.7717	0.7480

Table 1 presents a comparative analysis of the performance of U-NET and SAM4SIS on the PASO-SIS test dataset. U-NET, which employs semantic segmentation masks during supervised training, achieves a mDICE of 71.25% and a mIoU of 57.72%. These values are notably lower than the annotation variance, which stands at 84.73% for mDICE and 74.54% for mIoU. In contrast, SAM4SIS, utilizing data-efficient training with only class labels, records a mDICE of 60.62% and a mIoU of 49.67%. The metric most pertinent to small objects, the NSD, reveals that 93.7% of U-NET predictions achieve an NSD value of 0.75 or higher, whereas SAM4SIS attains 74.8% in this metric.

The relatively higher mDICE values compared to mIoU values suggest a substantial occurrence of false positive and false negative predictions. Qualitative analyses indicate that this disparity frequently arises from the predicted areas of surgical instruments being larger than the corresponding annotation masks. This phenomenon can be attributed to the variance in annotations and the ambiguous boundaries of instruments when visualized using OCT. Refer to Fig. 3 (b) and (c) for illustrative examples.

For SAM4SIS, successful cases demonstrate predicted masks that achieve a level of accuracy comparable to those generated by U-NET. However, it is noteworthy that 22.83% of SAM4SIS predictions fall below an NSD of 0.5, categorizing them as failure cases. These instances exhibit minimal to no overlap between the predicted masks and the reference masks, cf. Figure 3 (c), example 5.

5   Summary and Conclusion

PASO constitutes the first large-scale anterior segment dataset featuring both raw interferograms and reconstructed volumetric OCT images, opening avenues to a plethora of potential use cases related to OCT reconstruction and enhancement. The PASO-SIS dataset facilitates the development and evaluation of robust SIS models for automated scene understanding in ophthalmic surgery with the statistics provided in this work enabling insightful interpretation of the results. The performance of state-of-the-art SIS models leads to two key conclusions: First, the volume of available data supports the creation of effective SIS models. Secondly, there is still potential for further advancing research on SIS in OCT, which is now enabled by our pioneering dataset.

References

1. Briel, M., et al.: Intraoperative adaptive eye model based on instrument-integrated OCT for robot-assisted vitreoretinal surgery. Int. J. Comput. Assist. Radiol. Surg. **20**(5), 881–889 (2025). https://doi.org/10.1007/s11548-025-03325-0
2. Britten, A., et al.: Surgical microscope integrated MHz SS-OCT with live volumetric visualization. Biomed. Opt. Express **14**(2), 846–865 (2023). https://doi.org/10.1364/BOE.477386
3. Cuartas-Vélez, C., Restrepo, R., Bouma, B.E., Uribe-Patarroyo, N.: Volumetric non-local-means based speckle reduction for optical coherence tomography. Biomed. Opt. Express **9**(7), 3354–3372 (2018)
4. Dettelbacher, K., et al.: FrankenEYE: preparation, handling and multi-day storage of porcine eyes for WetLabs. Invest. Ophthalmol. Vis. Sci. **65**(7), 2031 (2024)

5. Devalla, S.K., Subramanian, G., Pham, T.H., Wang, X., Perera, S., Tun, T.A., Aung, T., Schmetterer, L., Thiéry, A.H., Girard, M.J.: A deep learning approach to denoise optical coherence tomography images of the optic nerve head. Sci. Rep. **9**(1), 14454 (2019)

6. Ehlers, J.P., et al.: The DISCOVER Study 3-Year results: feasibility and usefulness of microscope-integrated intraoperative OCT during ophthalmic surgery. Ophthalmology **125**(7), 1014–1027 (2018). https://doi.org/10.1016/j.ophtha.2017.12.037

7. Fercher, A.F., Hitzenberger, C.K., Sticker, M., Zawadzki, R., Karamata, B., Lasser, T.: Numerical dispersion compensation for partial coherence interferometry and optical coherence tomography. Opt. Express **9**(12), 610–615 (2001). https://doi.org/10.1364/OE.9.000610

8. Flouty, E., et al.: Cadis: cataract dataset for image segmentation. CoRR abs/1906.11586 (2019). http://arxiv.org/abs/1906.11586

9. Ghamsarian, N., et al.: Cataract-1K dataset for deep-learning-assisted analysis of cataract surgery videos. Sci. Data **11**(1), 373 (2024). https://doi.org/10.1038/s41597-024-03193-4

10. Hu, M., et al.: OphNet: a large-scale video benchmark for ophthalmic surgical workflow understanding. In: Leonardis, A., Ricci, E., Roth, S., Russakovsky, O., Sattler, T., Varol, G. (eds.) Computer Vision – ECCV 2024, pp. 481–500. Springer Nature Switzerland, Cham (2025)

11. Kirillov, A., et al.: Segment anything. arXiv:2304.02643 (2023)

12. Lee, W., Nam, H.S., Seok, J.Y., Oh, W.Y., Kim, J.W., Yoo, H.: Deep learning-based image enhancement in optical coherence tomography by exploiting interference fringe. Commun. Biol. **6**(1), 464 (2023)

13. Maier-Hein, L., et al.: Metrics reloaded: recommendations for image analysis validation. Nat. Methods **21**(2), 195–212 (2024). https://doi.org/10.1038/s41592-023-02151-z

14. Nienhaus, J., et al.: PASO: Porcine Anterior Segment OCT dataset (2025). https://doi.org/10.7910/DVN/HUCGAE

15. Peter, R., Moreira, S., Tagliabue, E., Hillenbrand, M., Nunes, R.G., Mathis-Ullrich, F.: Stereo reconstruction from microscopic images for computer-assisted ophthalmic surgery. Int. J. Comput. Assist. Radiol. Surg. (2024). https://doi.org/10.1007/s11548-024-03177-0

16. Peter, R., et al.: Domain-agnostic weakly supervised surgical instrument segmentation. Manuscript submitted for publication (2025)

17. Ronneberger, O., Fischer, P., Brox, T.: U-Net: convolutional networks for biomedical image segmentation. In: Navab, N., Hornegger, J., Wells, W.M., Frangi, A.F. (eds.) MICCAI 2015. LNCS, vol. 9351, pp. 234–241. Springer, Cham (2015). https://doi.org/10.1007/978-3-319-24574-4_28

18. Sanchez, I., Martin, R., Ussa, F., Fernandez-Bueno, I.: The parameters of the porcine eyeball. Graefes Arch. Clin. Exp. Ophthalmol. **249**(4), 475–482 (2011). https://doi.org/10.1007/s00417-011-1617-9

19. Shu, Y., et al.: Changing trends in the disease burden of cataract and forecasted trends in china and globally from 1990 to 2030. Clin. Epidemiol. **15**, 525–534 (2023). https://doi.org/10.2147/CLEP.S404049, place: New Zealand

20. Sommersperger, M., Weiss, J., Ali Nasseri, M., Gehlbach, P., Iordachita, I., Navab, N.: Real-time tool to layer distance estimation for robotic subretinal injection using intraoperative 4D OCT. Biomed Opt. Express **12**, 1085–1104 (2021)

21. Wang, M., et al.: GPU-accelerated iterative method for FD-OCT image reconstruction with an image-level cross-domain regularizer. Opt. Express **31**(2), 1813–1831 (2023)

22. Xi, J., Huo, L., Li, J., Li, X.: Generic real-time uniform k-space sampling method for high-speed swept-source optical coherence tomography. Opt. Express **18**(9), 9511–9517 (2010)
23. Zhang, Y., et al.: Neural network-based image reconstruction in swept-source optical coherence tomography using undersampled spectral data. Light: Sci. Appl. **10**(1), 155 (2021)

abVAE: Attribute-Based Booster Variational Autoencoder for Interpretable Latent Presentation in Optical Coherence Tomography of Glaucomatous Eyes

Pei-Hsin Chiu[1], Brett A. Johnson[2], Edward F. Linton[2,3], Andrew E. Pouw[2], Michael Wall[2], Young H. Kwon[2,3], Randy H. Kardon[2,3], Jui-Kai Wang[4], and Mona K. Garvin[1,2,3(✉)]

[1] Department of Electrical and Computer Engineering, The University of Iowa, Iowa City, IA, USA
pei-hsin-chiu@uiowa.edu
[2] Department of Ophthalmology and Visual Sciences, The University of Iowa, Iowa City, IA, USA
[3] Center for the Prevention and Treatment of Visual Loss, Iowa City VA Health Care System, Iowa City, IA, USA
mona-garvin@uiowa.edu
[4] Department of Ophthalmology, University of Texas Southwestern Medical Center, Dallas, TX, USA
Jui-Kai.Wang@UTSouthwestern.edu

Abstract. Glaucoma is a chronic optic neuropathy characterized by progressive retinal ganglion cell loss. To better visualize glaucomatous spatial patterns of nerve loss, we propose the attribute-based booster variational autoencoder (abVAE), which enables controllable latent representations without compromising reconstruction performance. Building upon the booster VAE (bVAE) framework and inspired by the attribute alignment loss introduced in Attri-VAE [1], the abVAE preserves reconstruction fidelity while enabling attribute-specific controllability over the inferior temporal (IT) and superior temporal (ST) sectors within the elliptical annulus of the retinal ganglion cell plus inner plexiform layer (GCIPL) thickness map from optical coherence tomography scans. By design, the latent space montage maps reveal that thicker regions are concentrated in the upper right corner, while thinner regions appear in the lower left. Quantitatively, the linear relationships between the latent variables and anatomical attributes (d_1–T_{IT}^* and d_2–T_{ST}^*) are reflected in the mean values of R^2: 0.95 ± 0.01 and 0.86 ± 0.04 for the abVAE model, 0.76 ± 0.06 and 0.45 ± 0.22 for the bVAE model, and 0.64 ± 0.21 and 0.23 ± 0.32 for the β-VAE model. The model also achieves high reconstruction quality, with a Dice score of 0.99 and a structural similarity index (SSIM) of 0.73. These results demonstrate that abVAE effectively balances anatomical interpretability and reconstruction accuracy, making it suitable for modeling spatial patterns of retinal thinning in glaucoma.

J.-K. Wang and M. K. Garvin—Joint senior authors.

© The Author(s), under exclusive license to Springer Nature Switzerland AG 2026
H. Fang et al. (Eds.): OMIA 2025, LNCS 16209, pp. 137–146, 2026.
https://doi.org/10.1007/978-3-032-10351-2_14

Keywords: Glaucoma · Optical coherence tomography · Ganglion cell-inner plexiform layer · Variational autoencoder

1   Introduction

Glaucoma, a leading cause of irreversible blindness worldwide, affects 80 million individuals and is projected to impact 111.8 million by 2040 [3,10]. Given its silent and irreversible progression, glaucoma requires early diagnosis and lifelong monitoring. Optical coherence tomography (OCT) is one of the most objective tools for early glaucoma detection, enabling precise measurements of retinal structures such as ganglion cell axons in the retinal nerve fiber layer (RNFL) and retinal ganglion cells and their dendrites in the ganglion cell plus inner plexiform layer (GCIPL) at the macula [2,4,8,14].

Variational autoencoders (VAEs) [7] are unsupervised generative models that encode images into compact latent variables (LVs), defining a latent space that captures statistically meaningful variations of spatial patterns in the data and enables image generation/synthesis. β-VAE [5] introduces a weighting factor β to encourage feature disentanglement in the latent space and has been used to extract retinal spatial patterns from OCT images and provide an intuitive visualization for distinguishing glaucoma from normal cases [12]. However, due to the stochastic nature of sampling in VAEs, decoders often fail to reconstruct input images with high fidelity. Additionally, β does not directly influence the data distribution of the distinct spatial patterns caused by optic nerve disease in the latent space. To address both limitations, the booster variational autoencoder (bVAE) [11] adds an auxiliary loss encouraging latent distributions aligned with target retinal features, while booster variables enhance reconstruction quality.

In this study, we present the attribute-based booster VAE (abVAE), which uses regional GCIPL thicknesses as explicit attributes to enforce anatomically meaningful spatial patterns and promote continuity in the latent space, enabling progressive glaucomatous pattern generation. While the bVAE reduces variability from random initialization, it does not explicitly organize disease-related spatial features of retinal nerve loss. abVAE incorporates an attribute-specific regularization term, inspired by the Attri-VAE [1], to align latent variables with GCIPL thickness in the inferior and superior temporal sectors, which are the regions most vulnerable to glaucomatous damage [6]. It consistently represents seed-independent and anatomically interpretable glaucomatous patterns.

2   Methods

2.1   Overview

The overall flow is shown in Fig. 1. Input data processing is described in Sect. 2.2. Model architectures and loss functions for β-VAE and bVAE (Fig. 1a) are presented in Sects. 2.3 and 2.4. The attribute constraint in abVAE (Fig. 1b) is discussed in Sect. 2.5. Data descriptions are provided in Sect. 3.1. Evaluation metrics and experimental settings (Fig. 1c) are covered in Sects. 3.2 and 3.3.

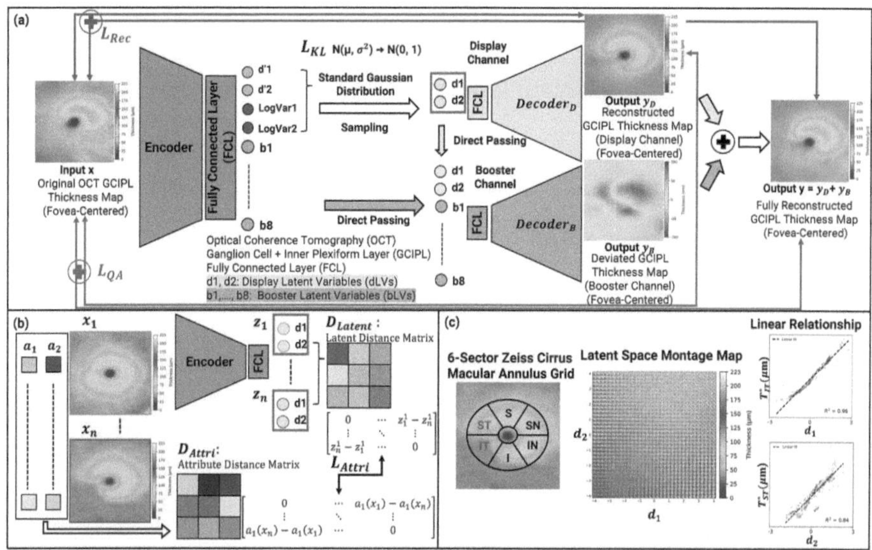

Fig. 1. Overview of this study. (a) Architecture shared by the bVAE and abVAE models. (b) Attribute constraint introduced in the abVAE model. Pairwise differences are computed along the attribute-aligned latent dimensions ($z_1 \leftrightarrow T_{IT}$, $z_2 \leftrightarrow T_{ST}$) to form D_{Latent}, which is compared with the corresponding attribute difference matrix D_{Attri} to compute L_{Attri} [1]. (c) Visualization of the latent space montage map and quantitative evaluation via linear regression fit with R^2.

2.2 Ganglion Cell – Inner Plexiform Layer (GCIPL) Thickness Map

To analyze structural patterns associated with glaucoma damage, we computed GCIPL thickness maps from Cirrus OCT volumes. Each volume was segmented by an existing hybrid deep-learning method [2]. Each GCIPL thickness map was then created and centered at the fovea. The map was cropped but still contained the standard Zeiss Cirrus macular annulus region [2]. This annulus grid was divided into six sectors (Fig. 1c): superior nasal (SN), superior (S), superior temporal (ST), inferior temporal (IT), inferior (I), and inferior nasal (IN). Given that glaucomatous damage more commonly affects the IT and ST optic nerve axon bundles [6,12,13], the thicknesses of these two sectors (T_{IT}, T_{ST}) were assigned as the aligned attributes corresponding to LVs d_1 and d_2.

2.3 β-VAE

The β-VAE shares the standard VAE architecture, consisting of an encoder (E) and a display decoder (D_D), shown in Fig. 1(a). The encoder estimates the mean ($\mathbf{d}_1'$, $\mathbf{d}_2'$) and log-variance (LogVar1, LogVar2) of two latent Gaussian distributions, from which the display latent variables (dLVs), d_1 and d_2, are sampled via the reparameterization trick. These dLVs are passed to D_D to reconstruct input images and generate latent space montage map visualizations. Reconstruction loss L_{Rec}, weighted with β_{Rec}, is computed as the mean squared error (MSE) between the input x and the output y. A Kullback-Leibler (KL) divergence term, scaled by β_{KL}, penalizes deviations from the standard normal prior and promotes disentangled latent representations. Equation 1 shows the full loss function.

$$Loss = \underbrace{\beta_{\text{Rec}} \cdot \text{MSE}(x, y)}_{L_{\text{Rec}}} + \underbrace{\beta_{\text{KL}} \cdot \text{KL}(E(\mathbf{d}|x), \mathcal{N}(0, 1))}_{L_{\text{KL}}} \tag{1}$$

2.4 Booster Variational Autoencoder (bVAE)

The bVAE extends the β-VAE by introducing additional booster latent variables (bLVs) and a second decoder (D_{B}) to improve reconstruction, as shown in Fig. 1(a). While the display latent variables (dLVs), d_1 and d_2, continue to support montage map visualization through D_{D}, the bLVs (b_1 to b_8), which are not sampled from a prior, are concatenated with the dLVs and input to D_{B} for enhanced reconstruction. The outputs of D_{D} and D_{B}, denoted as y_{D} and y_{B}, are summed to produce the final reconstructed image y. This one-encoder-two-decoder design enables both interpretable visualization and improved synthesis of GCIPL thickness map patterns.

The bVAE loss function incorporates four terms: reconstruction loss (L_{Rec}), reconstruction quality loss (L_{QA}), KL divergence loss (L_{KL}), and display alignment loss (L_{D}):

$$Loss = \underbrace{\beta_{\text{Rec}} \cdot [\text{MSE}(x, y) + \text{MSE}(x, y_{\text{D}})]}_{L_{\text{Rec}}} + \underbrace{\beta_{\text{QA}} \cdot [\text{SSIM}(x, y) + \text{SSIM}(x, y_{\text{D}})]}_{L_{\text{QA}}}$$
$$+ \underbrace{\beta_{\text{KL}} \cdot \text{KL}(E(\mathbf{d}|x), \mathcal{N}(0, 1))}_{L_{\text{KL}}} + \underbrace{\beta_{\text{D}} \cdot [(d_1 - c \cdot T_{\text{IT}}) + (d_2 - c \cdot T_{\text{ST}})]}_{L_{\text{D}}} \tag{2}$$

Here, β_{Rec}, β_{QA}, β_{KL}, and β_{D} denote the weighting coefficients for each corresponding loss term. The scalar c controls the alignment strength in the latent space montage, while T_{IT} and T_{ST} represent the GCIPL thicknesses in the inferior temporal and superior temporal sectors, respectively. MSE is computed between the input x and both the final output y and intermediate output y_{D} in L_{Rec}. Similarly, structural similarity index (SSIM) is employed in L_{QA} to evaluate perceptual similarity.

2.5 Attribute-Based Booster Variational Autoencoder (abVAE)

The abVAE shares the same one-encoder-two-decoder architecture and global loss design as the bVAE. However, the display alignment loss term is replaced with an attribute alignment term, L_{Attri}:

$$Loss = \underbrace{\beta_{\mathrm{Rec}} \cdot [\mathrm{MSE}(x, y) + \mathrm{MSE}(x, y_{\mathrm{D}})]}_{L_{\mathrm{Rec}}} + \underbrace{\beta_{\mathrm{QA}} \cdot [\mathrm{SSIM}(x, y) + \mathrm{SSIM}(x, y_{\mathrm{D}})]}_{L_{\mathrm{QA}}}$$

$$+ \underbrace{\beta_{\mathrm{KL}} \cdot \mathrm{KL}(E(\mathbf{d}|x), \mathcal{N}(0, 1))}_{L_{\mathrm{KL}}} + \underbrace{\beta_{\mathrm{Attri}} \cdot \|\tanh(\alpha \cdot D_{\mathrm{Latent}}) - \mathrm{sign}(D_{\mathrm{Attri}})\|_1}_{L_{\mathrm{Attri}}}$$

$$\tag{3}$$

where β_{Attri} is the weighting coefficient for the attribute loss term, α is a gradient scaling factor, D_{Latent} denotes the latent distance matrix, and D_{Attri} denotes the attribute distance matrix, as shown in Fig. 1(b).

Specifically, D_{Latent} is computed as pairwise differences along the attribute-aligned latent dimensions (z_1 and z_2, corresponding to T_{IT} and T_{ST}, respectively), and D_{Attri} is computed as the corresponding pairwise differences of these clinical attributes, following the formulation in Attri-VAE [1]. To emphasize relational structure rather than magnitude, $\mathrm{sign}(D_{\mathrm{Attri}})$ is applied to preserve ranking directions only. Similarly, $\tanh(\alpha \cdot D_{\mathrm{Latent}})$ transforms the latent distances to the same $[-1, 1]$ range for directional alignment and gradient stability. The L1 loss penalizes directional mismatches while avoiding overemphasis on large errors, following the design principles in [9].

3   Experimental Methods

3.1   Data Preparation

A total of 4,941 OCT scans from 256 subjects, collected at the University of Iowa Ophthalmology Clinics, were included in this study. Of these, 1,104 scans from 76 subjects belonged to the normal group, and 3,837 scans from 180 subjects belonged to the glaucoma group. All left eye scans were horizontally flipped to match the right eye orientation. Eyes with coexisting ocular conditions were excluded. The data was split into training, validation, and testing sets in a 3:1:1 ratio based on the subjects. There were 153 subjects in the training set, 51 subjects in the validation set, and 52 subjects in the test set.

3.2   VAE Models

Each GCIPL thickness map was a 2D single-channel image of size 180×180, where each pixel represented the GCIPL thickness in micrometers (μm). The images were preprocessed by normalizing the pixel values to the $[0, 1]$ range and resizing them to 112×112 pixels using bilinear interpolation. To reflect both localized and global GCIPL thickness changes, the attributes aligned with d_1 and d_2 were primarily based on the T_{IT} and T_{ST}, respectively, with an additional 10% contribution from the mean thickness across all six elliptical annulus sectors, denoted as T_{IT}^* and T_{ST}^*. This weighting was empirically chosen to introduce mild sensitivity to overall GCIPL variation without overpowering the dominant sector-specific alignment. The VAE models shared the same hyperparameter settings: 100 training epochs, a batch size of 36 images, a learning rate of 0.001, and the Adam optimizer with a weight decay of 10^{-5}. The loss weights for each model were as follows: For β-VAE, $\beta_{\mathrm{Rec}} = 1.0$ and $\beta_{\mathrm{KL}} = 0.5$; for bVAE, $\beta_{\mathrm{Rec}} = 0.7$, $\beta_{\mathrm{QA}} = 0.3$, $\beta_{\mathrm{KL}} = 0.5$, and $\beta_{\mathrm{D}} = 5$; for abVAE, $\beta_{\mathrm{Rec}} = 0.7$, $\beta_{\mathrm{QA}} = 0.3$, $\beta_{\mathrm{KL}} = 0.5$, and $\beta_{\mathrm{Attri}} = 5$. β_{QA} is considered as a component of β_{Rec} for bVAE and abVAE models. The bVAE scaling constant c was set to 0.02.

3.3 Model Evaluations

Both the reconstruction performance and attribute controllability were evaluated on the testing set. For reconstruction, SSIM and Dice coefficients were calculated for all models. To evaluate attribute controllability, we examined whether the latent space montage maps reflected the intended alignment of d_1 and d_2 with T^*_{IT} and T^*_{ST}. Ideally, a controllable montage map would display thicker regions concentrated in the upper right corner and thinner regions in the bottom left. In addition, latent-attribute correlation plots were generated with linear regression fits, and the corresponding R^2 values were reported.

4 Results

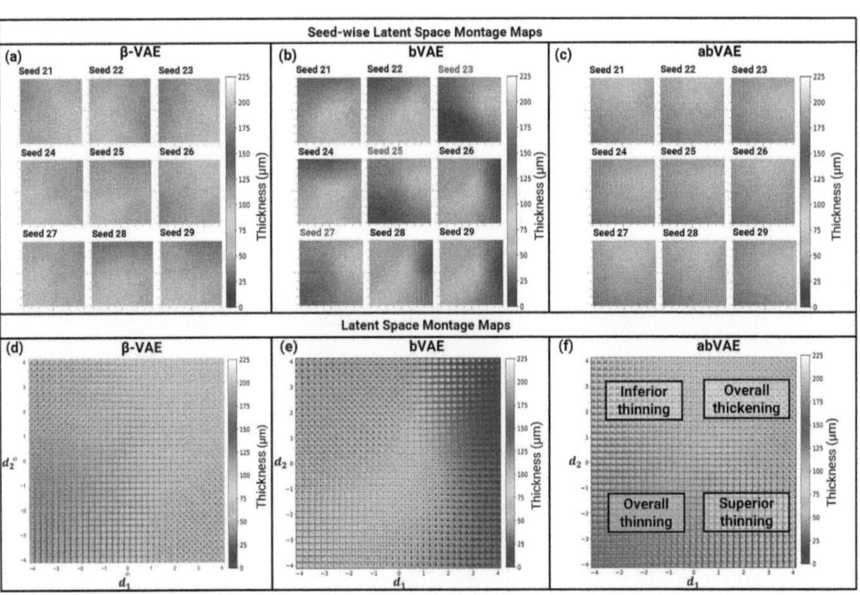

Fig. 2. Latent space montage maps of (a) β-VAE, (b) bVAE, and (c) abVAE across random seeds 21–29. The maps at seed 26 for (d) β-VAE (e) bVAE (f) abVAE models.

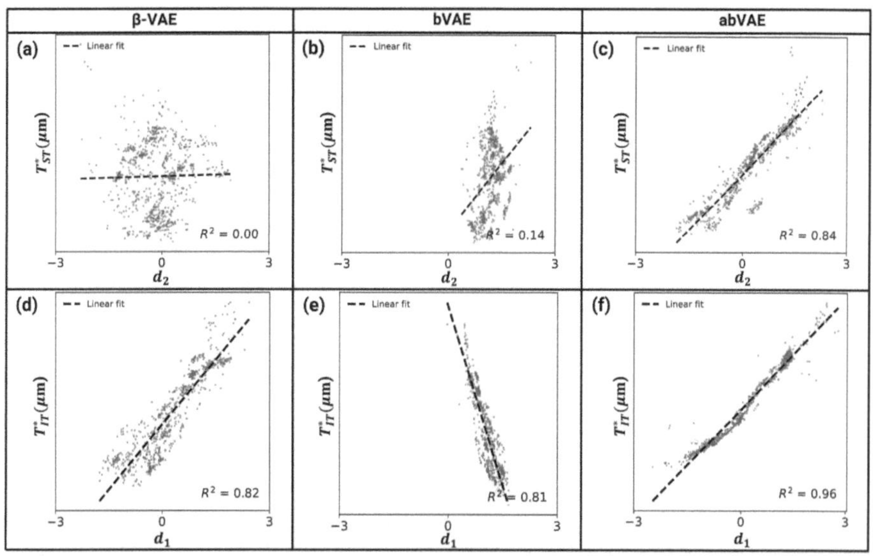

Fig. 3. Example relationships between d_2–T^*_{ST} and d_1–T^*_{IT} for the (a, d) β-VAE, (b, e) bVAE, and (c, f) abVAE models at seed 26. The best controllability (and associated relationship between desired sectoral thicknesses and associated latent values) is shown with the abVAE model.

Figure 2a-c present the latent space montage maps across different random seeds (21–29) for each experimental model. In the β-VAE model, where no attribute constraints were applied, the distribution of thick and thin regions appeared randomly across seeds. Introducing the display alignment loss L_D in the bVAE model led to partial attribute controllability, with some seeds (e.g., 23, 25, 27) exhibiting localized patterns. Replacing L_D with the attribute-specific loss term L_{Attri} in the abVAE model produced consistently structured montage maps across seeds, aligning well with the intended design. These findings suggest that the abVAE achieves more robust and consistent attribute controllability under random initialization. As shown in Fig. 2d–f, the zoomed-in montage maps at seed 26 further highlight differences in spatial alignment. The β-VAE model exhibited a disorganized thickness distribution with no clear directional structure. The bVAE model displayed a structured pattern, but in the opposite direction of the expected alignment. In contrast, the abVAE map closely matched the intended layout, with top right indicating overall thickening, top left showing inferior thinning, bottom right showing superior thinning, and bottom left reflecting overall thinning.

Quantitatively, the mean R^2 values were calculated across seeds 21 to 29 for the VAE models. The β-VAE model exhibits a mean R^2 of 0.64 ± 0.21 between d_1 and T^*_{IT}, and 0.23 ± 0.32 between d_2 and T^*_{ST}. The bVAE model shows moderately stronger associations, with 0.76 ± 0.06 and 0.45 ± 0.22 respectively,

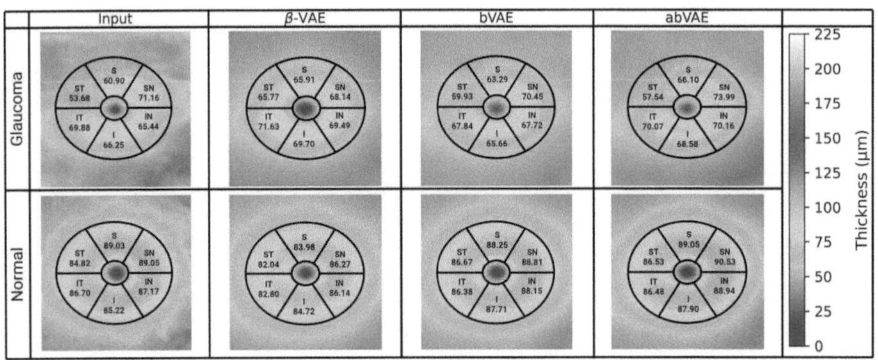

Fig. 4. Reconstruction across VAE models for an example glaucoma and normal case.

reflecting partial controllability. In contrast, the abVAE model demonstrates consistently strong linear relationships, achieving mean R^2 values of 0.95 ± 0.01 between d_1 and T^*_{IT}, and 0.86 ± 0.04 between d_2 and T^*_{ST}. An example linear fit at the seed 26 for each VAE model is shown in Fig. 3.

In contrast to the marked differences in latent space structure, the improvement in reconstruction fidelity is shown in Fig. 4. Although all models achieved similar average Dice scores on the testing set (0.99), differences in average SSIM values were observed: 0.69 for the β-VAE, 0.72 for the bVAE, and 0.73 for the abVAE. These results highlight the importance of incorporating the booster one-encoder-two-decoder structure to enhance reconstruction fidelity.

5 Discussion and Conclusion

This study demonstrated that the abVAE model achieved superior attribute controllability without compromising reconstruction performance, compared to the β-VAE and bVAE models. As shown in Fig. 2, the β-VAE model exhibited randomly distributed thickness-concentrated regions across different seeds, with mostly scattered spatial patterns. Although the bVAE model produced partially concentrated distributions of related spatial patterns, it remained sensitive to seed initialization. In contrast, the abVAE model consistently aligned the target attributes with strong linearity, regardless of seed variation. This resulted in truly controllable latent space montage maps, eliminating the need for specific seed selection. These montage maps offer an intuitive visualization of glaucoma-related changes in the spatial patterns of OCT thickness maps and may further aid in identifying structural progression patterns. An important advantage of this approach is that multiple latent maps, corresponding to different retinal layers (e.g. retinal ganglion cell complex layer vs. retinal nerve fiber layer) or latent maps of spatial patterns of visual field loss can be controlled so that the locations of spatial patterns are similar across the different latent maps.

Nonetheless, this study has limitations. First, the dataset was relatively small and imbalanced, with all data collected from a single clinical center location (Iowa), potentially introducing geographic bias. Second, limited progression was observed across longitudinal scans from the same patients in this dataset, which may have reduced the diversity of montage maps generated with attribute control and limited their usefulness for modeling disease progression over time. Third, the variability of the unexamined gradient scaling factor could potentially influence the robustness of the abVAE model and warrants further investigation. Finally, the current implementation of abVAE treats each attribute independently, which may overlook potential interactions between attributes. Future work will involve validating the proposed model on larger and more diverse eye disease datasets to further evaluate its generalizability and progression modeling capability.

Acknowledgements. This study was supported, in part, by the Department of Veteran Affairs (VA) Rehabilitation Research and Development (RR&D) I50RX003002, RR&D I01RX003797, UTSW RPB Challenge Grant, CTSA 1UL1TR003163-05, and NIH P30EY030413.

References

1. Cetin, I., Stephens, M., Camara, O., González Ballester, M.A.: Attri-VAE: attribute-based interpretable representations of medical images with variational autoencoders. Comput. Med. Imaging Graph. **104**, 102158 (2023). https://doi.org/10.1016/j.compmedimag.2022.102158
2. Chen, Z., et al.: Hybrid deep learning and optimal graph search method for optical coherence tomography layer segmentation in diseases affecting the optic nerve. Biomed. Opt. Express **15**(6), 3681–3698 (2024). https://doi.org/10.1364/BOE.516045
3. Flaxman, S.R., et al.: Global causes of blindness and distance vision impairment 1990–2020: a systematic review and meta-analysis. Lancet Glob. Health **5**(12), e1221–e1234 (2017). https://doi.org/10.1016/S2214-109X(17)30393-5
4. He, Y., Carass, A., Liu, Y., Calabresi, P.A., Saidha, S., Prince, J.L.: Longitudinal deep network for consistent OCT layer segmentation. Biomed. Opt. Express **14**(5), 1874–1893 (2023). https://doi.org/10.1364/BOE.487518
5. Higgins, I., et al.: beta-VAE: learning basic visual concepts with a constrained variational framework. In: International Conference on Learning Representations (2017). https://openreview.net/forum?id=Sy2fzU9gl
6. Hood, D.C., Raza, A.S., de Moraes, C.G.V., Liebmann, J.M., Ritch, R.: Glaucomatous damage of the macula. Prog. Retinal Eye Res. **32**, 1–21 (2013). https://doi.org/10.1016/j.preteyeres.2012.08.003
7. Kingma, D.P., Welling, M.: An introduction to variational autoencoders. Found. Trends Mach. Learn. **12**(4), 307–392 (2019). https://doi.org/10.1561/2200000056
8. Mishra, Z., Ganegoda, A., Selicha, J., Wang, Z., Sadda, S.R., Hu, Z.: Automated retinal layer segmentation using graph-based algorithm incorporating deep-learning-derived information. Sci. Rep. **10**, 9541 (2020). https://doi.org/10.1038/s41598-020-66355-5

9. Pati, A., Lerch, A.: Attribute-based regularization of latent spaces for variational auto-encoders. Neural Comput. Appl. **33**, 4429–4444 (2021). https://doi.org/10.1007/s00521-020-05270-2
10. Tham, Y.C., Li, X., Wong, T.Y., Quigley, H.A., Aung, T., Cheng, C.Y.: Global prevalence of glaucoma and projections of glaucoma burden through 2040: a systematic review and meta-analysis. Ophthalmology **121**(11), 2081–2090 (2014). https://doi.org/10.1016/j.ophtha.2014.05.013
11. Wang, J.K., et al.: Quantifying the spatial patterns of retinal ganglion cell loss and progression in optic neuropathy by applying a deep learning variational autoencoder approach to optical coherence tomography. Front. Ophthalmol. **4** (2025).https://doi.org/10.3389/fopht.2024.1497848
12. Wang, J.-K., Kardon, R.H., Garvin, M.K.: Representation and reconstruction of image-based structural patterns of glaucomatous defects using only two latent variables from a variational autoencoder. In: Fu, H., Garvin, M.K., MacGillivray, T., Xu, Y., Zheng, Y. (eds.) OMIA 2021. LNCS, vol. 12970, pp. 159–167. Springer, Cham (2021). https://doi.org/10.1007/978-3-030-87000-3_17
13. Wy, S., et al.: Comparison of patterns of structural progression in primary open angle glaucoma and pseudoexfoliation glaucoma. J. Glaucoma **33**(3), 155–161 (2024). https://doi.org/10.1097/IJG.0000000000002348
14. Yadav, S.K., et al.: Intraretinal layer segmentation using cascaded compressed U-Nets. J. Imaging **8**(5), 139 (2022). https://doi.org/10.3390/jimaging8050139

Early CHD Detection from Retinal Fundus Scans Using a Spatial Context-Aware Hierarchical Attention Framework

Sparsh Rastogi[1(✉)], Khushboo Modi[1], Sahil Thakur[2,3], and Vinay Arora[1]

[1] Computer Science and Engineering Department, Thapar Institute of Engineering and Technology, Patiala, Punjab, India
{srastogi_be22,kmodi_be22,vinay.arora}@thapar.edu
[2] MediWhale, Seoul, South Korea
sahil.thakur@mediwhale.com
[3] Singapore Eye Research Institute, Singapore, Singapore

Abstract. Retinal fundus imaging provides a non-invasive, cost-effective, and scalable modality for early detection of systemic diseases such as coronary heart disease (CHD). This study proposes a Swin Transformer-based deep learning framework for CHD classification from retinal fundus images, enhanced through vascular segmentation and model interpretability. A total of 17,242 images were curated from the UK Biobank, with class imbalance mitigated using optimal transport-based sampling. Retinal vasculature was segmented using LW-Net to extract both full vessel maps and isolated arteriolar structures, which served as anatomically enriched inputs to the Swin Transformer classifier. The model achieved an AUROC of 0.81 using raw fundus images, which improved to 0.90 with vessel maps and 0.87 with arteriole-only maps—highlighting the benefit of vessel-focused preprocessing. Grad-CAM visualizations revealed consistent attention around the optic disc and major arterioles, reinforcing clinical relevance and model transparency. These findings establish a robust and interpretable pipeline for CHD risk prediction and support the broader utility of retinal imaging for cardiovascular screening, especially in resource-constrained settings.

Keywords: Deep Learning · Cardiovascular Diseases · Retinal Fundus Scans · Oculomics · Image Processing · Coronary Heart Disease(CHD) · Digital Health · Atherosclerosis

1 Introduction

Coronary Heart Disease (CHD), also referred to as Ischemic Heart Disease or Coronary Artery Disease, remains the leading cause of cardiovascular mortality worldwide. It accounts for over 17.8 million deaths annually, including approximately 610,000 deaths each year in the United States alone, representing one in four deaths in the country [3]. The burden is especially high in low and middle

© The Author(s), under exclusive license to Springer Nature Switzerland AG 2026
H. Fang et al. (Eds.): OMIA 2025, LNCS 16209, pp. 147–157, 2026.
https://doi.org/10.1007/978-3-032-10351-2_15

income countries, where more than 75 % of CHD-related deaths occur due to limited access to early screening and timely interventions. With increasing rates of hypertension, diabetes, obesity, and aging populations, the global impact of CHD is expected to grow, with projected healthcare costs exceeding one trillion US dollars by the year 2030. CHD is primarily caused by progressive atherosclerosis, which leads to narrowing or obstruction of the coronary arteries, often without noticeable symptoms until acute cardiac events occur. This highlights the importance of early detection methods that can identify individuals at risk before the onset of clinical symptoms. Existing diagnostic tools such as echocardiography, computed tomography, and magnetic resonance imaging are expensive, complex, and require specialized infrastructure that is not always available in resource-constrained settings [14]. There is an urgent need for accessible and scalable alternatives for population-level risk assessment.

Recent progress in retinal imaging has given rise to the field of oculomics, which explores the potential of the retina as a biomarker for systemic health. As a visible extension of the central vascular and nervous systems, the retina provides a unique noninvasive view into microvascular function. Numerous studies have shown strong associations between retinal features, including arteriolar narrowing, venular dilation, vascular tortuosity, and altered fractal geometry, and systemic conditions such as hypertension, diabetes, stroke, and CHD [9,11,15]. Retinal fundus photography is safe, cost-efficient, and increasingly available through portable devices, making it a promising tool for early risk stratification in community or primary care settings. Motivated by these observations, this study investigates whether retinal fundus images can be used to predict the presence of CHD using deep learning. We employ the Swin Transformer, a hierarchical vision transformer architecture, to model disease-relevant morphological features in both raw color fundus photographs and segmented vascular representations [21]. To support interpretability and clinical translation, we also incorporate explainability techniques that visualize regions contributing to model decisions. The main contributions of this work could be summarized as follows:

1. We construct a high-quality dataset from UK Biobank retinal fundus images, balanced using optimal transport sampling and filtered through a rigorous image quality pipeline for CHD classification.
2. We introduce a novel Swin Transformer-based pipeline for CHD prediction, achieving benchmark performance on the UK Biobank dataset, where we systematically validate its efficacy across both raw images and anatomically enriched inputs derived from vessel segmentation. To the best of our knowledge, this is the first application of a hierarchical transformer architecture like Swin to this task, enhancing performance while substantially reducing training data requirements.
3. We provide model interpretability through gradient-based attention visualizations, which validate our model by confirming its focus on clinically relevant structures such as the optic disc and major arterioles.

2   Related Works

Retinal fundus imaging has emerged as a valuable non-invasive modality for cardiovascular risk assessment, offering insight into systemic vascular health through the microvascular structures of the eye. With growing interest in oculomics, numerous studies have explored predictive models that leverage retinal features to identify individuals at risk of cardiovascular disease (CVD). Broadly, the literature in this space can be categorized into two methodological paradigms: statistical and classical machine learning (ML) approaches, and deep learning-based models. Each has contributed significant insights, while also presenting several limitations in terms of robustness, generalizability and interpretability.

Classical approaches primarily rely on manually extracted retinal features such as vessel calibers, tortuosity, and choroidal thickness. These features are analyzed using interpretable models including logistic regression, support vector machines (SVMs), and decision trees. For instance, retinal vessel density measured via optical coherence tomography angiography (OCTA) has been shown to differ significantly between patients with and without coronary total occlusion (CTO), highlighting its diagnostic relevance for coronary artery disease (CAD) [20]. Similarly, Zhao *et al.* [19] demonstrated that central retinal artery equivalent (CRAE) and subfoveal choroidal thickness (SFChT) were significantly different in stroke patients versus controls. Expanding on these efforts, TShen *et al.* introduced Reti-CVD, a Cox regression model that improved 10-year CVD risk prediction, particularly when integrated with QRISK3 scores [16]. RNFL thinning, measured via OCT, has also been linked to elevated CVD risk in large-scale cohort studies such as the UK Biobank and GDES [4]. Despite the interpretability and statistical robustness of these approaches, they are constrained by several limitations. Manual feature extraction is time-intensive and requires expert oversight, introducing inter-observer variability and limiting reproducibility. Performance often varies across imaging devices and acquisition protocols, reducing generalizability. Moreover, these models tend to perform inconsistently across populations with diverse demographic or clinical characteristics, thereby restricting their applicability in real-world clinical settings.

To address these constraints, deep learning methods have been increasingly adopted for their ability to learn discriminative features directly from raw fundus images. Initial CNN-based models, such as Wu et al. [18], showed promising accuracy (82%) for binary CVD classification on the EyePACS dataset. Ma et al. [10] achieved a high AUROC of 0.97 on the BRAVE dataset, though these early architectures struggled with overfitting and domain transfer. Poplin et al. [13] introduced Inception v3 to handle multi-scale features in large scale datasets (300,000 images), reporting an AUROC of 0.70. However, the computational demands of such models posed challenges for clinical deployment. Residual networks offered a more scalable alternative. Dai et al. [5] used ResNet-50 for calcification prediction, while Munk et al. [12] scaled to ResNet-152 on 3.2 million images, achieving 83% accuracy. Yet deeper variants offered diminishing performance gains relative to computational cost, prompting exploration of more efficient architectures. DenseNets addressed this by enhancing feature reuse. Khan et al. [7] achieved an AUROC of 0.89 using DenseNet-201, and Lee et al. [8] reported robust results (AUROC: 0.78–0.87) across multiple cohorts with DenseNet-169. Kumar et al. [1] achieved 97.2% accuracy in CAD classification using DenseNet-121 with vessel segmentation. However, DenseNets remain memory intensive and prone to overfitting on small datasets. Simpler models like VGG-16 have been applied for efficiency (e.g., Barriada et al. [2], 67% accuracy), but often underperform on complex tasks. Ensemble approaches, such as Vaghefi et al. [17], offer improved robustness, with AUROCs of 0.89–0.90 reported across EyePACS and UK Biobank. More recently, transformer-based models have been explored. Hu et al. [6] applied Vision Transformers (ViT) for CVD prediction on 69,000 images, though the AUROC of 0.67 reflects challenges related to high data requirements and the absence of spatial inductive bias. Foundation models like RetFound have attempted to mitigate these limitations by pretraining ViT backbones on over 1.6 million unlabeled retinal images, achieving strong performance across diverse downstream tasks [22]. However, such approaches rely heavily on access to large-scale training data and remain limited by the inherent lack of spatial structure in standard ViTs, which can constrain their utility in modeling localized anatomical features relevant for clinical diagnosis.

This study addresses these limitations by employing a hierarchical Swin Transformer, which introduces multiscale processing and shifted window attention to enable efficient spatial context modeling. Crucially, we evaluate whether comparable performance to large-data ViT models can be achieved with significantly smaller training sets by leveraging spatially structured, domain-relevant information. We further differentiate our approach by integrating anatomically enriched inputs derived from vessel segmentation, thereby enhancing both predictive performance and clinical interpretability. Attention-activated heatmaps have been used to validate that the model consistently attends to diagnostically relevant vascular structures in alignment with established clinical literature, while also providing real-time visual outputs that support clinician decision making in practice.

3   Methodology and Experimental Setup

The overall methodological framework adopted in this study is presented in Fig. 1. The pipeline comprises four principal components: (i) cohort construction from a large-scale retinal imaging biobank, (ii) systematic image quality control and preprocessing, (iii) vascular feature enhancement through deep learning-based segmentation, and (iv) coronary heart disease (CHD) prediction using a hierarchical transformer model with integrated interpretability. During preprocessing, anatomical fidelity is enhanced via LW-Net-based vessel segmentation, producing both full vascular and arteriolar maps that suppress non-diagnostic background variation [23]. These refined representations are subsequently used as inputs to the Swin Transformer, which is trained to discriminate between CHD and control cases. To support clinical interpretability, Grad-CAM is employed to generate attention heatmaps, thereby localizing the retinal regions most influential to the model's predictions [25]. The individual components of this pipeline,

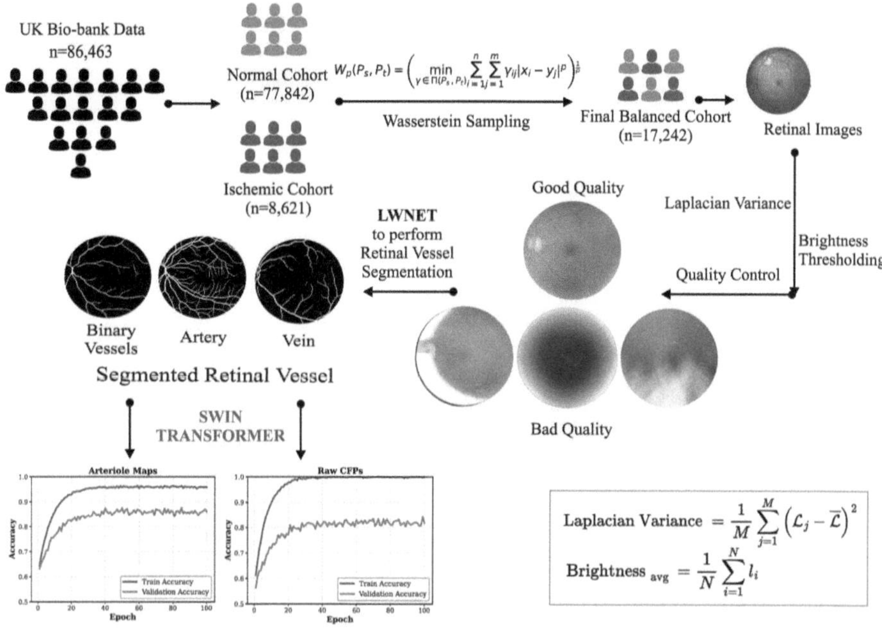

$$W_p(P_s, P_t) = \left(\min_{\gamma \in \Pi(P_s, P_t)} \sum_{i=1}^{n} \sum_{j=1}^{m} \gamma_{ij} |x_i - y_j|^p \right)^{\frac{1}{p}}$$

$$\text{Laplacian Variance} = \frac{1}{M} \sum_{j=1}^{M} \left(\mathcal{L}_j - \overline{\mathcal{L}} \right)^2$$

$$\text{Brightness}_{\text{avg}} = \frac{1}{N} \sum_{i=1}^{N} l_i$$

Fig. 1. An illustration of the overall methodology of the approach

along with their implementation details and design rationale, are elaborated in the following subsections.

Fig. 2. Demographic distribution of the dataset across CHD and control cohorts.

3.1 Data Creation and Preprocessing

This study leverages color fundus photographs (CFPs) from the UK Biobank, encompassing 172,926 images from 86,463 participants [24]. To enable binary classification of coronary heart disease (CHD), two distinct cohorts were constructed. The CHD-positive group included 8,621 individuals diagnosed with chronic ischemic heart disease (ICD-10 code I25), while the control group consisted of 77,842 individuals without any ICD-coded cardiovascular diagnosis.

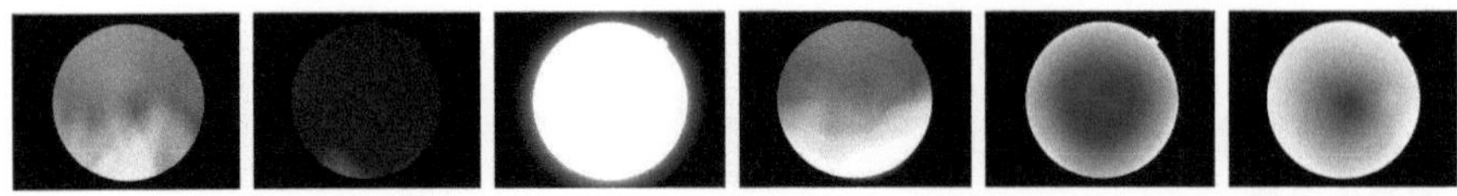

Fig. 3. Examples of retinal imaging artifacts: (a) Eye-blink motion, (b) Underexposure, (c) Illumination flash, (d) Corneal/eyelid reflection, (e) Defocus blur, (f) Vignetting.

This yielded a significant class imbalance (approximately 1:9) which necessitated robust sampling strategies.

To address this, we employed an optimal transport-based downsampling technique. Control samples were selected to minimize the Wasserstein distance between the distribution of the CHD cohort and the resampled control cohort (Eq. 1), resulting in a demographically balanced set of 17,242 images. To prevent data leakage, the dataset was split at the patient level, with the final partitions for training (70%), validation (15%), and testing (15%) containing no patient overlap. Figure 2 presents the demographic distribution, capturing age and sex disparities between disease and control groups, with CHD patients tending to be older and predominantly male, in line with known epidemiological patterns.

$$W_p(P_s, P_t) = \left(\min_{\gamma \in \Pi(P_s, P_t)} \sum_{i=1}^{n} \sum_{j=1}^{m} \gamma_{ij} |x_i - y_j|^p \right)^{\frac{1}{p}} \tag{1}$$

To ensure image quality and preserve vascular detail essential for downstream learning, we implemented a two-stage quality control pipeline. First, underexposed images, such as those caused by poor illumination or lens shading, were filtered using average brightness thresholds (Eq. 2). Second, images with defocus or motion blur were excluded by computing the variance of the Laplacian operator (Eq. 3). Figure 3 illustrates representative artifacts frequently encountered during retinal imaging, including eye blinks, corneal reflections, excessive illumination, and vignetting. These distortions degrade the visibility of retinal vessels and were carefully screened to retain only diagnostically viable images.

$$\text{Brightness}_{avg} = \frac{1}{N} \sum_{i=1}^{N} I_i \tag{2}$$

$$\text{Laplacian Variance} = \frac{1}{M} \sum_{j=1}^{M} \left(\mathcal{L}_j - \bar{\mathcal{L}} \right)^2 \tag{3}$$

Following quality control, images were resized to 224 × 224 pixels and augmented through random cropping, affine transformations, and histogram equalization. To enhance vascular clarity, CLAHE was used for local contrast enhancement, while Laplacian sharpening accentuated vessel edges. Retinal vessel segmentation was conducted using LW-Net, a lightweight convolutional architecture designed for accurate extraction of retinal vasculature. The model produced both complete vessel maps and arteriole-only segmentations. As shown in Fig. 4, segmentation helped isolate vascular morphology from the background, eliminating confounders such as pigmentation artifacts and macular texture. This preprocessing step yielded structured representations that made downstream classification more robust and anatomically grounded.

3.2   CHD Prediction and Explainability

We employed the Swin Transformer, a hierarchical vision transformer architecture optimized for long-range context modeling using shifted window attention. Its multi-scale processing enables efficient learning of vascular topologies essential for capturing subtle changes in tortuosity, caliber, and vessel branching patterns associated with CHD. The model was trained using binary cross-entropy loss and the Adam optimizer, with a cosine annealing learning rate schedule (1×10^{-4} to 1×10^{-6}). Dropout (0.2), weight decay (0.05), and early stopping based on validation AUROC (patience = 10) were applied for regularization. All experiments were conducted on an HPC cluster equipped with 8 NVIDIA H100 GPUs (80GB), using TensorFlow v2.18 and CUDA v12.5.

To ensure clinical relevance and transparency, we integrated Grad-CAM explainability into the pipeline. As seen in Fig. 4d), Grad-CAM visualizations consistently highlighted regions around the optic disc and major arterioles, areas previously implicated in cardiovascular risk. This attention alignment not only validates the model's focus on meaningful anatomical structures but also strengthens interpretability and trustworthiness for potential deployment in clinical screening systems. By combining vessel-centric preprocessing and attention-based interpretability, our approach ensures that CHD prediction from retinal images is both accurate and explainable. The segmentation-filtered input streamlines learning, while Grad-CAM offers post hoc validation of the model's decision rationale together forming a clinically informed, end-to-end oculomic pipeline.

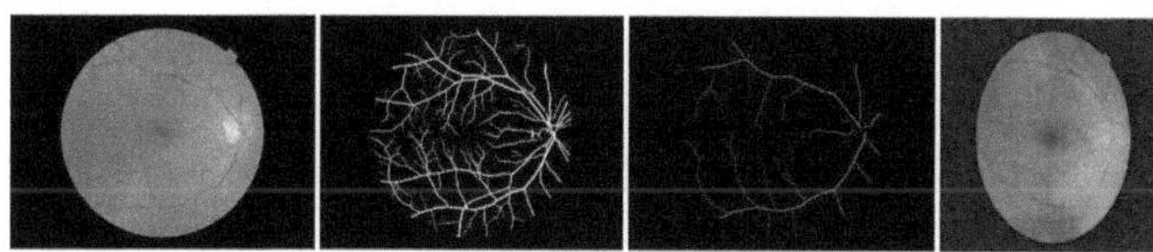

Fig. 4. Retinal vessel segmentation and attention visualization. (a) Original CFP, (b) segmented vessel map, (c) isolated arteriolar map, (d) Grad-CAM heatmap from the raw CFP model, showing focused attention on the optic disc and major arterioles

4   Results and Discussion

To evaluate the effectiveness of vessel-centric representations for coronary heart disease (CHD) prediction, the Swin Transformer was trained using three input modalities: raw color fundus photographs (CFPs), segmented vessel maps, and

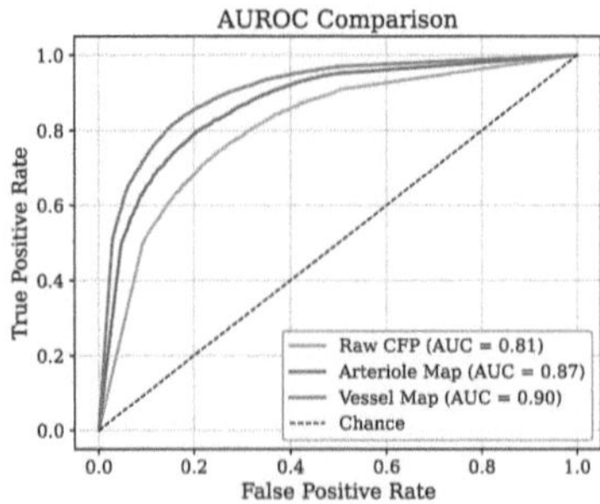

Fig. 5. Comparison of model performance using AUROC across three modalities for CHD prediction—raw CFPs (0.81), vessel maps (0.90), and arteriole maps (0.87).

arteriole-only maps. The comparative AUROC and accuracy values across these modalities are presented in Fig. 5 and Fig. 6. When trained on raw CFPs, the model converged rapidly during training, reaching over 99% training accuracy. However, validation performance plateaued at 82% accuracy with an AUROC of 0.81, indicating overfitting due to noise from non-vascular structures such as pigmentation variability, macular features, and imaging artifacts. In contrast, vessel maps yielded a significant improvement: 88% validation accuracy and an AUROC of 0.90. By isolating retinal vasculature, segmentation suppressed background variation and enhanced morphological signals, such as arteriolar narrowing and vessel tortuosity relevant to CHD pathology. This validates the hypothesis that vessel-focused preprocessing improves model generalization and robustness. Arteriole-only maps produced slightly lower performance (86% accuracy, 0.87 AUROC), suggesting that excluding venular information may result in partial loss of context. While arterioles are more directly affected by cardiovascular pathology, venular changes may still reflect systemic inflammatory and hemodynamic conditions relevant to prediction.

Finally, to enhance interpretability, Grad-CAM was used to generate attention heatmaps over input images. As shown in Fig. 4d, the model consistently localized attention to clinically meaningful regions, including the optic disc and primary arterioles. These areas are well-established correlates of systemic cardiovascular status, and their consistent highlighting indicates that the model is learning pathophysiologically relevant features. This dual-layered interpretability

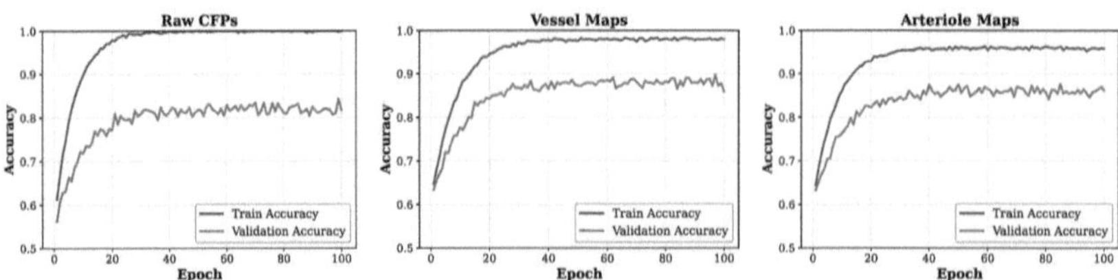

Fig. 6. Training and validation accuracy comparison across input modalities: (a) Raw fundus images, (b) Segmented vessel maps, (c) Arteriole-only maps

via anatomical segmentation and attention-based localization adds transparency and trust to the predictive pipeline. It enables both verification by clinicians and refinement of the model based on anatomical priors. Together, the results affirm the value of integrating segmentation and explainability into deep learning workflows for retinal image-based disease prediction.

5   Conclusion

This study establishes a clinically relevant and interpretable framework for coronary heart disease prediction using retinal fundus images, leveraging vascular segmentation and Swin Transformer-based classification. Vessel-focused preprocessing improved model generalizability and alignment with anatomical markers, while Grad-CAM visualizations reinforced the model's clinical plausibility by consistently highlighting the optic disc and arteriolar regions.

Looking ahead, expanding validation to diverse, multi-ethnic cohorts and imaging devices will be essential for broader applicability. Developing calibration strategies for demographic variations and robust preprocessing pipelines for cross-device generalization can further enhance clinical readiness. Integration of longitudinal retinal data, expert-guided interpretability benchmarking, and multimodal fusion with systemic biomarkers may also advance both accuracy and trust in real-world settings. Together, these directions build on the strong predictive performance and explainability demonstrated in this work, positioning the model as a scalable and transparent tool for population-level cardiovascular risk screening.

Acknowledgements. We would like to express our gratitude to the UK Biobank for providing access to their comprehensive data resource. This research has been conducted using the UK Biobank Resource under Application Number 142339. We also thank the Thapar Institute of Engineering and Technology for providing the GPU infrastructure used for conducting the experiments in this study.

References

1. Cardiovascular risk assessment with retinal images using densenet-121. Int. Res. J. Modernizat. Eng. Technol. Sci. (2024)
2. Barriada, R.G., Simó-Servat, O., Planas, A., Hernández, C., Simó, R., Masip, D.: Deep learning of retinal imaging: a useful tool for coronary artery calcium score prediction in diabetic patients. Appl. Sci. (Basel) **12**(3), 1401 (2022)
3. Brown, J.C., Gerhardt, T.E., Kwon, E.: Risk factors for coronary artery disease. In: StatPearls. StatPearls Publishing, Treasure Island (2024)
4. Chen, Y., et a.: Retinal nerve fiber layer thinning as a novel fingerprint for cardiovascular events: results from the prospective cohorts in UK and China. BMC Med. **21**(1), 24 (2023). https://doi.org/10.1186/s12916-023-02728-7
5. Dai, G., et al.: Exploring the effect of hypertension on retinal microvasculature using deep learning on East Asian population. PLoS ONE **15**(3), 1–13 (2020). https://doi.org/10.1371/journal.pone.0230111

6. Hu, W., et al.: Real-world feasibility, accuracy and acceptability of automated retinal photography and AI-based cardiovascular disease risk assessment in Australian primary care settings: a pragmatic trial. NPJ Digit. Med. **8**(1), 122 (2025)

7. Khan, N.C., et al.: Predicting systemic health features from retinal fundus images using transfer-learning-based artificial intelligence models. Diagnostics (Basel) **12**(7), 1714 (2022)

8. Lee, Y.C., et al.: Multimodal deep learning of fundus abnormalities and traditional risk factors for cardiovascular risk prediction. NPJ Digit. Med. **6**(1), 14 (2023)

9. Liang, C., Gu, C., Wang, N.: Retinal vascular caliber in coronary heart disease and its risk factors. Ophthalmic Res. **66**(1), 151–163 (2022). https://doi.org/10.1159/000526753

10. Ma, Y., et al.: Deep learning algorithm using fundus photographs for 10-year risk assessment of ischemic cardiovascular diseases in China. Sci. Bull. (Beijing) **67**(1), 17–20 (2022)

11. Matulevičiūtė, I., Sidaraitė, A., Tatarūnas, V., Veikutienė, A., Dobilienė, O., Žaliūnienė, D.: Retinal and choroidal thinning-a predictor of coronary artery occlusion? Diagnostics (Basel) **12**(8), 2016 (2022)

12. Munk, M.R., Kurmann, T., Márquez-Neila, P., Zinkernagel, M.S., Wolf, S., Sznitman, R.: Assessment of patient specific information in the wild on fundus photography and optical coherence tomography. Sci. Rep. **11**(1), 8621 (2021)

13. Poplin, R., et al.: Prediction of cardiovascular risk factors from retinal fundus photographs via deep learning. Nat. Biomed. Eng. **2**, 158–164 (2018). https://doi.org/10.1038/s41551-018-0195-0. https://www.nature.com/articles/s41551-018-0195-0

14. Skelly, A.C., Hashimoto, R., Buckley, D.I., et al.: Noninvasive Testing for Coronary Artery Disease. No. 171 in Comparative Effectiveness Reviews, Agency for Healthcare Research and Quality (US), Rockville (MD) (2016). https://www.ncbi.nlm.nih.gov/books/NBK361133/

15. Tedeschi-Reiner, E., Strozzi, M., Skoric, B., Reiner, Z.: Relation of atherosclerotic changes in retinal arteries to the extent of coronary artery disease. Am. J. Cardiol. **96**(8), 1107–1109 (2005). https://doi.org/10.1016/j.amjcard.2005.05.070. https://www.sciencedirect.com/science/article/pii/S0002914905011707

16. Tseng, R.M.W.W., et al.: Validation of a deep-learning-based retinal biomarker (Reti-CVD) in the prediction of cardiovascular disease: data from UK biobank. BMC Med. **21**(1), 28 (2023)

17. Vaghefi, E., et al.: Development and validation of a deep-learning model to predict 10-year atherosclerotic cardiovascular disease risk from retinal images using the UK biobank and EyePACS 10K datasets. Cardiovasc. Digit. Health J. **5**(2), 59–69 (2024)

18. Wu, J.H., Liu, T.Y.A.: Application of deep learning to retinal-image-based oculomics for evaluation of systemic health: a review. J. Clin. Med. **12**(1), 152 (2022)

19. Zhao, L., Wang, H., Yang, X., Jiang, B., Li, H., Wang, Y.: Multimodal retinal imaging for detection of ischemic stroke. Front. Aging Neurosci. **13** (2021). https://doi.org/10.3389/fnagi.2021.615813

20. Zhong, P., et al.: Retinal microvasculature changes in patients with coronary total occlusion on optical coherence tomography angiography. Front. Med. **8** (2021). https://doi.org/10.3389/fmed.2021.708491. https://www.frontiersin.org/journals/medicine/articles/10.3389/fmed.2021.708491

21. Liu, Z., Lin, Y., Cao, Y., et al.: Swin transformer: hierarchical vision transformer using shifted windows. In: Proceedings of the IEEE/CVF International Conference on Computer Vision, pp. 10012–10022 (2021)

22. Zhou, Y., Chia, M.A., Wagner, S.K., et al.: A foundation model for generalizable disease detection from retinal images. Nature 622(7981), 156-163 (2023). https://doi.org/10.1038/41586-023-06555-

23. Galdran, A., Anjos, A., et al.: State-of-the-art retinal vessel segmentation with minimalistic models. Sci. Rep. **12**(1), 6174 (2022). https://doi.org/10.1038/41598-022-09675-

24. Bycroft, C., Freeman, C., Petkova, D., et al.: The UK Biobank resource with deep phenotyping and genomic data. Nature **562**(7726), 203–209 (2018). https://doi.org/10.1038/41586-018-0579-

25. Selvaraju, R.R., Cogswell, M., Das, A., et al.: Grad-cam: Visual explanations from deep networks via gradient-based localization. In: Proceedings of the IEEE International Conference on Computer Vision, pp. 618–626 (2017). https://doi.org/10.1109/.2017.74

Dataset, Baseline and Evaluation Design for GAVE Challenge

Zhiwei Liu[1,4], Huihui Fang[2(✉)], Shandi Liu[5], Ping Zhang[3], Wenqun Xi[3], Changjian Wu[4], Zihao Zhong[4], Xinyu Fu[6], Qifan Yang[4], Xiangyu Chen[7], Mengxiong Luo[7], Xinya Hu[3], Jiongning Zhao[4], Mingkui Tan[1], Weihua Yang[3], and Yanwu Xu[4,8(✉)]

[1] School of Software Engineering, South China University of Technology, Guangzhou 510006, China
[2] College of Computing and Data Science, Nanyang Technological University, 639798 Singapore, Singapore
`huihui.fang@ntu.edu.sg`
[3] Shenzhen Eye Hospital, Shenzhen Eye Medical Center, Southern Medical University, Shenzhen 518040, China
[4] School of Future Technology, South China University of Technology, Guangzhou 510006, China
[5] Huaian Hospital, Huaian 223200, China
[6] School of Biomedical Sciences and Engineering, South China University of Technology, Guangzhou 510006, China
[7] Department of Ophthalmology, Affiliated Hospital of North Sichuan Medical College, Nanchong 637000, China
[8] Pazhou Lab, Guangzhou 510320, China
`yxwu@ieee.org`

Abstract. Retinal vessel characteristics serve as crucial biomarkers for screening and diagnosing various diseases. Retinal vessel segmentation, particularly arteriovenous (A/V) segmentation, is a key step in enabling AI-assisted disease screening and diagnosis. Fundus photography, a non-invasive retinal imaging technique, is widely accessible and cost-effective. To advance AI applications in screening and diagnosing conditions such as diabetes and cardiovascular diseases, we collaborated with Medical Image Computing and Computer Assisted Intervention (MICCAI) 2025 to launch the Generalized Analysis of Vessels in Eye (GAVE) Challenge. This initiative provides a dataset with expert annotations for three research tasks: vessel segmentation, A/V segmentation, and quantitative biomarker measurement in fundus images. In the annotation process of the dataset, the fluorescein fundus angiography(FFA) paired with color fundus photos are introduced, which can provide a clearer and more accurate annotation reference than relying on color fundus photos alone. This is the first and biggest dataset to incorporate paired FFA into the vascular annotation of the artery/vein and provides arteriovenous ratio (AVR) parameter annotations. This paper describes the released dataset of 150 color fundus images with corresponding annotations, baseline methods for the three subtasks, and evaluation protocols. The GAVE Challenge is accessible at https://aistudio.baidu.com/competition/detail/1315.

Keywords: Retinal vessel segmentation · Artery/Vein Segmentation ·
Biomarker · GAVE Challenge

1   Introduction

Color fundus photography offers an efficient non-invasive approach for observing
the human retinal vasculature [5]. Alterations in the retinal vessels are associated with numerous diseases: arterial narrowing indicates hypertension [17],
while venous dilation suggests diabetic retinopathy [15]. Diabetes and cardiovascular diseases impose a substantial global healthcare burden [18]. Deep learning
models enables disease screening and diagnosis assistance using color fundus
photographs [14,21], where accurate vascular segmentation and measurement of
vascular morphological parameters (e.g., vessel diameter [8], AVR [1]) are critical
steps [10]. Because different artery/vein changes represent distinct pathologies,
the precise segmentation of vessels into arteries and veins is important, which
enables biomarkers quantification, enhancing the models prediction performance
and interpretability [4,9,20].

Currently, the number of publicly available color fundus arteriovenous vessel segmentation datasets is limited, like DRIVE [13], HRF [3], LES-AV [12],
RITE [7], less than 50 color fundus images. Moreover, the manual annotation
process is fraught with uncertainties [19], especially when annotators rely solely
on color fundus photographs to identify and annotate vessels. These challenges
have severely restricted the development of related fields. To advance research
on arteriovenous vessel segmentation and index measurement, we in collabora-
tion with MICCAI 2025, organized the GAVE Challenge. The aim is to provide
a rich and accurately annotated dataset of color fundus photographs for arteriovenous annotation, which can be used for research on vessel segmentation,
arteriovenous segmentation, and vascular biomarkers measurement. This paper
primarily introduces the 150 color fundus photographs dataset released in the
GAVE Challenge, including three subtasks (vessel segmentation, arteriovenous
segmentation, and AVR measurement), and the method of using color fundus
photos paired with FFA for labeling is described in detail. Then we provide
baselines and elaborate on the evaluation methods.

2   Dataset

The 150 color fundus photographs are derived from a dataset collected during
a previous fundus disease study at Shenzhen Eye Hospital in China. This study
spanned six years and included individuals aged 18âĂŞ60 years without obvious
ocular pathologies. From the original dataset, a subset featuring high-quality
imaging and comprehensive data modalities was carefully selected to serve as
the annotated dataset. Each data instance encompasses a color fundus photo-
graph of one subject's eye, a FFA image depicting the complete arterial filling of
the corresponding eye, and at least one FFA image demonstrating the complete
filling of all fundus blood vessels of the same eye. The objective is to utilize the

FFA images in these two states to facilitate the discrimination and labeling of arteries and veins in the fundus. In contrast to color fundus photographs, FFA images exhibit superior imaging quality. They can clearly image the boundary of vessel, the morphology of arterioles and venule, and the relative positional relationships among near vessels. In addition, the principle underlying fluorescein angiography allows physicians to acquire color fundus photographs with exclusive arterial filling and those with the complete filling of both arteries and veins during the angiography procedure. This approach, compared to relying solely on color fundus photographs, enables annotating physicians to more precisely and effortlessly distinguish arterial and venous vessels, particularly in the case of minute vessels and those regions that are challenging to differentiate due to imaging - related factors. The images were acquired using a variety of ophthalmic devices, including the Topcon NW400, Canon CR - 2 AF, KeHe VX - 10i, Zeiss VIUCAM200, and other commonly employed fundus cameras in ophthalmic hospitals. This study was approved by Institutional Review Board of Shenzhen Eye Hospital (Approval 2024KYPJ013) and adhered to the Declaration of Helsinki. The original acquired images were stored in JPG format at a resolution of 1536 × 1024. The dataset images are saved in PNG format at the same resolution of 1536 × 1024. An illustrative example of one such image is presented in Fig. 1.

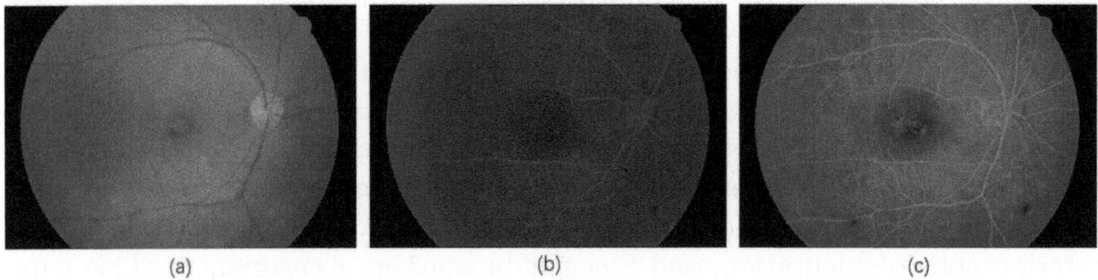

Fig. 1. Illustration of color fundus photography and paired FFA angiography process. (a) represents the color fundus photo, (b) represents the FFA images with filled arteries, and (c) represents the FFA image with both arteries and veins filled

The GAVE dataset provides segmentation masks for retinal vessels in color fundus images, arterial and venous classification labels, and average AVR measurement values for the top 4 vessels around the optic disc. The manual annotation team consists of one quality control doctor with higher seniority, three primary annotating doctors, and five image annotation support personnel. These 150 images were randomly divided into three subsets, each annotated by one doctor, supported by assistants and supervised throughout by the quality control doctor. During annotation, the three annotating doctors used the color fundus images and FFA images in each case to assist and followed a unified annotation standard and specification. Specifically, each image included color fundus images, corresponding FFA images with arteries filling and the FFA with both arteries and veins filled, and a pre-segmented mask using a fine-tuned pre-trained deep learning model. The FFA images and the pre-segmented mask were used to help the doctors make judgments and annotations. The annotating doctors first observed the FFA filled arteries images and those with both arteries and veins filled, identified venous vessels, especially the tiny vessels at the ends, the interlaced vessels, and the parts that are difficult to observe and distinguish in the color fundus images. For some occlusions due to imaging or lesions, the FFA images could also assist the doctors in identifying and annotating the vessels. Then the annotating doctors used the annotation tools to draw the edges of the venous vessels and obtained the vessel masks by filling the contours. The same process was completed for the annotation of arteries with the cooperation of annotating doctors and annotation support personnel, and the doctors supervised and checked the annotations. The separately annotated arterial and venous vessel masks were merged and processed further after being checked and verified by the doctors. For overlapping areas of arterial and venous vessels, separate annotations were made to ensure the continuity of the single class vessel masks, and the overlapping parts were handled separately in the final annotation results. In the final segmentation masks, red represents arteries, blue represents veins, and green represents the overlapping parts of the vessels, we present three examples in Fig. 2.

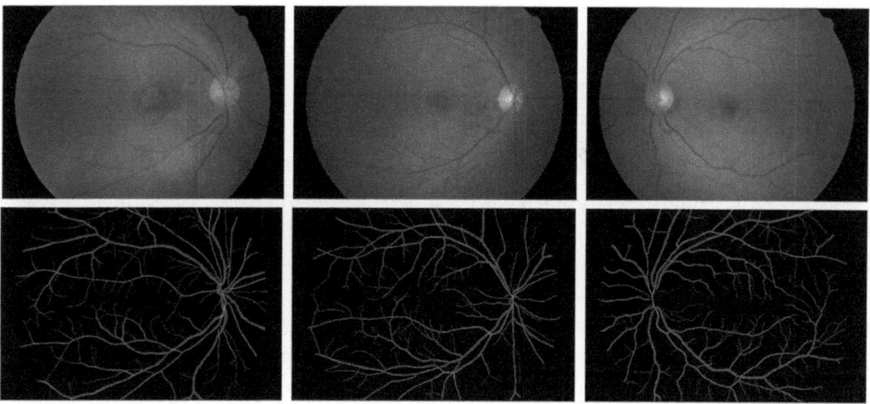

Fig. 2. Three examples of color fundus images with their corresponding pixel-wise manual annotations in GAVE dataset.

The data on the ratio of arteriovenous diameters is based on the labels made by doctors on the arteriovenous vessels and the optic disc. By using both labels, the diameters of the arteriovenous vessels around the optic disc are obtained, and the diameters of the largest arteries and veins are calculated. Finally, the AVR of the top four groups of vessels are calculated as the final reference standard. An example optic disk label and its corresponding AVR annotation are shown in Fig. 3. Finally, in the released dataset, 150 color fundus photos and corresponding arteriovenous labels, AVR measurements are included. The 150 images in the dataset will be randomly divided into three groups. In the preliminary stage, 50 labeled images will be provided for model training, another 50 labeled images will be used for validation, and the remaining 50 images will be used for the final test.

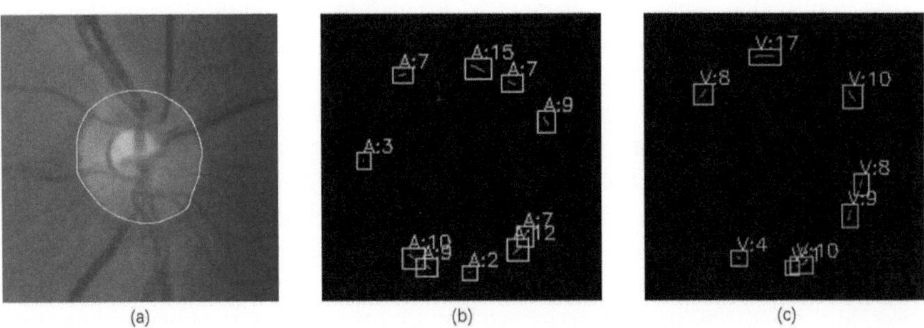

Fig. 3. Measurment process of AVR. Figure (a) presents manually labeled optic disc contour with 1 pixel width, (b) and (c) show arterial diameter section surface and venous diameter section obtained based on optic disc contour and vascular labeling, respectively. Numbers around bounding box represent the number of pixels of the blood caliber width.

3   Baseline

We design a baseline model for all three challenge sub-tasks. Inspired by [11], we propose a U-shaped model with recursive framework for vessel segmentation and arteriovenous segmentation simultaneously. As shown in Fig. 4, we introduce dense skip-connection and Vision Transformer(ViT) for better multiscale representative fusion and enhancing global context extraction, respectively. Through dense skip links, patches of different sizes from other layers can be aggregated together to serve as supplementary, thereby reducing information loss. To compensate for the limited receptive fields of convolutional layers, we incorporate a pre-trained ViT module in the deepest network stage to capture long-range dependencies. The recursive framework allows the model to continually improve the segmentation results of the previous model by correcting classification errors in the input results; we set the recursion depth 7 in experiment. During training, the weight of the loss of the first layer is the highest because the subsequent iterations are all based on its results. A decaying weight scheme is applied to the loss terms of deeper network layers during iterative training, which the weight equals to the ratio of its layer index to the cumulative sum of preceding layers.

The baseline is implemented in PyTorch and trained on an NVIDIA A6000 GPU (48GB memory). Input images are resized to 70% of their original dimensions to accommodate GPU memory constraints. We use pre-processing following [11]. For GAVE dataset, 50 images were used for training and 50 for testing.

During training, we use an Adam optimizer with learning rate $= 10^{-4}$ and early stopping.

Following clinical practice experience, the diameters of the four largest vessels around the optic disc are used as the source for calculating the AVR. To measure AVR, we first use the pre-trained optic disc segmentation model [6] to segment the color fundus photo to obtain the contour of the optic disc, and then process it with the segmentation results of the second task to obtain the artery and vein diameters at the boundary of the optic disc, and calculate the average diameter of the top 4 arteries and veins to obtain the final AVR. The codes of our baseline are available at https://github.com/liuzw20/GAVE.

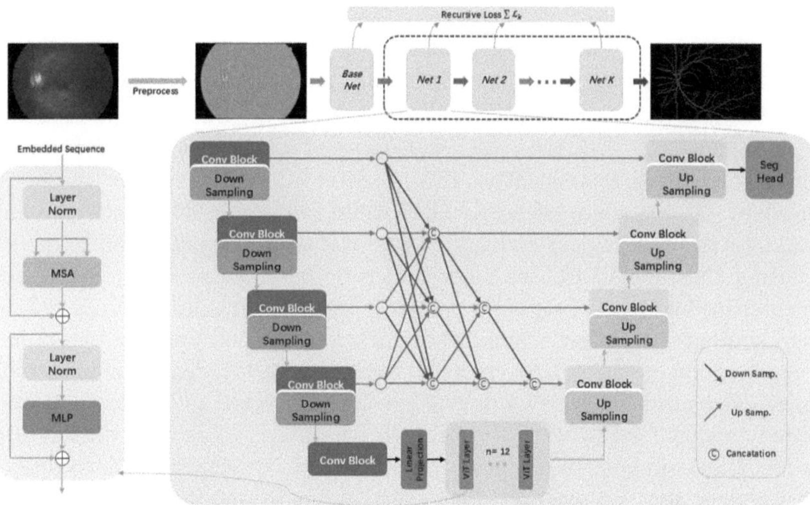

Fig. 4. The model structure of baseline

4   Evaluation

4.1   Task 1: Retinal Vessel Segmentation

To measure the accuracy of the segmentation region, we use the Dice Similarity Coefficient(DSC), which is a commonly used metric for evaluating segmentation tasks. $\text{DSC} = \frac{2 \cdot |X \cap Y|}{|X| + |Y|}$, where X represents the set of segmented target pixels in the ground truth, Y represents the set of segmented pixels in the prediction result, $|X \cap Y|$ denotes the number of pixels in the intersection between X and Y, $|X|$ and $|Y|$ denote the number of elements (i.e., pixels) in X and Y, respectively. To assess the accuracy of the segmentation results on vascular boundaries, we use the 95% Hausdorff Distance (HD95) as the evaluation metric. $\text{HD95}(X, Y) = \max\left\{\sup_{x \in X} \inf_{y \in Y} d(x, y), \sup_{y \in Y} \inf_{x \in X} d(x, y)\right\}_{95\%}$, where X and Y denote boundary points sets of the groundtruth and the prediction, respectively. $d(x,y)$ is the Euclidean distance between the points $x \in X$ and $y \in Y$. $\inf_{y \in Y} d(x,y)$ represents the minimum distance from the point x to the set Y. In addition, to evaluate tubular structure segmentation, such as blood vessels, the centerline Dice (clDice) index [16] is applied to assess topological connectivity. Our baseline achieves DSC of 0.7369, HD95 of 2.2361 and clDice of 0.2611. When designing the scoring calculation, we set the proportions of Dice score, HD95 score, and clDice score to 0.4, 0.3, and 0.3 according to the importance of metrics, respectively.

$$\text{Score}_{\text{task1}} = 10 \times \left(0.4 \times \text{DSC} + 0.3 \times \frac{3}{3 + \text{HD95}} + 0.3 \times \text{clDice} \right) \tag{1}$$

4.2 Task 2: Artery/Vein Segmentation

For artery/vein segmentation, we also choose DSC. Three evaluation indicators from different perspectives of vascular classification attributes are selected, $\text{Sen} = \frac{TP}{TP+FN}$, $\text{Spe} = \frac{TN}{TN+FP}$, $\text{Acc} = \frac{TP+TN}{TP+FN+FP+TN}$, where TP, TN, FP, and FN denote true positive, true negative, false positive and false negative, respectively. Inspired by [2], we used infeasible (INF) and correct (COR) path percentage to evaluate the topological connectivity of the A/V segmentation map. When calculating INF and COR, the algorithm randomly samples two points on the real centerline and finds their nearest corresponding points in the predicted mask. It then compares whether the shortest path lengths between the two pairs are consistent (allowing for a 10% error) to evaluate the topological connectivity of the predicted mask. If the two points are not connected in the prediction, it is recorded as an infeasible path. If the path length is significantly deviated(more than 10%), it is judged as an incorrect connection; otherwise, it is considered a correct connection. Because too long paths indicate missing links, whereas too short ones indicate hallucinated connections. We randomly sample 100 paths during the testing phase. Finally, by statistically analyzing the proportions of the three types of paths (infeasible, shorter/larger, and correct), the topological consistency of the prediction results is quantified. The higher value of COR and the lower value of INF implies better performance. The results of each specific evaluation metric are shown in Table 1. When designing the score calculation, we set the proportions of the segmentation evaluation indicators, classification evaluation indicators, and topological connectivity evaluation indicators in the total score to 0.3, 0.3, and 0.4, respectively.

$$\begin{aligned} \text{Score}_{\text{task2}} = 10 \times \big(&0.3 \times \text{DSC} + 0.1 \times (\text{Sen} + \text{Spe} + \text{Acc}) \\ &+ 0.2 \times (1 - \text{INF}) + 0.2 \times \text{COR} \big) \end{aligned} \tag{2}$$

4.3 Task 3: Arteriovenous Ratio Automatic Measurement

In order to assess the performance of regression task, We adopt the Mean Absolute Error (MAE), which is a commonly used metric for evaluating regression

Table 1. Evaluation results for artery and vein segmentation.

	DSC	Sen	Spe	Acc	INF ↓	COR
Artery	0.6009	0.4981	0.9952	0.9807	0.8478	0.1511
Vein	0.7383	0.7448	0.9879	0.9775	0.7048	0.2924

tasks. We also used the Symmetric Mean Absolute Percentage Error (SMAPE) to calculate the difference between the predicted values and the target values. $\text{MAE} = \frac{1}{n} \sum_{i=1}^{n} |y_i - \hat{y}_i|$, $\text{SMAPE} = \frac{100\%}{n} \sum_{i=1}^{n} \frac{|y_i - \hat{y}_i|}{(|y_i| + |\hat{y}_i|)/2}$, where n is the number of samples, y_i is the groundtruth value, and $\hat{y}_i$ is the predicted value. The baseline achieves MAE of 0.2511 and SMAPE of 34.02%. When designing the score calculation, we set the ratio of the MAE score to the SMAPE score to 0.5 and 0.5 respectively.

$$\text{Score}_{\text{task3}} = 10 \times (0.5 \times \frac{0.37665}{0.37665 + \text{MAE}} + 0.5 \times (1 - \frac{\text{SMAPE}}{2})) \tag{3}$$

Based on the evaluation criteria, our baseline achieves a score of 5.4605 for the vessel segmentation task, a score of 5.4918 for the artery vein segmentation task and a score of 7.1495 for the final AVR measurement task. Arteriovenous segmentation has a higher level of task complexity and clinical value. Therefore, when calculating the total score of the task, we give task 2 a higher weight:

$$\text{Score}_{\text{round}} = 0.3 \times \text{Score}_{\text{task1}} + 0.4 \times \text{Score}_{\text{task2}} + 0.3 \times \text{Score}_{\text{task3}} \tag{4}$$

where round $\in \{\text{preliminary}, \text{final}\}$. Based on the task total score formula, the score of our baseline model on the preliminary set is 5.9797. Since the leaderboard of the preliminary competition is visible to all players, players can adjust the model parameters or strategies to obtain the best prediction on the preliminary set. To prevent players' results from overfitting on the preliminary dataset and obtaining higher scores, we assign a lower weight to the preliminary score when calculating the total challenge score. Therefore, the total score is:

$$\text{Score}_{\text{total}} = 0.3 \times \text{Score}_{\text{preliminary}} + 0.7 \times \text{Score}_{\text{final}} \tag{5}$$

5   Conclusion

In this article, we introduce the GAVE challenge at MICCAI 2025. We designed three subtasks based on the new GAVE dataset, including color fundus image vessel segmentation, arteriovenous segmentation, and automatic measurement of the AVR. In the dataset annotation process, we innovatively introduced two paired FFA images for accurate annotation, which represented the state of FFA images arteries filled and both arteries and veins filled, respectively. To the best of our knowledge, this is the first and largest vessel segmentation dataset which is annotated in this way and provides AVR labels as well. We further proposed a novel recursive framework and measurement method as baseline for GAVE dataset. Finally, we illustrate specific metrics for the evaluation of three tasks.

References

1. Akbar, S., Hassan, T., Akram, M.U., Yasin, U.U., Basit, I.: AVRDB: annotated dataset for vessel segmentation and calculation of arteriovenous ratio. In: Proceedings of the International Conference on Image Processing, Computer Vision, and Pattern Recognition (IPCV), pp. 129–134. The Steering Committee of The World Congress in Computer Science, Computer Engineering and Applied Computing (WorldComp) (2017)
2. Araújo, R.J., Cardoso, J.S., Oliveira, H.P.: A deep learning design for improving topology coherence in blood vessel segmentation. In: Shen, D., et al. (eds.) MICCAI 2019. LNCS, vol. 11764, pp. 93–101. Springer, Cham (2019). https://doi.org/10.1007/978-3-030-32239-7_11
3. Budai, A., Bock, R., Maier, A., Hornegger, J., Michelson, G.: Robust vessel segmentation in fundus images. Int. J. Biomed. Imaging **2013**(1), 154860 (2013)
4. Chen, W., et al.: TW-GAN: topology and width aware GAN for retinal artery/vein classification. Med. Image Anal. **77**, 102340 (2022)
5. Fogel-Levin, M., et al.: Advanced retinal imaging and applications for clinical practice: a consensus review. Surv. Ophthalmol. **67**(5), 1373–1390 (2022)
6. Fu, H., Cheng, J., Xu, Y., Wong, D.W.K., Liu, J., Cao, X.: Joint optic disc and cup segmentation based on multi-label deep network and polar transformation. In: Medical Image Computing and Computer-Assisted Intervention – MICCAI 2018. LNCS, vol. 11071, pp. 1597–1605. Springer, Cham (2018). 10.1007/978-3-030-00934-2_177
7. Hu, Q., Abràmoff, M.D., Garvin, M.K.: Automated separation of binary overlapping trees in low-contrast color retinal images. In: Mori, K., Sakuma, I., Sato, Y., Barillot, C., Navab, N. (eds.) MICCAI 2013. LNCS, vol. 8150, pp. 436–443. Springer, Heidelberg (2013). https://doi.org/10.1007/978-3-642-40763-5_54
8. Ikram, M.K., et al.: Are retinal arteriolar or venular diameters associated with markers for cardiovascular disorders? The Rotterdam study. Invest. Ophthalmol. Vis. Sci. **45**(7), 2129–2134 (2004)
9. Kang, W., et al.: An interpretable machine learning model with deep learning-based imaging biomarkers for diagnosis of Alzheimer's disease. In: Celebi, M.E., et al. (eds.) International Conference on Medical Image Computing and Computer-Assisted Intervention, pp. 69–78. Springer (2023). https://doi.org/10.1007/978-3-031-47401-9_7
10. Mookiah, M.R.K., et al.: A review of machine learning methods for retinal blood vessel segmentation and artery/vein classification. Med. Image Anal. **68**, 101905 (2021)
11. Morano, J., Aresta, G., Bogunović, H.: RRWNet: recursive refinement network for effective retinal artery/vein segmentation and classification. Expert Syst. Appl. **256**, 124970 (2024)
12. Orlando, J.I., Barbosa Breda, J., van Keer, K., Blaschko, M.B., Blanco, P.J., Bulant, C.A.: Towards a glaucoma risk index based on simulated hemodynamics from fundus images. In: Frangi, A.F., Schnabel, J.A., Davatzikos, C., Alberola-López, C., Fichtinger, G. (eds.) MICCAI 2018. LNCS, vol. 11071, pp. 65–73. Springer, Cham (2018). https://doi.org/10.1007/978-3-030-00934-2_8
13. Qureshi, T.A., Habib, M., Hunter, A., Al-Diri, B.: A manually-labeled, artery/vein classified benchmark for the drive dataset. In: Proceedings of the 26th IEEE International Symposium on Computer-Based Medical Systems, pp. 485–488. IEEE (2013)

14. Rahman, A.U., Alsenani, Y., Zafar, A., Ullah, K., Rabie, K., Shongwe, T.: Enhancing heart disease prediction using a self-attention-based transformer model. Sci. Rep. **14**(1), 514 (2024)
15. Safi, H., Safi, S., Hafezi-Moghadam, A., Ahmadieh, H.: Early detection of diabetic retinopathy. Surv. Ophthalmol. **63**(5), 601–608 (2018)
16. Shit, S., et al.: CLDICE-a novel topology-preserving loss function for tubular structure segmentation. In: Proceedings of the IEEE/CVF Conference on Computer Vision and Pattern Recognition, pp. 6560–16569 (2021)
17. Tapp, R.J., Owen, C.G., Barman, S.A., Welikala, R.A., Foster, P.J., Whincup, P.H., Strachan, D.P., Rudnicka, A.R., Eye, U.B., Consortium, V.: Associations of retinal microvascular diameters and tortuosity with blood pressure and arterial stiffness: united kingdom biobank. Hypertension **74**(6), 1383–1390 (2019)
18. Wong, N.D., Sattar, N.: Cardiovascular risk in diabetes mellitus: epidemiology, assessment and prevention. Nat. Rev. Cardiol. **20**(10), 685–695 (2023)
19. Wu, J., et al.: Multi-rater prism: learning self-calibrated medical image segmentation from multiple raters. Sci. Bull. **69**(18), 2906–2919 (2024)
20. Zhao, Y., et al.: Retinal vascular network topology reconstruction and artery/vein classification via dominant set clustering. IEEE Trans. Med. Imaging **39**(2), 341–356 (2019)
21. Zhou, Y., et al.: A foundation model for generalizable disease detection from retinal images. Nature **622**(7981), 156–163 (2023)

UncEGA-Net: Uncertainty-Guided Edge Attention for Optic Nerve Segmentation in Ultrasound Images

Wenhui Li[1,2], Yalin Zheng[2,3], Gregory Y. H. Lip[2,4,5], Mark Kelson[6], and Yanda Meng[1(✉)]

[1] Computer Science Department, University of Exeter, Exeter, UK
`y.m.meng@exeter.ac.uk`
[2] Liverpool Centre for Cardiovascular Science at University of Liverpool, Liverpool John Moores University and Liverpool Heart and Chest Hospital, Liverpool, UK
[3] Department of Eye and Vision Sciences, University of Liverpool, Liverpool, UK
[4] Department of Clinical Medicine, Aalborg University, Aalborg, Denmark
[5] Medical University of Bialystok, Bialystok, Poland
[6] Institute of Data Science and Artificial Intelligence, Department of Mathematics, University of Exeter, Exeter, UK

Abstract. Accurate segmentation of the optic nerve and surrounding structures in transorbital ultrasound (TOS) imaging is essential for non-invasive assessment of elevated intracranial pressure and other neuro-ophthalmic conditions. However, inherent low contrast, speckle noise, and ambiguous anatomical boundaries in ultrasound images pose significant challenges. In this work, we propose UncEGA-Net, a novel encoder-decoder architecture designed to robustly segment the optic nerve (ON) and optic nerve sheath (ONS) from TOS images. The backbone employs a ConvNeXtV2-Tiny encoder to extract high-level semantic features while maintaining computational efficiency. Most importantly, we introduce the EGA-U module (Edge-Guided Attention with Uncertainty), which exploits a Bernoulli-based proxy approximation to predict uncertainty, thus dynamically regulating the inverse attention and enhance the feature representation near the uncertainty boundary. Extensive experiments on a public multicenter dataset demonstrate that UncEGA-Net achieves state-of-the-art performance, outperforming strong baselines in terms of Dice coefficient and other boundary-based metrics. Furthermore, we validate the model's clinical utility by estimating optic nerve diameters that show a moderate correlation with ground-truth measurements. Our approach highlights the value of integrating uncertainty modelling with edge-guided attention for precise and reliable segmentation in challenging ultrasound settings.

Keywords: Ultrasound segmentation · Optic nerve ·
Uncertainty-guided learning

H. Fang et al. (Eds.): OMIA 2025, LNCS 16209, pp. 168–177, 2026.
https://doi.org/10.1007/978-3-032-10351-2_17

1   Introduction

Transorbital ultrasound (TOS) is a non-invasive imaging technique, and widely used to assess the optic nerve and its surrounding sheath. Measurement of the optic nerve diameter (OND) and optic nerve sheath diameter (ONSD) from ultrasound images plays an important role in the detection of elevated intracranial pressure (ICP) [8] and other neurological conditions [8,14]. Compared to invasive methods, ultrasound-based assessments are safer, faster, and more suitable for emergency and bedside evaluations [16].

Recent studies on automatic segmentation and diameter measurement of the optic nerve in TOS images have primarily relied on convolutional neural network (CNN) architectures. U-NetâĂŞbased systems trained on multicenter datasets have demonstrated moderate segmentation performance [9]. Variants such as ResNet encoded U-Nets and fully convolutional networks have been used to enhance structural accuracy, particularly for diameter measurement tasks [10,19]. More advanced approaches have incorporated hybrid architectures, such as YOLOv5s [2] combined with transformer-based modules, which improve boundary localisation in low-contrast or low-signal noise ratio (SNR) regions. A recent narrative review [4] summarised that automated ONSD measurement techniques has highlighted key challenges in both classical and machine learningâĂŞbased methods. These include a high sensitivity to image quality and uncertainty in boundary delineation, particularly under variable acquisition conditions. The review emphasises the importance of developing robust boundary-aware segmentation frameworks, which motivates our focus on edge enhancement strategies in the context of ultrasound segmentation.

However, automatically segmenting the optic nerve and its sheath in ultrasound images is a challenging task. The ultrasound images are often affected by speckle noise, low contrast, and poorly defined anatomical boundaries [12]. Those limitations not only hinder the accuracy of locating the position of the region of interest but also directly impact the reliability of OND and ONSD measurements derived from the segmentation masks. Since optic nerve diameters are typically measured within a fixed anatomical zone, any inaccuracy in boundary localisation may lead to clinically significant measurement errors.

To address the limitations of existing segmentation approaches in capturing precise and robust boundaries in noisy ultrasound images, we propose a novel boundary-aware framework named UncEGA-Net. This architecture is built upon two key innovations. **First, we adopt ConvNeXtV2 as the encoder backbone to replace conventional CNN-based feature extractors.** ConvNeXtV2 [15] offers improved representational capacity and a larger effective receptive field while maintaining the efficiency of pure convolutional networks. These properties are particularly beneficial for capturing the anatomical variability and low-contrast structures that are often present in TOS images. **Second, we introduce an uncertainty-guided edge attention module, referred to as EGA-U.** Unlike previous edge-guided attention mechanisms [1], where they treat all edge signals equally, our EGA-U dynamically modulates attention weights using a pixel-wise uncertainty map derived from the segmentation

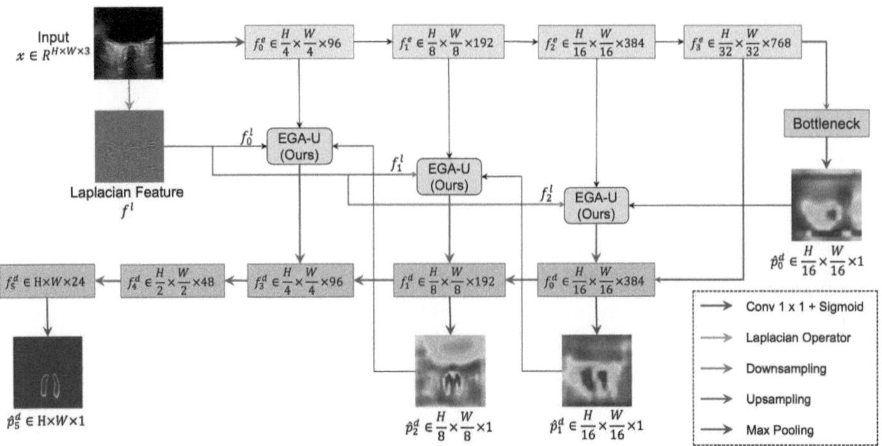

Fig. 1. Overall architecture of our proposed UncEGA-Net, consisting of a ConvNeXtV2-based encoder and a decoder with three EGA-U modules. Each EGA-U integrates decoder predictions, Laplacian edge priors, and encoder features to enhance boundary localisation. In this context, H, W denote the input height and width.

output. This mechanism allows the model to emphasise edge information in confident regions while suppressing misleading signals in ambiguous or noisy areas. By combining structural priors with uncertainty-aware modulation, UncEGA-Net achieves more accurate and robust boundary delineation, which is critical for downstream tasks such as optic nerve diameter measurement.

2   Methods

We propose UncEGA-Net, a boundary-aware segmentation framework designed to improve optic nerve and sheath delineation in TOS images. The overall architecture of our proposed UncEGA-Net is illustrated in Fig. 1. The architecture builds upon a U-NetâĂŞlike encoderâĂŞdecoder structure, where the encoder is replaced with a ConvNeXtV2 [15] backbone for enhanced feature extraction. To address the challenges of imprecise and noisy boundaries, we introduce a novel uncertainty-guided edge attention module (EGA-U) into the decoder path. This module adaptively fuses static edge priors with model-predicted uncertainty to improve boundary localisation.

The network accepts 3-channel B-mode ultrasound images as input and outputs binary segmentation masks, indicating the optic nerve sheath region. Multiscale features from the encoder are successively fused in the decoder through skip connections. At each stage, the decoder is guided by EGA-U modules that incorporate Laplacian edge maps and an internally derived pixel-level uncertainty map. The model is trained end-to-end; intermediate predictions serve as a guidance mechanism within the EGA-U modules but are not directly supervised. The final output is used for diameter measurement.

2.1 ConvNeXtV2 Encoder

We use ConvNeXtV2-Tiny [15,17] as the encoder backbone in our UncEGA-Net architecture. ConvNeXtV2 is a pure convolutional network that incorporates key design principles from vision transformers, such as large kernel sizes, GELU activation, inverted bottlenecks, and hierarchical depth. Compared to traditional ResNet or VGG-style encoders used in standard U-Net models, ConvNeXtV2 offers a stronger ability to capture both local and global context while maintaining high computational efficiency.

The encoder consists of four stages with progressively downsampled feature maps. These multiscale features serve as the foundation for subsequent boundary-aware decoding. In our setting, ConvNeXtV2 [15] is initialised with pretrained weights from ImageNet-22K [3] and fine-tuned end-to-end on the ultrasound segmentation task. This enables the network to extract rich semantic features even under low contrast and noisy imaging conditions.

2.2 EGA-U Module

Overview of the original EGA module. Our design builds on the edge-guided attention (EGA) mechanism introduced in MEGANet for boundary-aware segmentation [1]. The original EGA module enhances decoder features by integrating three inputs: (1) the encoder feature at a given scale, (2) a static edge map extracted using a Laplacian operator, and (3) a coarse prediction from the previous decoder stage. The prediction is inverted to form a reverse attention map, which suppresses foreground regions and redirects focus to boundaries. These maps are fused with encoder features via convolution and refined using a Channel Spatial Attention Module (CBAM), which produces enhanced features for segmentation.

Motivation. While the original EGA [1] guides attention to boundaries, it treats all edge signals equally, ignoring their reliability. In ultrasound, static Laplacian edge maps may contain noisy or weak boundaries due to low contrast and anatomical ambiguity. To address this, we introduce uncertainty-guided edge attention (EGA-U), which modulates reverse attention using a pixel-wise uncertainty estimate computed as a scaled Bernoulli proxy (peaking at prediction probability 0.5). This uncertainty map relaxes suppression in ambiguous regions, enabling adaptive attention to uncertain yet informative boundaries.

Module Design and Implementation. The overall structure of our proposed EGA-U module is shown in Fig. 2, which illustrates the interaction among three attention pathways: uncertainty-modulated reverse attention, boundary attention, and high-frequency guidance.

The module refines decoder features using three inputs: the encoding feature from stage i, denoted as $f_i^e \in \mathbb{R}^{H_i \times W_i \times N_i}$; the guidance map from the higher-level prediction of decoder stage $i + 1$, denoted as $\hat{p}_{i+1}^d \in \mathbb{R}^{H_i \times W_i \times 1}$; and the Laplacian edge map from the input image, $f_i^l \in \mathbb{R}^{H_i \times W_i \times 1}$.

The design includes three parallel attention branches:

1. **Reverse attention branch.** The guidance map $\hat{p}^d_{i+1}$ is first obtained by applying a sigmoid activation to the decoder output $\hat{f}^d_{i+1}$:

$$\hat{p}^d_{i+1} = \sigma(\hat{f}^d_{i+1}) \tag{1}$$

To estimate the confidence of the model, we compute a pixel-wise uncertainty map based on a Bernoulli entropy proxy:

$$U(x) = 4\hat{p}(x)(1 - \hat{p}(x)) \tag{2}$$

This uncertainty peaks when $\hat{p}(x) = 0.5$, indicating maximum ambiguity. We use it to soften the reverse attention mask. The reverse gate is defined as:

$$G_{\mathrm{RA}}(x) = (1 - \hat{p}(x)) + U(x) \tag{3}$$

This gate is applied to the input feature f^e_i, producing the reverse attended feature with uncertainty.
2. **Boundary attention branch.** To emphasize edge-localized activation, we apply a Laplacian filter to the predicted probability map $\hat{p}^d_{i+1}$, producing a boundary map $f^b_i = \mathcal{L}(\hat{p}^d_{i+1})$ that highlights sharp transitions. This boundary map gates the input feature to produce the boundary-aware response.
3. **Edge feature guidance.** The static Laplacian edge map f^l_i extracted from the input image is passed through a 1×1 convolution to match the channel dimension of the encoder feature. It is then used to modulate f^e_i as a third pathway of attention.

The outputs of the three attention branches—reverse attention, boundary attention, and edge feature guidance—are first concatenated and fused via a 3×3 convolution to form an intermediate feature representation:

$$f^c_i = \mathrm{Conv}\left(\left[f^e_i \otimes G_{RA}(x),\ f^e_i \otimes f^b_i,\ f^e_i \otimes \mathrm{Conv}_{1\times1}(f^l_i)\right]\right) \tag{4}$$

To suppress background noise and emphasize salient regions, we compute an attention mask by applying a 1×1 convolution followed by a sigmoid activation. The attention map A_i is then used to modulate the input feature f^e_i via a residual connection:

$$f^a_i = f^e_i + (f^e_i \otimes A_i),\ where A_i = \sigma(\mathrm{Conv}_{1\times1}(f^c_i)) \tag{5}$$

Finally, the modulated feature f^a_i is passed through a Convolutional Block Attention Module (CBAM) [18] to further refine spatial and channel-level information:

$$f^d_i = \mathrm{CBAM}(f^a_i) \tag{6}$$

This fusion process strengthens spatial focus and boundary precision while maintaining robustness to ambiguous and noisy regions.

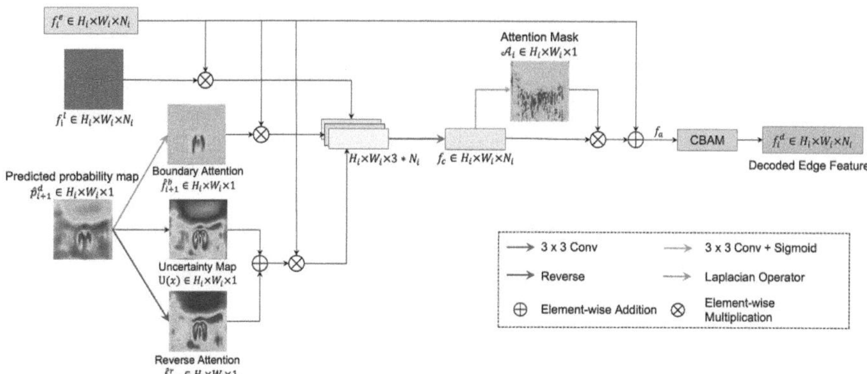

Fig. 2. The architecture of the proposed EGA-U module. The input includes the encoding feature $f_i^e \in \mathbb{R}^{H_i \times W_i \times N_i}$, Laplacian edge map $f_i^l \in \mathbb{R}^{H_i \times W_i \times 1}$, and sigmoid-activated prediction $\hat{p}_{i+1}^d \in \mathbb{R}^{H_i \times W_i \times 1}$. Uncertainty is computed as $U(x)$ and added to reverse attention. Three attention-enhanced features are fused and refined via CBAM to obtain f_i^d.

3   Experiments

Dataset. We conduct experiments on the public TOS dataset released by Marzola et al. [9], containing 464 B-mode images from 110 subjects across four centres using five ultrasound systems. All images are pre-cropped to 256 × 256 and manually annotated for optic nerve (ON) and optic nerve sheath (ONS).

Evaluation Metrics. We evaluate segmentation using Dice score, boundary IoU (BIoU), Hausdorff Distance (HD), and Average Symmetric Surface Distance (ASSD). Dice assesses region-level agreement. HD, ASSD, and BIoU reflect boundary accuracy—crucial for diameter estimation reliability, which is more important in this work. Metrics are computed on the optic nerve sheath between the manual masks and the automatic ONS masks.

Implementation Details. All models are implemented in PyTorch and trained on an NVIDIA RTX A5000 GPU. Input images are resized to 256 × 256 pixels and normalized to the [0, 1] range. We adopt ConvNeXtV2-Tiny pretrained on ImageNet-22K [3] as the encoder backbone. Training uses Adam optimiser (lr = 1e-4, batch size = 4), a polynomial learning rate schedule with warmup, and standard data augmentation for 200 epochs. The segmentation network is optimized using a combination of Dice loss and binary cross-entropy (BCE), which balances region overlap and pixel-level prediction accuracy.

We follow five-fold cross-validation and evaluate predictions on the combined test sets. During inference, we apply test-time augmentation [7,11] using four flip variants and average the outputs. Diameter measurements for OND and ONSD are computed using the provided MATLAB script within a 3 mm zone posterior to the optic disc.

4 Results and Discussion

4.1 Quantitative Results

The performance comparison of our model on the optic nerve dataset is shown in Table 1. We compare UncEGA-Net with the original U-Net [13], the implementation from Marzola et al. [9], U-Net++ [20], and SE-UNet [6]. Our UncEGA-Net achieves the best overall results across all metrics, with a Dice score of **0.7365** and a aHD of **20.31**. Notably, the BIoU reaches **0.3532**, reflecting improved boundary precision. These results demonstrate the effectiveness of our uncertainty-guided attention mechanism.

Table 1. Segmentation performance comparison on the optic nerve dataset. Metrics are calculated on the combined predictions from all five cross-validation test folds. Values are reported as global mean (standard deviation).

Methods	HD $\downarrow$	BIoU $\uparrow$	ASSD $\downarrow$	Dice $\uparrow$
U-Net (Marzola et al.)	21.93 (13.09)	0.3335 (0.1128)	3.80 (2.11)	0.7186 (0.1388)
Simple U-Net	25.27 (19.04)	0.3447 (0.1166)	4.02 (2.66)	0.7205 (0.1437)
U-Net++	25.20(18.54)	0.3408 (0.1180)	4.11 (2.84)	0.7179 (0.1484)
SE-UNet	22.90 (13.52)	0.3447 (0.1101)	3.76 (2.14)	0.7238 (0.1379)
UncEGA-Net (Ours)	**20.31 (13.46)**	**0.3532 (0.1197)**	**3.61 (2.24)**	**0.7365 (0.1373)**

4.2 Qualitative Visualization

To further assess the visual consistency of segmentation boundaries, we overlay predictions from multiple models on the original ultrasound image. A representative comparison is shown in Fig. 3. It shows a qualitative comparison of segmentation contours overlaid on the ultrasound image for a representative case. The ground truth and model predictions are shown in different colours. UncEGA-Net achieves better alignment with anatomical boundaries compared to U-Net variants, particularly along the lateral sheath edges, where boundary ambiguity is higher.

4.3 Ablation Study

To evaluate the contribution of each component, we conduct a series of ablation experiments summarised in Table 2. Starting from a baseline U-Net, introducing the EGA module improves Dice by 0.47% and reduces ASSD, indicating more precise boundary localisation. Replacing the backbone with ConvNeXtV2 brings a larger gain in overall accuracy, with Dice increasing to 0.7332. Finally, incorporating the uncertainty-guided reverse attention (UncEGA-Net) achieves the best results across most metrics, particularly in boundary-aware measures such as BIoU and HD. These findings highlight the effectiveness of our uncertainty-enhanced attention design.

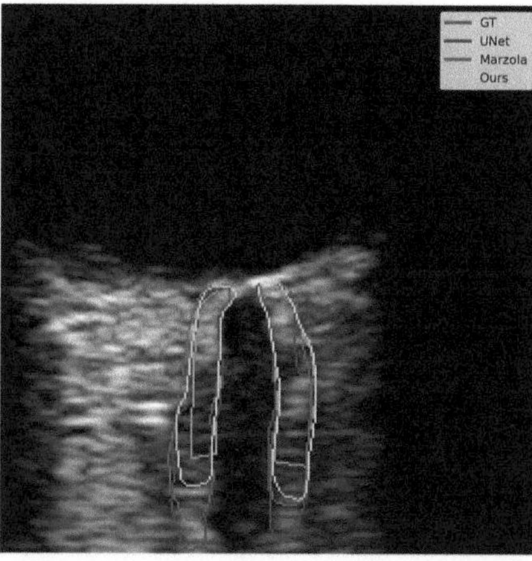

Fig. 3. Overlay of segmentation contours on a representative TOS image. Ground truth is shown in green, U-Net (Marzola et al. (Color figure online)) in red, U-Net in blue, and UncEGA-Net (ours) in yellow. Our method better aligns with GT boundaries in challenging regions.

Table 2. Ablation study of the proposed components.

Method	HD ↓	BIoU ↑	ASSD ↓	Dice ↑
Baseline U-Net	25.27	0.3447	4.0165	0.7205
U-Net + EGA	23.51	0.3419	3.8511	0.7252
ConvNeXtV2 + EGA	22.68	0.3450	3.8432	0.7332
UncEGA-Net (Ours)	**20.31**	**0.3532**	**3.6110**	**0.7365**

4.4   OND and ONSD Estimation

To assess whether the proposed segmentation improvements translate into better clinical measurements, we evaluate both optic nerve diameter (OND) and optic nerve sheath diameter (ONSD) using the official MATLAB protocol provided with the dataset. Following prior studies [9], diameters are automatically extracted from predicted masks and compared against manual annotations.

Table 3 presents the results. Our UncEGA-Net model achieves a mean absolute error (MAE) of 0.240 mm for OND and 0.402 mm for ONSD. Compared to the baseline UNet50 [9] model (OND: 0.323 mm, ONSD: 0.394 mm), our method yields significantly lower OND error, while maintaining comparable ONSD accuracy. For both diameters, the intraclass correlation coefficients (ICC) are high (OND: 0.661, ONSD: 0.664), suggesting reliable agreement with expert measurements.

In terms of correlation, UncEGA-Net achieves a Pearson coefficient of $r = 0.691$ for OND and $r = 0.678$ for ONSD. These results indicate strong linear alignment between predicted and reference diameters. Interestingly, despite

Table 3. ONSD and OND measurement results using automated segmentation. MAE: mean absolute error (mm), icc: intraclass correlation coefficient, r: Pearson correlation against manual annotations.

Method	OND Err	ONSD Err	OND MAE	ONSD MAE	iccOND	iccONSD	rOND	rONSD
U-Net (Marzola et al.)	-0.253 ± 0.318	0.027 ± 0.507	0.323 ± 0.246	0.394 ± 0.319	0.518	0.661	0.686	0.692
UncEGA-Net (Ours)	0.095 ± 0.318	0.018 ± 0.525	0.240 ± 0.228	0.402 ± 0.338	0.661	0.664	0.691	0.678

having a slightly lower correlation for OND compared to UNet50 ($r = 0.686$), UncEGA-Net achieves a lower MAE, indicating more precise predictions with less variability.

Both OND and ONSD are considered clinically relevant biomarkers, especially for detecting raised intracranial pressure [5,8]. Our results confirm that the proposed boundary-aware architecture enhances segmentation quality and supports accurate, automated quantification of both anatomical structures from TOS images.

5   Conclusion

We propose UncEGA-Net, a novel segmentation network for TOS images of the optic nerve, addressing the challenge of blurry and ambiguous boundaries. Our model combines a powerful encoder (ConvNeXtV2-Tiny) with a novel edge attention module guided by uncertainty (EGA-U) that adjusts attention strength by predicting an uncertainty proxy. Extensive experiments on a multicenter optic nerve dataset demonstrate that UncEGA-Net consistently outperforms standard and enhanced U-Net variants across multiple segmentation metrics. Furthermore, the diameter measurement based on our predicted masks yields strong agreement with the expert annotations, validating the clinical applicability of our approach.

References

1. Bui, N.T., Hoang, D.H., Nguyen, Q.T., Tran, M.T., Le, N.: MegaNet: multi-scale edge-guided attention network for weak boundary polyp segmentation. In: Proceedings of the IEEE/CVF Winter Conference on Applications of Computer Vision, pp. 7985–7994 (2024)
2. Chu, Y., et al.: Optic nerve sheath ultrasound image segmentation based on CBC-YOLOV5S. Electronics **13**(18), 3595 (2024)
3. Deng, J., Dong, W., Socher, R., Li, L.J., Li, K., Fei-Fei, L.: ImageNet: a large-scale hierarchical image database. In: 2009 IEEE Conference on Computer Vision and Pattern Recognition, pp. 248–255. IEEE (2009)
4. Escamilla-Ocañas, C.E., Morales-Cardona, N.C., Sagreiya, H., Akhbardeh, A., Hirzallah, M.I.: Automation of ultrasonographic optic nerve sheath diameter measurement: a scoping review. J. Neuroimaging **35**(1), e70017 (2025)

5. Helmke, K., Hansen, H.: Fundamentals of transorbital sonographic evaluation of optic nerve sheath expansion under intracranial hypertension: I. experimental study. Pediatric Radiol. **26**, 701–705 (1996)

6. Hu, J., Shen, L., Sun, G.: Squeeze-and-excitation networks. In: Proceedings of the IEEE Conference on Computer Vision and Pattern Recognition, pp. 7132–7141 (2018)

7. Kimura, M.: Understanding test-time augmentation. In: Mantoro, T., Lee, M., Ayu, M.A., Wong, K.W., Hidayanto, A.N. (eds.) ICONIP 2021. LNCS, vol. 13108, pp. 558–569. Springer, Cham (2021). https://doi.org/10.1007/978-3-030-92185-9_46

8. Lochner, P., et al.: Optic nerve sheath diameter: present and future perspectives for neurologists and critical care physicians. Neurol. Sci. **40**(12), 2447–2457 (2019). https://doi.org/10.1007/s10072-019-04015-x

9. Marzola, F., Lochner, P., Naldi, A., Lemor, R., Stögbauer, J., Meiburger, K.M.: Development of a deep learning-based system for optic nerve characterization in transorbital ultrasound images on a multicenter data set. Ultrasound Med. Biol. **49**(9), 2060–2071 (2023)

10. Meiburger, K.M., Naldi, A., Lochner, P., Marzola, F.: Automatic segmentation of the optic nerve in transorbital ultrasound images using a deep learning approach. In: 2021 IEEE International Ultrasonics Symposium (IUS), pp. 1–4. IEEE (2021)

11. Moshkov, N., Mathe, B., Kertesz-Farkas, A., Hollandi, R., Horvath, P.: Test-time augmentation for deep learning-based cell segmentation on microscopy images. Sci. Rep. **10**(1), 5068 (2020)

12. Noble, J., Boukerroui, D.: Ultrasound image segmentation: a survey. IEEE Trans. Med. Imaging **25**(8), 987–1010 (2006). https://doi.org/10.1109/TMI.2006.877092

13. Ronneberger, O., Fischer, P., Brox, T.: U-Net: convolutional networks for biomedical image segmentation. In: Navab, N., Hornegger, J., Wells, W.M., Frangi, A.F. (eds.) MICCAI 2015. LNCS, vol. 9351, pp. 234–241. Springer, Cham (2015). https://doi.org/10.1007/978-3-319-24574-4_28

14. Sallam, A., et al.: The diagnostic accuracy of noninvasive methods to measure the intracranial pressure: a systematic review and meta-analysis. Anesthesia & Analgesia **132**(3), 686–695 (2021)

15. Woo, S., et al: Convnext V2: co-designing and scaling convnets with masked autoencoders. arXiv preprint arXiv:2301.00808 (2023)

16. Soliman, I., et al.: New optic nerve sonography quality criteria in the diagnostic evaluation of traumatic brain injury. Crit. Care Res. Prac. **2018**(1), 3589762 (2018)

17. Wightman, R.: PyTorch image models (2019). https://doi.org/10.5281/zenodo.4414861, https://github.com/huggingface/pytorch-image-models

18. Woo, S., Park, J., Lee, J.Y., Kweon, I.S.: CBAM: convolutional block attention module. In: Proceedings of the European Conference on Computer Vision (ECCV), pp. 3–19 (2018)

19. Xiao, Y.: Automatic optic nerve assessment from transorbital ultrasound images: a deep learning-based approach. Curr. Med. Imaging **20**(1), e15734056293608 (2024)

20. Zhou, Z., Rahman Siddiquee, M.M., Tajbakhsh, N., Liang, J.: UNet++: a nested U-Net architecture for medical image segmentation. In: Stoyanov, D., et al. (eds.) DLMIA/ML-CDS -2018. LNCS, vol. 11045, pp. 3–11. Springer, Cham (2018). https://doi.org/10.1007/978-3-030-00889-5_1

Author Index

H. Fang et al. (Eds.): OMIA 2025, LNCS 16209, pp. 179–180, 2026.
https://doi.org/10.1007/978-3-032-10351-2